18-23, 46

NAVY DEPARTMENT
OFFICE OF NAVAL RECORDS AND LIBRARY
HISTORICAL SECTION

Publication Number 5

HISTORY
OF
THE BUREAU OF ENGINEERING
NAVY DEPARTMENT

DURING THE WORLD WAR

Published under the direction of
The Hon. EDWIN DENBY, Secretary of the Navy

WASHINGTON
GOVERNMENT PRINTING OFFICE
1922

NAVY DEPARTMENT
OFFICE OF NAVAL RECORDS AND LIBRARY
HISTORICAL SECTION

Publication Number 5

HISTORY

OF

THE BUREAU OF ENGINEERING NAVY DEPARTMENT

DURING THE WORLD WAR

Published under the direction of
The Hon. EDWIN DENBY, Secretary of the Navy

WASHINGTON
GOVERNMENT PRINTING OFFICE
1922

ADDITIONAL COPIES
OF THIS PUBLICATION MAY BE PROCURED FROM
THE SUPERINTENDENT OF DOCUMENTS
GOVERNMENT PRINTING OFFICE
WASHINGTON, D C
AT
60 CENTS PER COPY

ENGINEER IN CHIEF ROBERT S. GRIFFIN, U. S. NAVY.
Chief of Bureau of Steam Engineering.

INTRODUCTION.

This description of the operations of the Bureau of Engineering (formerly Bureau of Steam Engineering) during the World War was prepared at the request of the Historical Section by Rear Admiral Robert S. Griffin, Engineer in Chief, U. S. Navy, Chief of Bureau, the distinguished officer on whom rested the responsibility for the varied and extensive duties and activities of the Bureau and its branches, so ably and efficiently performed

W. D. MacDougall,
Captain, U. S. Navy, Officer in Charge,
Office of Naval Records and Library, and Historical Section.
July 20, 1921.

PREFACE.

In preparing this narrative of the operations of the Bureau during the war, I have been embarrassed on account of the fact that most of it was written so long after the events recorded—when the officers intimately associated with the work had either been ordered to sea duty or placed on inactive duty—that it has been almost impossible to give adequate space to many matters that deserve recognition. In some cases the records of important undertakings were so condensed, on account of war conditions, as to give all too brief mention of events that are deserving of extended notice. However, the entire story is submitted in the belief that the facts recorded have in them sufficient merit to be of general interest to all officers of the Navy, as well as to engineers either directly or remotely interested in the activities of that Bureau of the Navy Department which is responsible for the efficient operation of the motive power of our ships.

To Commander William L. Catheart, U. S. Naval Reserve Force, I am under special obligation for assistance in preparing and in editing the manuscript.

R. S. GRIFFIN,
Engineer in Chief, U. S. Navy,
Chief of Bureau.

May 8, 1921

ACTIVITIES OF THE BUREAU OF STEAM ENGINEERING
DURING THE WORLD WAR.

In order that the scope of the work performed by the Bureau of Steam Engineering[1] may be clearly understood, there is submitted below a brief summary of its functions during the war.

The Navy Regulations state in broad terms that the duties of the Bureau comprise, amongst others, "all that relates to designing, building, fitting out, and repairing machinery used for the propulsion of naval ships," the word "ships" including all floating craft of whatever description. The Bureau's field is, therefore, largely that of dynamical engineering, covering the design, construction, maintenance, and repair of all steam and internal combustion engines used for propelling vessels of the Navy, as well as the electric motors and generators used in the case of "electric drive" ships, and the storage batteries and electric motors for submarines. This includes not only the main engines and boilers but also all the auxiliaries and accessories necessary for the successful operation of the engines and for their maintenance in efficient condition.

The electrical engineering work of the Bureau comprises a great variety of duties besides those connected with the propulsion of ships. These duties are defined by regulation as "the entire system of interior communications * * * interior and exterior signal communications (except range finders and battle order transmitters and indicators), and of all electrical appliances of whatsoever nature on board naval vessels, except motors and their controlling apparatus used to operate the machinery belonging to other bureaus." This means that the Bureau supplies the electric generators, switchboards and wiring, the call bells and buzzers, voice tubes, telephones, engine and steering telegraphs and transmitters, searchlights and electric lighting generally, and supplies electric current for all purposes for which it is used, whether it be for operating a turret turning motor, a feed pump, a flat iron, or a cigar lighter. It also supplies portable ventilating fans for use in officers' quarters and in those portions of the ship which are not easily reached by the ship's ventilating system.

---

[1] Title changed June 4, 1920, to Bureau of Engineering.

In radio engineering, the Bureau's field is a wide one, and during the war comprehended the radio installation on every ship that flew the American flag, as well as the design and supply of the equipment for all shore stations in the United States and in our island possessions, and also for a large station just completed at Bordeaux, France.

A new duty that devolved on it during the war was the provision of devices for detecting the presence of submarines and of aircraft

In the aeronautic field, the Bureau's duties cover the same kind of work as for surface vessels, i. e., it supplies the machinery and its accessories, and is also charged with responsibility for the generation and supply of gas for observation balloons and for dirigibles.

Besides the duties mentioned, which may be considered as relating chiefly to the material features necessary for operating the ship, many others devolve on the Bureau relating to the health and comfort of the crew. Chief among these is the provision of a supply of salt water for sanitary purposes, and of fresh water for drinking and bathing, which in a battleship of 2,500 men rises to the proportion of the waterworks of a small town. The allowance of fresh water is liberal, and finds its return in the health, the comfort, and the contentment of the crew. Next in importance to this is the provision of machinery and appliances for making ice, and for cooling the refrigerating rooms so that fresh provisions may be always available and thus contribute to the reputation which the Navy enjoys of being the best fed Navy in the world.

The Bureau also heats the ship by steam and by electric power and supplies the same power for cooking

With so much machinery and so many appliances to care for, it is necessary that the ships be provided with engineering supplies and with hand and machine tools for keeping this equipment in serviceable condition. To accomplish this the Bureau provides a machine shop on each ship with facilities suited to her ordinary needs. For heavier work it equips the shops of the repair ships which accompany the fleet so that any work within reason may be undertaken. Similarly, at navy yards, it decides upon and supplies the equipment of the shops of the Machinery Division, and is held responsible for the adequacy of that equipment.

For engineering supplies, the Bureau decides on the allowance of each kind which shall be issued to each ship, and on the quantity to be carried in stock; it draws the specifications for their purchase, inspects during manufacture those of a technical character, and passes upon the award of contract for them.

It maintains at each shipbuilding establishment that has a contract for building ships for the Navy an inspection force presided over by an officer of experience, whose duty it is to see that the requirements of the specifications are faithfully observed, and that when ready for delivery to the Government the ship is in all respects complete and ready for service. A like organization for the inspection of engineering material is maintained in a number of districts into which the country has been divided, whose function it is to see that the chemical and physical characteristics of material comply with the specified requirements before it is shipped to the building yards for incorporation in the ship. Where completely fabricated articles are manufactured the inspection extends to the completed article.

The inspection of fuel is also under the Bureau

At Annapolis it maintains an experiment station where special problems are investigated and tests made of engineering devices which appear to possess merit and whose installation in naval vessels would be desirable

It will be seen then that the Bureau's field is most extensive with regard to the material of the fleet, both in its provision and operation In sum, it covers everything necessary for propulsion, whether the vessel operates on the surface of the water, beneath it, or in the air. It provides such "public utilities" as a central power plant furnishing light, heat, and power for a multitude of activities necessary for the military efficiency of the ship and the comfort of her crew, a cold-storage plant, telephone service, telegraphic service by radio, and an aqueduct in miniature It provides also everything necessary for the maintenance in efficient operation of all these services and for many others of less importance

Just what this represents in figures may be judged from a consideration of a few facts bearing on these activities. During the fiscal year ending June 30, 1918, the expenditures of the Bureau reached the sum of $283,742,767, which is nearly six times those of the preceding year, during three months of which we were at war.

The motive power of the fleet, including that of all the new vessels authorized, the ex-German ships, the patrol and other vessels reached the enormous figure of 11,000,000 horsepower. An appreciation of this power may be had from a consideration of the fact that it is more than twenty times as great as the horsepower of our fleet during the Spanish-American War. It is about eighteen times the power developed on both sides of Niagara Falls, and is also equal to about one-fourth the primary fuel and water power now employed in land service in the United States, not including the locomotives

ORGANIZATION AND ADMINISTRATION.

The administration of the Bureau is vested in a chief of bureau, an assistant to the bureau and a chief clerk and to various duties, clerical and technical division being presided over by an officer specially qualified by experience for the performance of the duties pertaining thereto. These are:

    The Clerical Division
    The Division of Design.
    The Electrical Division.
    The Radio Division.
    The Division of Aeronautics.
    The Division of Repairs
    The Inspection Division.
    The Supply Division.
    The Fuel and Personnel Division.
    The Division of Logs and Records.

The Clerical Division is in charge of the chief clerk and has supervision of all clerical activities, financial returns and records, and of the file room, and maintains a record of the classified employees of the Bureau and of inspection offices.

The Division of Design has control of the design of machinery and of alterations therein, and prepares the specifications for new machinery It has supervision of the construction of machinery, as well as of the contracts and payments therefor. It also has under its direction the engineering experiment station and the oil-fuel testing plant.

The Electrical Division has charge of the design and specifications for all electrical apparatus, for interior communication and wiring systems, searchlights, storage batteries, and motors for submarines

The Radio Division has similar control over the design and supply of all radio apparatus for ship and shore installations and for aircraft, and also of sound detection matters though during the war this activity was with the Electrical Division.

The Division of Aeronautics has in a general way the same control over aircraft machinery that the Division of Design has over surface craft, but there is necessarily close cooperation between the two divisions respecting certain features of design.

The Division of Repairs has charge of all repairs to machinery of vessels of the fleet, whether done at a navy yard or elsewhere. It also is charged with the manufacture of steam and gasoline engines for power boats, and of records pertaining thereto. Technical questions arising are referred to the division concerned for comment. It prepares allowance lists for all ships.

The Inspection Division is charged with supervision of the inspection of material, of the preparation of specifications, the conduct of tests, and the records of tests.

The Supply Division handles requisitions from ships and navy yards, prepares Bureau requisitions, analyzes bids received for material, and makes recommendations regarding award of contracts It also has charge of production matters and of cost of work

The Fuel and Personnel Division, as its designation implies, handles two widely different subjects. It prepares specifications for fuel and supervises its inspection, and has general supervision of the naval petroleum reserves. In conference with the Bureau of Navigation, it suggests the detail of officers for certain duty of an engineering character.

The Division of Logs and Records prepares and issues blank forms for use in the engineer department of ships, reviews and analyzes the steam logs, and prepares for issue to the naval service engineering information of interest and value.

The chief of bureau determines questions of Bureau policy, authorizes expenditures, and decides important matters of detail as well as many minor ones

The assistant to the bureau, in the absence of the chief of bureau, assumes his duties and responsibilities In general he handles routine business in technical and administrative affairs, and has general supervision of the equipment of shops of the Machinery Division of navy yards.

In the absence of the chief of bureau and the assistant to the bureau, the chief clerk acts as chief of bureau.

This organization was not one created for the war or under war conditions, but was one that had been built up during the preceding 30 years, and is the development of one inaugurated about that time by Mr. Asa M Mattice, at that time an engineer officer of the Navy That it stood the test of war conditions and required no change whatever in its basic principle is the best evidence that can be given of its excellence. Additions and extensions were made as conditions dictated the necessity therefor, but no change was made in the system.

PERSONNEL.

Prior to the beginning of the war, the officer personnel of the Bureau consisted of 35 commissioned officers, a number insufficient even under peace conditions to satisfactorily conduct the diversified duties for which the Bureau was responsible To meet the greatly enlarged demands that would come with war, when every officer who could possibly be spared would be wanted for sea duty, was not a pleasant situation to contemplate, and in preparing for this condition relief was naturally sought from the retired list of the Navy, where officers of naval education and training could be found who would be capable of filling some of the most important positions, and who would bring to the performance of their duty knowledge of naval conditions and demands which it would have taken a civilian months and in some cases years to acquire

Accordingly, in the preparation of the mobilization scheme which was prepared far in advance of our entrance into the war, certain officers of engineering education and training were selected for duty in the Bureau, and in offices of inspectors of machinery and of engineering material, on boards, and for special duty; and but for the fortuitous circumstance that these experienced officers were available, it would have been well-nigh impossible to have handled the enormous business that fell to the lot of the Bureau to administer.

Some of these officers had been retired for age, others for physical disability which did not prevent the performance of shore duty, and all had been notified in advance of the duty to which they would be assigned, so that a telegram directing them to report was all that was necessary to have them on duty again. One served as assistant to the Bureau for nearly a year during the war and for a considerable period thereafter; another, who had previously been in charge of the Division of Design, cheerfully took up the duty of a subordinate in that division; while a third, whom the Bureau intended to utilize in an advisory capacity, became a member of the Priorities Committee of the War Industries Board Others served either as heads of divisions or as subordinates in the Bureau, and as inspectors One of the former relinquished a very lucrative position in civil life to resume his naval status All served with a spirit and an enthusiasm that merit the highest commendation.

But retired officers were far too few in number to fill the demand, and the next step was to survey the list of former officers of the Navy who had resigned and all of whom were eager to return to the service. Many of them were enrolled in the Naval Reserve, but many others occupied such important positions in educational and industrial fields as to make it almost obligatory upon the Government to insist that they continue the work upon which they were engaged

The next class from which it seemed most desirable to recruit engineering talent was the shipbuilding establishments and the engineering firms who specialized in naval equipment, but here again arose the question of priority. These establishments were daily becoming busier and more necessary than ever to the successful prosecution of the war, and to weaken their organization would be suicidal In fact it was felt that everything possible should be done to keep those several organizations intact and, if possible, to strengthen them It was clear that assistance from this field could not be thought of

Meanwhile many offers of service were made by patriotic engineers who were eager to volunteer in any capacity and while the services of some were accepted, it was felt that in most cases the applicants were either too advanced in years for the subordinate positions to which they would necessarily have to be assigned or that the industrial field offered better opportunity for the exercise of their ability.

With all these conditions confronting us, recourse was eventually had to transferring from the Naval Reserve young officers whose training had been along engineering lines and who were favorably reported on by the district commandant or commanding officer under whom they were serving. In addition the Bureau of Navigation had, upon recommendation of the Bureau of Steam Engineering and approval of the Secretary of the Navy, conducted an examination for the enrollment as ensigns of 100 electrical engineers selected from a list of 250 applicants who had been recommended by the Naval Consulting Board, the National Research Council, and the American Institute of Electrical Engineers. Capt. R. H. Leigh, the assistant to the bureau, was the president of the board. The officers thus appointed rendered excellent service, and several of them were, after limited experience afloat, assigned to duty in the Bureau.

Qualified aviation personnel did not exist, and it was necessary to find men who were known to have a bent toward mechanical engineering problems, and in most cases send them to the Massachusetts Institute of Technology for an intensive course in aviation engineering that had been established there, thence to the airplane or engine factories for a short tour under the inspection officer, and then to duty in the Bureau, where they specialized on one particular part of the power plant of aircraft. This method was also followed in building up the inspection force, some selections being made every three months from each class that passed through the school. The men were awarded a commission in class 5 of the Naval Reserve Force after successfully passing through the weeding-out process and a probationary period of actual service. A few reserve officers were also obtained from the air stations for inspection duty. An excellent class of men who worked loyally and earnestly at all times was obtained.

Advantage was also taken of the transfer of the Coast Guard to the Navy to secure the assignment of some officers of that service to duty in the Bureau and for inspection. It is no less a duty than a pleasure to state that they rendered excellent service.

From these various sources, the officer personnel of the Bureau was recruited until at the time of the armistice it numbered 143, distributed as follows: Officers of the active list, 21; retired officers 10, temporary officers, 6, reserve officers, 99, Coast Guard officers, 6, Army officers 1

These offi... ... ... Office hours were forgotten, night work and work on Sundays and holidays, though not continuous, was so generally pursued as to make it almost routine. A night detail was always in effect, one officer being specially detailed for a certain period and his name and telephone number registered so that he might be available at an instant's notice

Shortly after the declaration of war, Admiral Sims advised that officers qualified in mechanical and electrical engineering be sent to London where the British Admiralty had expressed a willingness to give the fullest information regarding technical matters which had developed during the war and which should be known to all the Allies Advantage was taken of this offer to send Commander G. W S. Castle and Commander S M Robinson, who were not only given the widest opportunity for investigation at the Admiralty, but also were permitted to visit vessels of the Grand Fleet at Scapa Flow. The information they acquired was of great value, especially in fire-control work

Later Lieut Commander W A Smead, U. S. Navy, and Lieut. G M. Brush, U S Naval Reserve Force, were sent to France and England in connection with aircraft material, and Commander J O Fisher, U S. Navy, in connection with submarines. In each case much information of value was obtained.

Early in 1917 the French and the British Governments sent commissions to this country who contributed exceptionally valuable information respecting the methods in vogue abroad for the detection of submarines. The French Commission, composed of Majs. Fabry and Abrahams, brought samples of detection devices and other apparatus which were of great assistance in the development work we were then undertaking. Commander Bridge, R. N. and Sir Ernest Rutherford gave the fullest information respecting the work of the British, which enabled us to begin with the best information obtainable

Additional assistants for the offices of inspectors of machinery and inspectors of engineering material were obtained through district commandants from the list of enrolled officers and petty officers. In special cases, such as the production officers, who were specially selected men above draft age and of extensive experience, enrollment was made directly by the Navy Department

For a time inspection of material was seriously hampered because many of our trained assistant inspectors were lured to service under the War Department by offers of a commission and much higher pay than was possible of attainment under the Navy Department. This obtained also to a certain extent amongst civilian employees of the Bureau.

The administrative officers of the Bureau during the period from April 6, 1917, to November 11, 1918, were:

Rear Admiral Robert S. Griffin, Engineer in Chief, U. S. Navy
Assistant to bureau, Capt. R H Leigh, U. S. Navy.
Assistant to bureau, Capt. O. W. Koester, U S Navy (retired)
Chief clerk, Mr. A. C. Wrenn.
Special duty, Lieut Commander W. L. Cathcart, U S Naval Reserve Force.
Rear Admiral A. V Zane, U S Navy (retired), representing Bureau of Steam Engineering on Priorities Committee, War Industries Board.

CIVILIAN PERSONNEL.

While the conditions affecting the filling of the complement of technical officers were such as to cause no little concern, the situation with respect to the civilian working force was one that required unceasing attention.

In January, 1917, this force consisted of 50 clerks and messengers and 37 draftsmen and technical employees, a total of 87. The preparations that were made between that date and the declaration of war were such as to require a considerable increase in the technical force, which increase it was not possible to secure in the orthodox manner through the Civil Service Commission because the appropriation fixed by Congress limited the amount that might be expended for such service and also the number of employees All bureaus were experiencing the same difficulty, and relief finally came through the Bureau of Navigation, which enrolled in the Naval Reserve in the various grades of yeoman a number of female clerks (reservists F), who were assigned to duty in the Bureau But for this assignment, it would not have been possible to carry out the preparations that were made before the declaration of war, at which time the total number of employees engaged in clerical work numbered 84, an increase of 34.

The demand for additional civilian assistants increased by leaps and bounds and greatly exceeded the supply of competent availables. Even with a reduction in the requirements, it was difficult to obtain the desired employees Every means was used to increase the number, such as appeals to business colleges outside of Washington; and though difficulty was experienced, it is gratifying to state that all immediately urgent needs were met and that the efficiency of the Bureau was at no time impaired by lack of adequate civilian force.

On armistice day this force had grown to the following proportions:

Civilians (clerks)	170
Civilians, draftsmen and technical employees	103
Naval reservists	282
Total	555

Twenty-five of the civilian employees entered the military or naval service, as follows:

Brady, John B., ensign, U S Naval Reserve Force.
Brandon, Valentine N., corporal, 335th Machine Gun Battalion
Conrad Amos W., jr, corporal, Headquarters, 372d Infantry
Dean William R., jr, corporal, 164th Depot Brigade
Dickson, Walter S., carpenter's mate, second class, U S Naval Reserve Force
Elliott, Charles A., private, U S Marine Corps
Gladmon, Cassin G., private, Sanitary Detachment, Camp Meade
Goldstein, Bernard S, chief yeoman U. S Naval Reserve Force
Hill, Guy, captain, Signal Corps, U S. Army
King, Benedict J, musician, Headquarters, 371st Infantry
Lanigan, Arthur L, Students Army Training Corps
Laning, Benjamin A., ensign, U S Naval Reserve Force
McCutcheon, Ross, private, Tank Corps
Manitsky, Benjamin P, sergeant, Headquarters, Camp Upton
Martin, William L, private, Tank Corps
Reubenbaum, Samuel P, Headquarters, 79th Division
Roberts, Daniels Q, chief yeoman, U S. Naval Reserve Force
Rundorff, Robert L, Officers Material School, U S Naval Reserve Force
Sparrow, Marion C, private, Tank Corps
Spring, Arlington C, second lieutenant, Engineer Corps U S Army
Stein, Anders C, chief yeoman, U S Naval Reserve Force
Tallman, Henry W, second lieutenant, Aviation Corps, U S Army
Volinsky, Harry, corporal, 67th Infantry
Woulfe, Robert E, chief yeoman, U S Naval Reserve Force

The principal civilian employees of the Bureau during this period were:

Name	Rating
Wrenn, A C	Chief clerk
Moran, F S	Clerk to Engineer in Chief
Christman, A L	Financial clerk and accountant
Warman, F C	Chief of Files Division.
Biggers, A B	Principal clerk, Electrical Division
Haslett, L J	Principal clerk, Radio Division.
Hughes, M G	Principal clerk, Supply Division
Fessenden, A G	Principal clerk, Ships' Repairs Division
Orrison, A M	Miscellaneous furniture and supplies
Sicard, W F	Chief machinery draftsman
Thurston, P K	Assistant chief machinery draftsman
Gatchel, T L	Chief electrical draftsman
Trogner, A M	Chief radio draftsman
Carter, G O	Consulting engineer, hydrogen gas
Williams, Karl D	Metallurgical engineer
Herndon, E G	Machine tool expert

Throughout the entire period of the war this force worked with an enthusiasm which bespoke their loyalty to the country and their personal interest in winning the war

KEY TO OFFICERS, ENLISTED PERSONNEL AND CIVILIAN EMPLOY

Coincident with this great increase in the personnel of the Bureau came a demand for additional office space. This had been found to be too restricted even for the business of peace times, and the first step in acquiring more was by permission of the Secretaries of State, War, and Navy, to close the southeast driveway of the State, War, and Navy Building, in which the Bureau was then quartered, and to construct therein a one-room frame structure. Later, two additional rooms were acquired by inclosing two balconies leading off the quarters of the Bureau. Then followed occupancy of the hall on the third floor, the renting of three rooms in one building, and two upper floors of two old remodeled buildings at the corner of Seventeenth and G Streets NW. In July, 1917, two divisions of the Bureau were removed to the latter quarters, and in March, 1918, sufficient space was secured in the temporary Government buildings erected at Seventh and B Streets NW. to provide quarters for another division.

While the acquisition of this additional space gave the divisions that remained in the building a little more elbow room, the relief was only temporary, and in a short time the crowded condition again prevailed, and it was not until August, 1918, when the new Navy Building at Seventeenth and B Streets was completed that the Bureau really had sufficient space to transact business properly.

The delays incident to having the work of the Bureau carried on in so many buildings were vexatious to a degree; for while a good telephone and messenger force was established, the chief of Bureau lost that personal contact with the officers in charge of the work of the outlying divisions which is so necessary to satisfactory and expeditious conduct of business.

As a corollary to the increase in personnel and quarters, there came also a big demand for office equipment and supplies. This demand was successfully met, due in no small measure to the splendid cooperation of the Supply Division of the Department, which rendered every assistance in obtaining these necessities in the most direct manner possible.

It will be seen then that when the armistice was declared the Bureau's force comprised a total of 698 officers and employees and occupied about 2 acres of office space in the new Navy Building.

PRELIMINARY PREPARATIONS FOR WAR.

The first work done by the Bureau of Steam Engineering after the outbreak of the war in August, 1914, in order to keep in touch with the general situation and to make such preparations as might be necessary to insure the readiness of the material under its cognizance to meet any emergency was to request the Department to

Coincident with this great increase in the personnel of the Bureau came a demand for additional office space. This had been found to be too restricted even for the business of peace times, and the first step in acquiring more was by permission of the Secretaries of State, War, and Navy, to close the southeast driveway of the State, War, and Navy Building, in which the Bureau was then quartered, and to construct therein a one-room frame structure. Later, two additional rooms were acquired by inclosing two balconies leading off the quarters of the Bureau. Then followed occupancy of the hall on the third floor, the renting of three rooms in one building, and two upper floors of two old remodeled buildings at the corner of Seventeenth and G Streets NW. In July, 1917, two divisions of the Bureau were removed to the latter quarters, and in March, 1918, sufficient space was secured in the temporary Government buildings erected at Seventh and B Streets NW, to provide quarters for another division.

While the acquisition of this additional space gave the divisions that remained in the building a little more elbow room, the relief was only temporary, and in a short time the crowded condition again prevailed, and it was not until August, 1918, when the new Navy Building at Seventeenth and B Streets was completed that the Bureau really had sufficient space to transact business properly.

The delays incident to having the work of the Bureau carried on in so many buildings were vexatious to a degree; for while a good telephone and messenger force was established, the chief of Bureau lost that personal contact with the officers in charge of the work of the outlying divisions which is so necessary to satisfactory and expeditious conduct of business.

As a corollary to the increase in personnel and quarters, there came also a big demand for office equipment and supplies. This demand was successfully met, due in no small measure to the splendid cooperation of the Supply Division of the Department, which rendered every assistance in obtaining these necessities in the most direct manner possible.

It will be seen then that when the armistice was declared the Bureau's force comprised a total of 698 officers and employees and occupied about 2 acres of office space in the new Navy Building.

PRELIMINARY PREPARATIONS FOR WAR.

The first work done by the Bureau of Steam Engineering after the outbreak of the war in August, 1914, in order to keep in touch with the general situation and to make such preparations as might be necessary to insure the readiness of the material under its cognizance to meet any emergency, was to request the Department to send abroad an officer qualified to investigate the radio situation. This action was taken August 17, 1914, as shown by the following letter.

132447-787-W

NAVY DEPARTMENT,
BUREAU OF STEAM ENGINEERING,
Washington, August 17, 1914

From Bureau of Steam Engineering
To Department (Material and Personnel)
Subject Assignment of specially qualified officer as observer of radio operations in European war

1 The Bureau invites the Department's attention to the opportunity that is presented in connection with the proposed employment of Army transports in European waters of obtaining information of great value to the naval service A trained observer having authority to transfer from one of these ships to another, or to United States naval ships in the war zone, could, by simply listening in to the radio communication carried on, acquire information not only as to foreign material equipment but also as to principles of organization and tactical operation in regard to which our service has never received any information and which probably never can be acquired by any other method. It is essential, however, that the officer selected for this duty be one whose qualifications embrace not only expert operating ability but also special training in radio organization as applied to the intricate requirements of tactical use It happens conveniently that Lieut S C Hooper has just been relieved as fleet radio officer, Atlantic Fleet, and should now be available for this duty This officer has been engaged during the last two years in establishing an efficient radio organization in the fleet and he is preeminently qualified for the duty suggested In fact, his special training for this particular work could not have been improved upon by design The Bureau recommends that the necessary arrangements be made with the War Department and that orders be issued to Lieut Hooper giving him the largest allowable discretion in obtaining the data desired

(S) *Griffin*

Orders were issued in accordance with the above recommendation and Lieut. Hooper sailed on the *Olympic* the latter part of August, 1914, and remained abroad until January, 1915, returning on the *St. Paul*. The time was spent in England, France, Ireland, Belgium, and Holland. At the time of Lieut. Hooper's visit to Belgium it was occupied by the Germans, but he was, nevertheless, able to obtain information of value.

It was difficult to obtain information regarding radio matters from the Allies on account of the strict censorship that prevailed, but Lieut. Hooper's practical knowledge enabled him to listen in at various places and thus to acquire complete knowledge regarding the system employed by them and the use to which radio was put This information was later found to be correct when we entered the war He also inspected the apparatus under manufacture for the British Government and visited the principal high-power station at Carnarvon, Wales, which, at that time, was the largest station in existence The information of most value that he obtained was in regard to the distant control of radio stations, a system which was later adopted for our Navy

As a result of the complete information acquired, a board was appointed with a view to improving the communication service of our Navy. The general plan outlined by this board was the foundation of the present organization of the Naval Communication Service and has remained practically unchanged

On March 13, 1915, the General Board submitted to the Department an outline of a plan of preparedness This was approved by the Department May 28, 1915, and the Bureau was directed to make the first report in compliance with this outlined plan in one month following the date of its approval, and subsequent reports quarterly This was followed by a letter from the Chief of Naval Operations, June 10, 1915, directing the inspection of merchant ships to determine their suitability for use by the Navy, and calling for a report regarding the alterations and additions that would be necessary in order to make them suitable for Navy service.

The *first report* of the Bureau, dated June 28, 1915, stated that nearly all merchant ships except those for repair and supply ships could be put in service without delay, or without great expenditure, that plans were under way for the conversion of two merchant ships to repair ships; that conferences had been had with the Bureau of Supplies and Accounts respecting supply ships and refrigerating ships; that all auxiliaries could be immediately supplied with searchlights and blinker sets, and with auxiliary radio sets. General comment was made on other features of the order affecting the supply of engineering material. It was stated that the Bureau of Navigation had been furnished with a list of retired officers required for duty under the Bureau; that the Bureau would be ready to make specific recommendations regarding merchant ships as soon as reports of the Board of Inspection and Survey were received. This was followed, on October 8, 1915, by a report that plans had been prepared for the conversion of two repair ships, and attention was invited to the fact that no reports of inspection of merchant ships had yet been received.

October 28, 1915 —A letter was addressed to the commander in chief, Atlantic Fleet, requesting that supply officers of two ships of the fleet be directed to fill in, opposite certain items of the allowance list, the quantity of such material that had been used during six months or a year—this to enable the Bureau to prepare a stock list.

November 9, 1915 —The commandants of all navy yards and stations were directed to submit a detailed plan for the expansion on short notice of the facilities of the machinery divisions of the several yards and stations, and to submit an estimate of the time and cost for accomplishing this. A similar letter was sent to the naval station, Guantanamo, on January 8, 1916.

November 12, 1915.—The commanders in chief of the Atlantic, Pacific, and Asiatic fleets, Torpedo Flotilla commander, and the commander of the Cruiser Squadron, Atlantic Fleet, were directed to report the engineering material they considered desirable to keep on hand in order to secure a state of preparedness for war. Suggestions were requested as to the engineering material which it was desired to carry on fighting ships, repair ships, and tenders under war conditions, and what similar material should be kept in store for emergency shipment of the fleets.

November 13, 1915.—Letters were addressed to all inspectors of engineering material directing them to report the extent to which the capacity of manufacturing plants in their several districts who were engaged in the manufacture of important engineering material could be increased in case of emergency to meet a sudden demand. A list of the important material was given, and in a letter of December 1, 1915, the inspectors were directed to include machine tools in the list. Similar letters were addressed under date of January 25, 1916, to the inspectors of machinery at the Busch-Sulzer Co., St. Louis, Mo., and at the Babcock & Wilcox Co., Bayonne, N. J., to report on manufacturing plants in the vicinity of their headquarters.

November 22, 1915.—A similar letter was addressed to inspectors of engineering material for a report on articles of electrical equipment.

November 23, 1915.—Letters were addressed to the two principal manufacturers of submarine storage batteries and to the one manufacturer of submarine signaling apparatus asking that they submit a list of the articles, or component parts thereof, which they usually carried in stock, and to keep the Bureau advised of changes as they occurred. A similar letter, dated January 5, 1916, was addressed to the manufacturers of searchlights.

November 30, 1915.—Letters were addressed to the inspectors of machinery at all principal shipyards to report on the machinery repair and building work that could be undertaken in an emergency at the works to which they were assigned, and also of other ship and engine plants in the vicinity that could be relied upon to assist in the preparation for service of the auxiliary fleet.

December 3, 1915.—Letters were addressed to the commandants of all navy yards and stations directing them to submit lists of material which they considered it desirable to carry in stock.

December 7, 1915.—A letter was addressed to the industrial manager, navy yard, Portsmouth, directing him to submit a report on the maximum quantity of articles that could be manufactured with present facilities by an increase in the number of employees, and similar information regarding the output after 30 days by an increase in the facilities as well as in the number of employees. (The Portsmouth Navy Yard specializes in the manufacture of electrical fittings.)

The *second report* was dated December 31, 1915, and contained specific recommendations regarding improvements necessary in the machinery divisions of navy yards in order to increase their capacity for work. Difficulty in obtaining machine tools was pointed out. Report was made of the facilities of a number of shipyards and repair plants. Special attention was called to the desirability of increasing the stock of engineering material at navy yards, and much information given regarding sources of supply and available material of an engineering character. A list was given of the auxiliaries to be taken over or chartered, and recommendation made in each case as to the changes that would be required.

Special attention was directed to the inadequacy of the war detail of officers and technical employees under the Bureau, and to the duplication of work by the Navy Department and the War Department, and by different bureaus of the Navy Department, in collecting information to carry out the Department's order. Recommendation was made for obtaining funds to prepare navy yards so that they might quickly increase their facilities.

This report, which might be considered the first report under the operation of the plan outlined by the General Board, covered detailed reports on 10 navy yards and stations, on 22 shipbuilding and repair establishments, and on 300 manufacturing plants which might be called upon to supply engineering material. The report was of such a comprehensive character as to evoke a commendatory letter from the Chief of Naval Operations. Its preparation, as also that of subsequent ones, was under the special supervision of Capt. R. H. Leigh, assistant to the Bureau.

January 4, 1916.—Inspectors of machinery were directed to report the changes they considered necessary in their office force and office space in order to meet war conditions. The detail of officers assigned for each office under the mobilization plan was forwarded and suggestions requested regarding any modifications that might be considered necessary. A similar letter was sent to the inspectors of engineering material on January 5, 1916.

January 15, 1916.—The Bureau reported to the Department on the difficulty of obtaining engineering supplies and the delay occasioned thereby, cited numerous cases, and recommended that Congressional action be secured in order to assure procurement of such material.

January 28, 1916.—A letter was addressed to the commandants of all navy yards and stations expressing appreciation of the work that had been done in connection with the Bureau's report of December 31, 1915, and quoted the commendatory letter received from the Chief of Naval Operations. The opinion of the commandants was requested regarding personnel, and a statement called for as to whether the detail fixed in the mobilization scheme was considered satisfactory. Similar letters were addressed to the inspectors of engineering material and inspectors of machinery.

January 31, 1916.—The commandant of the navy yard, New York, was directed to report on the engineering work that could be undertaken by ship and engine building and repair plants in the vicinity of New York and Jersey City in connection with the alteration, repair, and outfit of vessels that might be taken over for auxiliary service. A similar letter was addressed to the inspector at the Babcock & Wilcox Co., under date of January 25, 1916; to the Maryland Steel Co., January 29, 1916; to 21 other ship and engine establishments on February 4, 1916; to 10 others on February 8, 1916; and to three others on March 7, 1916.

February 5, 1916.—The inspectors of engineering material were directed to ascertain the usual output and also the emergency capacity of manufacturing establishments in their districts for the manufacture of 20 different articles of equipment, which were enumerated by the Bureau.

The *third report* was dated March 31, 1916, and followed the general line of the preceding one. It gave an estimate of the cost to equip the machinery divisions of navy yards for building battleships, and noted the addition of certain large tools at Mare Island Navy Yard costing $133,000. It gave details of the building and repair facilities of 45 private yards and the principal details of 66 merchant ships then under construction, besides information from 80 manufacturing establishments for the supply of engineering material; a summary was given of the recommendations made in the case of 38 ships which had been inspected by the Board of Inspection and Survey.

Special attention was invited to the difficulty in obtaining material, and the Bureau's recommendation previously made that authority be obtained from Congress to place an embargo on the export of certain material was quoted. Note was made of the increased cost of material.

A suggestion was made for the employment of *store ships* as distinguished from *supply ships*, and a list given of engineering supplies which should be carried by *supply ships*. A list was also given of the personnel of the offices of inspectors of machinery and inspectors of engineering material recommended as "war personnel."

Under date of April 19, 1916, a memorandum was addressed to the Assistant Secretary of the Navy, giving the organization of the material branch of the radio service, which is under the direction of the Bureau of Steam Engineering, in which it was stated that there existed in the Bureau a list of the material which various manufacturers were capable of furnishing promptly in the event of war, and also what they could do in a specified time. The Department was also advised that the active cooperation of the Marconi company had been secured for installation of radio apparatus.

The *fourth report* was dated June 30, 1916, and contained estimates for equipping submarine bases. Information similar to that contained in preceding reports was given on 2 shipbuilding and repair establishments and 14 manufacturing plants. A list was given of 43 merchant ships for which new equipment necessary to be installed was given. This report also contained a summary of what had been done during the year and noted that detailed plans had been submitted to the Department for the expansion of the facilities of navy yards; that reports had been made on 71 shipbuilding and repair plants, and that the inspection reports of merchant ships numbered 112. Difficulty in securing material was emphasized, and the organization of the inspection service submitted.

The *fifth report* was dated September 30, 1916, and contained details of 2 shipbuilding and repair plants and of 6 engineering supply establishments. It recommended that a reserve stock of important engineering material be kept on hand, and that estimates be submitted to Congress for the purchase of it. A list of material required to equip merchant ships was given, amounting to $495,000. It was noted that the Department approved the Bureau's recommendation regarding the civilian personnel in inspection offices.

The *sixth report* was dated December 31, 1916, and contained further details of shipbuilding and repair plants of 15 additional establishments for the supply of engineering material. It gave a list of engineering material that should be provided, amounting to $2.262,500.

The *seventh report*, dated March 31, 1917, noted the allotment of $267,000 under this Bureau from the appropriation of $18,000,000 for the improvement of navy yards, and stated that additional allotments of $2,744,000 were required. It gave a summary of material required to meet war requirements, to cost $19,115,000. Recommendations were made for the conversion of 28 merchant ships and 35 patrol boats.

THE DESIGN AND CONSTRUCTION OF MACHINERY.

The Act of August 29, 1916, provided for the largest building program that was ever authorized by any Congress. It included 10 first-class battle-ships, 6 battle cruisers, 10 scout cruisers, 50 destroyers, 9 fleet submarines, 58 coast submarines, 1 special submarine, 3 fuel ships, 1 repair ship, 1 transport, 1 hospital ship, 2 destroyer tenders, 1 fleet submarine tender, 2 ammunition ships, 2 gunboats, the construction of 66 of which was directed to be commenced as soon as practicable.

The design of machinery for these latter was well under way when war was declared; that for the 4 battleships had been completed and contracts awarded, but the design for the 4 battle cruisers was not far advanced. Decision had, however, been reached to install electric motor driven machinery in all the capital ships, and as the decision in the case of the battle cruisers was the subject of much comment, it would seem that this is a proper place to give a short history of the Navy's adoption of this type of machinery for its capital ships.

ELECTRIC DRIVE

In 1909, Mr W. R L. Emmet, the consulting engineer of the General Electric Co. represented to the Navy Department the great advantage which would be derived by equipping one of our old battleships with electrically operated machinery, and submitted a tentative proposition for such an equipment. As the number of our battleships at that time, even including the old one under consideration, was too small to admit of assigning one to purely experimental work, the Navy Department declined to enter into the scheme proposed, which was substantially that the Government should buy the machinery and experiment with it. The Navy Department and the Bureau of Steam Engineering were, however, rather favorably impressed with the general idea contained in the proposition, and a year or two later, under the administration of my predecessor, Rear Admiral (now captain) Hutch I Cone, when the machinery of two colliers was under consideration, it was decided to equip one of them with electric drive and the other with turbine reduction gear, which had been strongly recommended by Rear Admiral Melville, formerly Engineer in Chief of the Navy.

The collier *Jupiter* was the one designated to be equipped with electric drive. Her machinery was of about 7,000 horsepower, transmitted through two shafts; but, so far as the electric generator was concerned, she was in fact no better than a single-screw ship, because her entire power was concentrated in one generator. The machinery was built by the General Electric Co and installed on a "no-cure. no-pay" basis—i e, the General Electric Co. agreed to remove the electric machinery if it did not prove satisfactory on trial and in service for a limited period, and so carefully was this provision kept in mind that the propeller shafting and the steam piping, which were installed by the Government, were so arranged that no change would be necessary in them in case it should have been necessary to remove the electric machinery and install reciprocating engines

The *Jupiter* has now been in service more than seven years, and has never been inactive one day on account of her electric machinery. So much importance did the Navy Department attach to this installation that she was officered and manned by a naval instead of by a merchant crew, and was brought from the Pacific to the Atlantic in order that the most reliable information might be obtained in regard to the working of this machinery. So great was the interest of the Bureau of Steam Engineering in the success of this first installation that the chief of the bureau consented to the temporary detail of the assistant to the bureau, Capt. S. S. Robison, to command her in order that upon his return to the Bureau first-hand information might be available in a consideration of questions that might arise regarding this or future installations. For the same reason, Commander U. T. Holmes, at the time in charge of the Division of Design, was detailed as a member of the board to witness the final trials of the ship.

In this way the Navy Department had accumulated a mass of valuable information regarding the operation of electric machinery; and so satisfactorily had this first installation on the *Jupiter* proved that the Department, in 1914, decided that the information then available was sufficient to justify the installation of electric machinery in the battleship *New Mexico* (formerly *California*) building at the New York Navy Yard. Subsequent experience with the *Jupiter* confirmed the earlier impressions, and the decision of the Navy Department to continue such installations was the best kind of evidence that no difficulty had been experienced with her installation.

When it came to the design of the battle cruisers, for which the speed and power contemplated were far in excess of the speed and power of any ship afloat, the question as to the kind of machinery which should be installed was naturally one of the greatest concern. Information which had been received from abroad had shown the paramount necessity of giving under-water protection to ships such as had never been contemplated before. Fortunately, electrically operated machinery lent itself admirably to the conditions imposed by protection, besides which it also possessed other military advantages. It was therefore decided that electric machinery was the only type that could be installed and make these ships what it was desired they should be, and it may be safely said that the protection provided in their design is the greatest that human ingenuity c'ld devise without encroaching upon the space for the installed machinery

For similar reasons, the same type of machinery was included in the design for the four battleships that were carried in the act of August 29, 1916, and of the six authorized in the acts of March 3, 1917, and July 1, 1919 When bids were received for the four of the 1916 act, it was clear that the shipbuilders were unwilling to give the usual guaranties regarding the satisfactory operation of the machinery, but so confident was the Department of the great advantage to be secured by the use of electrical machinery that, after conference between the shipbuilders and the electrical firms, it was decided to make a change in the usual form of contract, whereby the Navy Department relieved the shipbuilder of responsibility for the machinery subsequent to a successful dock trial, and entered into a contract with the electric companies covering responsibility and performance during the usual contract period.

While these preliminaries were under discussion, and after the bids for the battle cruisers had been received, the inventor of the Curtis turbine sent the Secretary of the Navy a long telegram representing to him that a great mistake would be made if electric machinery were put in the battleships; that Great Britain was using geared turbine machinery, and that a commission should be appointed to investigate the whole subject before final decision was reached This was followed by a letter amplifying his telegram, and later by another letter addressed to the President of the United States covering practically the same ground Mr. Curtis also put in print substantially the same arguments that he advanced in his letter to the Secretary of the Navy.

The identical arguments used by Mr. Curtis were advanced by a prominent manufacturer of electrical apparatus who interviewed the Secretary of the Navy on the subject, and who later approached other officers of the Department and the chairman of the Naval Committees of Congress. Appeals were made to engineers of prominence to urge the Department to adopt mechanical reduction gear or at least to refer the question to a board of "impartial expert" engineers for decision as to the type of machinery to be used. Just where such a board could be found was not stated, and as the Navy Department was of opinion that the most expert electrical engineers were in the employ of the two big electrical companies to whom the construction of the machinery must necessarily be intrusted, it could hardly be held that representatives from those firms, however "expert" they might be, could be classed as "impartial." For the same reason, those who were behind the propaganda to compel the installation of mechanical reduction in these ships could not be put in this category. Obviously, the question was one for the Secretary of the Navy to decide, and the attitude of the Department is well expressed in Secretary Daniels's letter of March 26, 1917, to a prominent mechanical engineer who had yielded to importunities to address the Navy Department on the subect. The letter follows:

SIR: Receipt is acknowledged of your letter of March 21, in regard to the use of electric drive in our battle cruisers, from which I note that you do not consider that you are in a position either to commend or condemn the type of machinery that has been adopted.

For the past five months an industrious propaganda has been waged, by parties interested in mechanical reduction gear to have that type of machinery substituted for the electric drive, and it is a noteworthy fact that during that time only seven people other than you have yielded to the importunity of the propagandists to write to the Navy Department in protest of its action. Of those who have written, one was a chemist, one an editor, two electrical engineers, one a college professor, one a mechanical engineer, and one whose name can not be found in the list of members of the mechanical or electrical engineers and who seems to be unknown to prominent engineers—not one "eminent" engineer among them. I make this statement because of your prominence as an engineer, and in order that you may know how slow the engineers of the country have been to yield to the clamor of people who see fat royalties escaping them with the use of electric drive.

It is clear from your letter that you have not been fully informed in the matter, and in order that you may have better information than you now possess, I will say that the Navy Department has a number of competent engineers in its employ, that their method of approaching an untried scheme is the same as yours, and that it was followed to the letter in this case. In addition to this, we have the benefit and advice of the best engineering talent and experience of the large shipbuilding establishments and of the large electric companies, and the fact that every shipbuilding company that bid made a proposal for electric drive and only one a proposal for geared as well as electric drive, would seem to be abundant evidence that they have no doubt of the satisfactory operation of the latter. Even Mr ———, whom you quote (and whose experience in large undertakings I feel sure you would not substitute for that of the engineers of the large electric companies), when asked by me if he had any doubt of the satisfactory working of the electric machinery, answered that he had not.

I have given this full consideration to your letter because it so happens that you are the *only* mechanical engineer of prominence who has written me in regard to it, and also because I want you and the American people generally to know that I and the officers of the Navy concerned in the design of these ships are just as anxious that they shall be a success as you or anybody else, and probably more so than some of the interested people behind this propaganda. We feel confident that the ships will be a pronounced success, and that they will confound the very people who would deny to us the great advantage that will come from the experimental work that we have conducted during the last three years. They will have electric drive.

Very respectfully,

JOSEPHUS DANIELS,
Secretary of the Navy

A member of the Naval Consulting Board suggested to the chief of bureau that the matter be referred   opinion as to whether electric drive   these ships, but it was pointed out to him that nearly all the electrical engineers on the board were in the employ of one or the other of the two big companies who would be called upon to build the machinery, and that an opinion from the board in such a case would be open to the criticism that it was not unbiased. He was also informed that the Navy Department was satisfied, and that the only people who were not satisfied were those who were interested in the adoption of another type of machinery, and that as they were not in any manner responsible for the success of the ships as a military unit, the decision might well be left with those upon whom responsibility rested.

The type of machinery adopted is the only one that could be installed in the space available, and the only one that could give the protection which is considered a necessary feature of the design of the ship.

It should be remembered that when this decision was reached we had only the experience of one installation in a collier, but since then the *New Mexico* has been completed, and every report from her shows how superior her electric drive is to that of any other arrangement of turbine equipment that could have been devised.

The technical side of the question in its application to naval ships is of such interest and importance as to justify a brief recital. It is clearly recognized that in order to obtain economy in a turbine it must be operated at high rotational speed, and that to obtain the greatest efficiency from a propeller it should run at low speed. In order, therefore, to secure the most efficient combination an intermediate reducing mechanism must be introduced between the turbine and the propeller. Those that admit of application are either mechanical, electrical, or hydraulic, but there are so many objections to the latter that it may be dismissed from consideration.

With mechanical reduction gear for the large installations, such as those of battleships, the high-pressure and low-pressure turbines for each screw are arranged in series and mounted on separate shafts, each shaft carrying a pinion that engages a single reducing gear of large diameter keyed to the propeller shaft. Each low-pressure turbine shaft carries also an astern or backing turbine. The principal objection to this arrangement is the necessity for the backing turbine, which gives at best only about 40 per cent of full power, as considerations of weight and space forbid the use of a backing turbine of the same power as the ahead turbine. The result is a short turbine operating at low economy.

Consider now the electric combination, where the turbine is, as before, the primary source of power, but wherein instead of operating a screw propeller it operates an electric generator. The electric power thus developed is transmitted to motors attached to the propeller shafts, and the motors operated to turn the propellers ahead or astern. In other words, there is a central power plant for generating current, and this current is transmitted to the point of application of the power. There is no backing turbine, the reversal being accomplished with ease and certainty through the motors, and with this great advantage over the mechanical reduction—full power is always available.

In large installations it is possible to distribute the power amongst several units in such manner as to secure high economy at both full and cruising speeds.

The advantage which electric reduction gives over other types may be summed up in these:

Greater flexibility and control in the use of power.

Improved economy in every-day service and good economy at full speed.

Less liability to serious derangement.

Less likelihood of speed of ship being seriously affected in the event that turbines are injured.

Military superiority that comes from greater maneuvering power.

Military superiority due to improved underwater protection.

This extended statement is given because of the importance of the subject and because the design of machinery for these battleships and battle cruisers, authorized to meet war emergencies, represented a power equipment of no less than 1,560,000 horsepower, the battle cruisers alone accounting for 1,080,000 horsepower.

While activities of the Design Division were concerned chiefly with other types of ships, work on the battle cruiser design was carried on as opportunity offered, but no work was done on the ships themselves.

Work was prosecuted on the battleships *Mississippi* and *Idaho*, building by contract, and on the *Tennessee* and *California*, building at the navy yards, New York and Mare Island, respectively. The *Mississippi* was delivered December 18, 1917, but the *Idaho* was not completed until some time after the signing of the armistice.

The officers of the Design Division were:

In charge of division: Rear Admiral C. W. Dyson, U. S. Navy.

Computing section: Rear Admiral F. H. Bailey, U. S. Navy, retired.

Surface vessels except destroyers: Commander J. O. Richardson, U. S. Navy[2]; Commander S. M. Robinson, U. S. Navy; Lieut. Commander W. C. Owen, U. S. Navy; Lieut. (j g) T. M Brodie, U. S. Naval Reserve Force.

Destroyers: Lieut. Commander A. T. Church, U. S. Navy; Lieut. Commander F. W. Sterling, U. S. Navy, retired. Succeeded by Commander N. H Wright, U. S. Navy; Ensign P. L. Emerson, U. S. Naval Reserve Force.

Internal combustion engines. Commander J. O. Fisher, U. S. Navy; Lieut (j g.) G S Diehl, U S Naval Reserve Force; Lieut (j. g) R. P. Sanborn, U S Naval Reserve Force

Contracts Lieut. Commander F. W. Sterling, U. S. Navy, retired

SCOUT CRUISERS

That a design of machinery which is desirable in one type of ship may not be suited to the conditions that must be met in a different type is exemplified by the fact that the design for the scout cruisers, the contracts for six of which were let in July and August, 1917, is mechanical reduction gear and not electric reduction Although the horsepower of these ships is 90,000, the conditions of design and the limitations of space necessary to permit of all the military features to be embodied in the design made it impossible to install anything but a mechanically geared turbine The conditions were, in fact, almost identical with those met in destroyers.

Although the contracts were awarded a few months after the declaration of war, the urgent necessity for building destroyers and patrol vessels made it impossible to do any work of consequence on the machinery of these vessels until after the signing of the armistice.

DESTROYERS

Immediately upon the entry of the United States into the war it was determined to concentrate construction upon such types as were most necessary, taking into consideration the time required to construct such vessels The reports from our representative at the seat of war emphasized in the strongest terms possible the urgent need of destroyers and generally of small craft that might be utilized in combating the submarine It was, therefore, early determined that this emergency construction should consist of:

Destroyers,
Submarine chasers,
Small destroyers (eagles),
Cargo vessels,
Submarines,
Conversion of troop ships,
Conversion of repair ships,
Mine sweepers,
Seagoing tugs,
Harbor tugs,

and that the precedence should be as given above

---

[2] Until June 20, 1917
[3] Until June 1, 1917.

In order that there might be the maximum possible production, the following principles of action were formulated

1. The adoption of standard design covering general features of construction

2 The adoption of the smallest practicable number of detail designs of propelling machinery and auxiliaries, taking into consideration expansion of existing facilities

3. Study of materials of construction to determine where substitution of material could be made with the least possible sacrifice of efficiency

The act of August 29, 1916, authorized the immediate construction of 20 destroyers, the design of which had been well advanced at that date. The speed contemplated was 35 knots. This was an increase of 5 knots over that of preceding destroyers and involved the solution of many difficult problems before the design was finally determined upon

The contracts for these 20 vessels were let in November and December, 1917, and were quickly followed by additional orders as fast as building facilities permitted, until a total of 270 were under order whose construction was authorized subsequent to August 29, 1916, and prior to October 10, 1917. Of this number the order for 120 had been given prior to the act of October 6, 1917.

As additional orders were placed from time to time, propositions were made to build 30-knot and also 28-knot destroyers all with a view to increasing production; but as the design of those under construction was well standardized this Bureau insisted upon adhering to the 35-knot boat as involving the least element of delay When, however, in July, 1917, the Bethlehem Shipbuilding Corporation submitted a tentative proposition for the construction of 150, serious consideration was given to the adoption of a 28-knot boat, as Admiral Sims had reported that any speed in excess of 25-knots would be satisfactory The 28-knot speed was considered from the fact that the destroyers under contract could make that speed with two boilers instead of four. After closer investigation however, it was found that the construction of boilers was not the time-controlling factor, and in general consideration of the subject several conferences were held with shipbuilders and manufacturers of forgings, boilers, machinery, and equipment, at which all phases of the problem were discussed.

As a result of these conferences it was determined that the most difficult situation to be faced was the one of forgings for shafting. For 28-knots solid forgings could be used and forging facilities utilized which would not be available if hollow forgings were insisted upon. There were only two large forging establishments that could handle all the material that would be needed for 35-knot vessels, and a third that could make only the shaft forgings, but the two firms with facilities for making all the forgings were not keen to undertake their manufacture Both had large munition orders and preferred to continue that class of work. In fact great difficulty had been experienced in getting one of the companies to supply the forgings for which they had contract, for the destroyers building at Cramps and at the New York Shipbuilding Co., and it required some decisive action on the part of the chairman of the War Industries Board before the prompt completion of these contracts was assured. As it was contemplated to build the 150 destroyers in 18 months, it was clear that additional forging facilities would have to be provided to carry out this program.

The proposition submitted by the Bethlehem Shipbuilding Corporation contemplated the erection of a turbine building shop at Buffalo, a boiler shop at Providence, and extensions of the works of other firms closely affiliated with the successful completion of this unprecedented undertaking It was apparent that Bethlehem could not handle the entire number of vessels, and equally so that, if completed at all, the work would have to be done by those firms that were then building destroyers, and whose organization and experience were such as to justify confidence in the successful completion and operation of the vessels assigned them But every one of these establishments was working to full capacity, and some of them were subletting important portions of the machinery which ordinarily are completed in their own shops. In some cases, these subcontracts were given to people who were unfamiliar with the class of work they had undertaken, and this resulted in a reduced output from the scheduled requirement No assistance could be expected from other shipbuilders of experience as they were fully occupied with merchant work and with mine sweepers

After full consideration of all the difficulties that had to be overcome, the Department decided to ask authority of Congress to build 150 additional destroyers. This authority was granted in the act of October 6, 1916, and the distribution was made as follows:

 85 to Bethlehem Shipbuilding Corporation, of which 45 were to be built at Quincy and Squantum, Mass, and 40 at the Union Iron Works, San Francisco, Calif.
 25 to the William Cramp & Sons Ship and Engine Building Co
 20 to the Newport News Shipbuilding & Dry Dock Co, Newport News, Va
 20 to the New York Shipbuilding Corporation, Camden, N. J

Later on six more destroyers were assigned to the Mare Island Navy Yard and three to the Norfolk Yard Six had previously

CURTIS TURBINE FOR DESTROYERS, GENERAL ELECTRIC COMPANY.

CURTIS L. P. AND REVERSE TURBINE, BETHLEHEM SHIPBUILDING CORPORATION.

CRUISING TURBINE, GENERAL ELECTRIC COMPANY.

BLADING I. P. TURBINE, BETHLEHEM SHIPBUILDING CORPORATION.

TURBINE BLADING, BETHLEHEM CORPORATION.

TURBINE BLADING, BETHLEHEM CORPORATION.

L. P. TURBINE WHEEL, BETHLEHEM SHIPBUILDING CORPORATION.

been assigned to Mare Island and one to Charleston. The first consideration in the design of the machinery was reliability coupled with speedy construction, and next to that was simplification of design in order to meet the condition that was fast confronting us of a very much lower standard of efficiency in both commissioned and the enlisted personnel. The destroyer force, as it existed in April, 1917, had most efficient personnel, and the encomium heaped upon their performance bore ample testimony to this happy condition. As additional destroyers were built, the majority of the crews had, of necessity, to be made up of inexperienced men, and everything that was possible was done to make the machinery installation simple and easy of operation.

Standardization, where possible, was insisted upon and successfully accomplished with propellers, propeller shafts, turbine units, pumps, blowers, safety valves, evaporators and distillers, ice machines, electric generators, searchlights, and even in smaller details. Much credit is due the shipbuilders, who set aside many of their own standards in order to cooperate fully with the Bureau in reducing the number of types to a minimum.

The 45 destroyers assigned to be built at Fore River and at Squantum—which latter place, in the language of the architect of the buildings, existed originally only as "a good marsh"—were to be duplicates of other destroyers building by Bethlehem. The engines for some were to be constructed at Fore River, but the majority were assigned to the new shop at Buffalo, the erection of which proceeded under great difficulty on account of the unprecedentedly cold winter of 1917–18. So far as concerned machinery, Squantum was simply an assembly plant. The castings for the turbine casings were made at other points and shipped to Buffalo. About two-thirds of the boilers for the entire lot were built in the new shop at Providence, which was specially equipped for the manufacture of Yarrow boilers, and the remainder at Quincy.

In the case of the Union Iron Works destroyers, a new shop had been erected at Alameda in order to facilitate the construction of the destroyers already under contract, and it was hoped that this shop would also be able to handle the machinery of the 40 additional destroyers, but it soon became apparent that this source of supply could not be depended upon. Fortunately, the General Electric Co. had just completed at Erie, Pa., the erection of a building which would admirably serve the purpose of a turbine shop, and a contract was accordingly entered into with them for equipping the shop and for building the turbines for the entire lot of 40 destroyers. It is of interest to note that the order for this work was given 10 days before Congress authorized the construction of these vessels.

In order to make possible the construction of the boilers at San Francisco, it was necessary to rent for this purpose the old Risdon Iron Works, and to equip and incorporate it as a part of the Union Iron Works. All the boilers were of the Yarrow type.

The turbines for the Cramp destroyers were built by that company, and this construction was made possible only by the purchase on account of the Navy Department of the stock of the De La Vergne Machinery Co., of New York City, and of the transfer of the operation of the works to the Cramp company. For the turbines for the Newport News and the New York Shipbuilding Corporation destroyers, a contract was entered into with the Westinghouse Machinery Corporation, which sublet a large portion of the work to the Allis-Chalmers Co. Thus were enlisted the combined facilities of those two big engineering establishments in the production of these engines. The Newport News Co. had, in the case of previous destroyers, found it necessary to place contracts for important portions of the turbines with firms in the Middle West, but the results that had attended the production of this work had not been of such a character as to justify an extension of these contracts, and for that reason the last 20 destroyers built by this firm, as well as those built by the New York Shipbuilding Corporation, have turbines differing from those of preceding ones.

The Bath Iron Works was not assigned any of the last 150 destroyers, as they were fully occupied with the orders in hand at the time the new destroyers were authorized.

Boilers.—The boilers for the Cramp company, as also those for the Newport News company and the New York Shipbuilding Corporation, which were of the White Forster type, were built by the Babcock & Wilcox Co., Bayonne, N. J., whose works had to be greatly enlarged to meet the schedule of 20 boilers a month, which output was finally improved to such a degree that the production of a boiler a day was reached. This was accomplished only after overcoming many difficulties, and even necessitated the manufacture in their own works of certain machine tools which could be obtained by purchase only after a delay too great to be considered in the execution of the contract. It also necessitated the calling into service of a portion of the facilities of their works at Barberton, Ohio.

Pumps.—When it came to a consideration of the pumps required for so many vessels, it was found that all manufacturers were working to capacity on existing orders for the Navy Department and for the Shipping Board, and that the only way in which it would be possible to secure this equipment in time would be either to create new facilities or to enlarge existing plants. After a thorough survey of the situation, it was decided that the Blake & Knowles Works of the Worthington Pump Co. offered the best source of supply. These

PARSONS TURBINES IN COURSE OF MANUFACTURE AT CRAMP'S.

PARSONS TURBINES AT THE WILLIAM CRAMP & SONS SHIP AND ENGINE BUILDING COMPANY.

PARSON'S TURBINES AND REDUCTION GEARS AT CRAMP'S.

WESTINGHOUSE H. P. TURBINE.

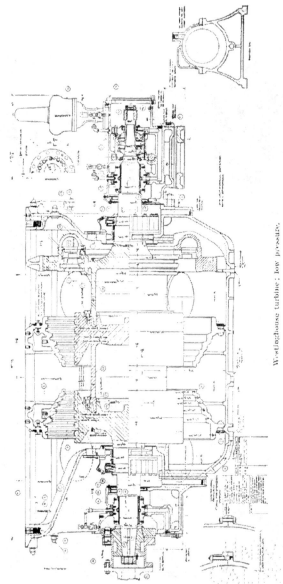

Westinghouse turbine; low pressure.

WHITE-FOSTER BOILERS, BABCOCK & WILCOX COMPANY.

WHITE-FOSTER BOILERS READY FOR INSTALLATION IN DESTROYERS.

PUMPS FOR DESTROYERS.

MANUFACTURING WORTHINGTON PUMPS FOR DESTROYERS.

PARTS OF PUMPS FOR DESTROYERS.

ASSEMBLING PUMPS, WORTHINGTON PUMP CO.

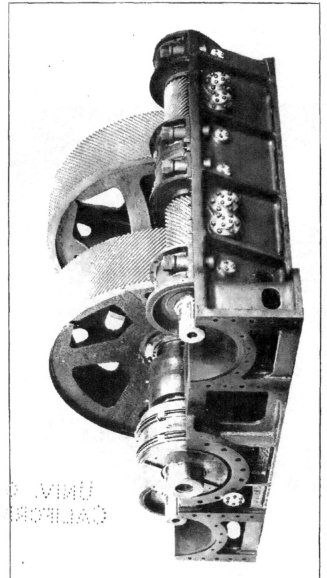

REDUCTION GEAR FOR DESTROYERS, THE FALK COMPANY.

WESTINGHOUSE REDUCTION GEAR UNDER TEST.

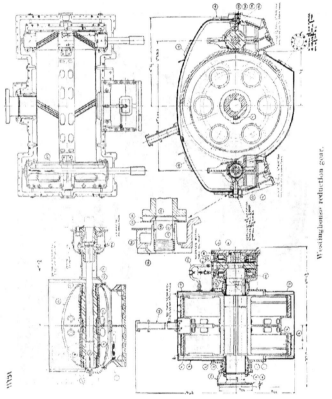

Westinghouse reduction gear.

REDUCTION GEAR FOR DESTROYERS, GENERAL ELECTRIC COMPANY.

works, in East Cambridge, Mass., were accordingly almost entirely remodeled and the order for all the pumps placed with that firm.

Reduction gear.—There is probably no other part of the machinery equipment that gave cause for greater concern during the construction of the entire destroyer program than did the reduction gears. So serious was the situation in this regard considered that immediately after the declaration of war our naval attaché in London was directed to make inquiry regarding the possibility of securing these gears in Great Britain. The reply was so unsatisfactory, involving the shipment of forgings from this country with consequent risk of loss of the rough material or of the finished gears during transport through the war zone, that the Bureau decided that the best results would be secured by obtaining abroad plans of the Parsons gear hobbing machine and building the machines in this country. The William Sellers Co., of Philadelphia, volunteered to undertake the work, but before the negotiations were concluded it was found possible, through the good offices of the British Commission, headed by Admiral de Chair, and the efforts of Admiral Sims, to secure entire machines in Great Britain. Even with these machines in prospect the time of delivery was so uncertain as to make necessary an enlargement of the works of the Falk Co., at Milwaukee, for cutting the gears of the destroyers allotted to the Fore River branch of the Bethlehem Corporation. At one time it was also contemplated to make a similar enlargement of the De Laval Steam Turbine Co.'s works at Trenton, N. J., where gears were cut for all the Cramp destroyers and for the first 10 assigned the New York Shipbuilding Corporation, but it was ultimately found possible to meet the required dates by slight additions to and modifications of existing equipment, and the plans for extension were therefore abandoned. The General Electric Co. and the Westinghouse company each cut the gears for the turbines which they manufactured, as did also Mare Island for the turbines built at that yard. For the earlier destroyers at Newport News, direct-driven turbines with cruising turbines were designed in order to lessen the demand for reduction gear, even though it involved a slight decrease in maximum speed.

Forced-draft fans.—Neither of the principal suppliers of fans could, with existing equipment, handle anything like the entire order, but it was found that by making slight additions and extensions to the works of the Sturtevant Co., at Hyde Park, Mass., this firm could supply fans for 105 destroyers, and that those for the remaining 45 could be furnished by the Terry Steam Turbine Co., of Hartford, Conn.

Evaporators and distillers.—The order for the entire outfit was placed with the Griscom-Russell Co., whose plant at M⸺ton, Ohio, had to be greatly enlarged to handle this work as well as the great volume intrusted to them for the account of the Shipping Board.

Propellers.—All propellers were manufactured by the William Cramp & Sons Ship and Engine Building Co, whose foundry was enlarged for their construction.

Boiler and condenser tubes.—For more than a year before we entered the war boiler tubes could be obtained only with difficulty In fact, there was only one firm on which the Department could rely to meet current demands The situation at one time became so acute that serious consideration was given to the advisability of requesting the President to place an embargo on the exportation of tubes. After war was declared, however, other firms were brought into line and a schedule established for delivery based on the capacity of each mill, so that a supply was assured for the earlier destroyers. This schedule was continued in effect for the new program, and little or no delay was experienced To accomplish this and at the same time meet the large demands of the Army and of the Allies, it became necessary for several of the larger mills to practically double their capacity.

A similar situation existed in regard to condenser tubes, but there was never that difficulty in obtaining them that prevailed with boiler tubes.

Forgings.—Because of the conditions previously mentioned, it was clear that the lot of 150 destroyers could not be built unless an enormous increase was made in the forging facilities of the country. There were many firms that could make solid forgings, and a few, besides the large ones referred to, who could make the smaller of the hollow forgings, but these few were so tied up with ordnance contracts for both the Army and the Navy that no assistance from them was to be thought of Accordingly the Department entered into contract with the Erie Forge Co. for the construction and equipment of an entirely new plant adjacent to their existing plant at Erie, Pa, and of capacity sufficient for handling the largest forgings for destroyers and also to manufacture gun forgings for the Bureau of Ordnance. This work was completed in the face of the most exasperating difficulties caused by weather, labor conditions, and delay in obtaining tool equipment, but the part it played in the construction of destroyers amply justified its erection

Lesser extensions of a similar character were made at the forge plant of the Allis-Chalmers Co., Milwaukee, at the Pollak Steel Co, Cincinnati, and at the Camden Forge Co., Camden. N. J., each of which did its part in supplying forgings for this big undertaking.

Miscellaneous.—All the safety valves were manufactured by the Consolidated Safety Valve Co., and a large number of the gate valves

CONDENSERS FOR DESTROYERS.
Wellman-Seaver-Morgan Co.

by the Edward Valve Co, Chicago, Ill Another firm in the Middle West, the Wellman-Seaver-Morgan Co, contributed to the manufacture of condensers and a great deal of sheet-metal work.

The electric generators, 25-kilowatt, were supplied by the General Electric Co. and the Westinghouse company, and the 24-inch high-power searchlights by the General Electric Co Loud speaking telephones of the Cory, Collophone, or Stentor type were installed in all these vessels.

The refrigerating apparatus was the product of the Clothel Co and of the Johns-Manville Co.

In what has preceded, mention has been made of some of the firms that contributed to the completion of the major portions of the work on the destroyers To mention all would be to mention many of the large as well as a large number of the small manufacturers of this country. The machine-tool manufacturers played a very important part, for the order for the last 150 destroyers came at a time when these establishments were working to capacity on war orders, and when the placing of an order with priority of delivery meant the displacing of another for war work, and the consequent interruption of orderly procedure in the shops Under the circumstances, it was but natural that conflict should arise regarding priority, but such cases were always decided by the Priorities Committee of the War Industries Board, upon which the Navy was represented by Rear Admirals N. E Mason and A V. Zane, and harmonious relations were preserved, though somebody was always disappointed

To Mr. S. W. Vauclain, the chairman of the War Industries Board, is due special mention for the vigorous manner in which he handled every important question that was brought to his attention, and especially for his untiring efforts in overcoming difficulties at some of the forging plants and in meeting what at one time threatened to be a serious situation in the production of boring lathes necessary in the manufacture of shafting

Production.—Forty-one destroyers were delivered between April 6, 1917, and November 11, 1918, of which the Bethlehem Shipbuilding Corporation delivered 20, 16 from Fore River, and 4 from the Union Iron Works. Cramp delivered 8, Bath Iron Works 5, Newport News 4, and Mare Island 4 At the time of the armistice, the destroyer production program was in full swing, and had the war lasted, the next three months would have witnessed their completion at the rate of at least 10 a month; but as soon as the armistice was signed working hours were reduced and every endeavor made to return to normal conditions An idea of the rate of production that had been reached may be inferred from the fact that 7 destroyers were delivered during the 19 days in November, 1918, that followed the signing of the armistice. In the number was the

Delphy, the first destroyer built at Squantum, which was delivered in a little more than 13 months from the time work was begun on constructing the shipyard where she was built, a record of which any firm might well be proud.

While all the shipbuilders that delivered destroyers worked with a will and cooperated to the fullest in the production of these terrors of the submarine, it is felt that on account of the magnitude of the work undertaken by the Bethlehem Shipbuilding Corporation, in supervising the construction and operation of the special plants and in the extension of their own plants, that firm is entitled to special mention, and that to Mr. J. W. Powell, the vice president, is due the credit for these undertakings.

This sketch of what was an unprecedented undertaking and performance would not be complete without mention of the names of the naval inspectors of machinery and of the chief engineers of the shipbuilding firms, as also those of the inspectors in the districts where material was fabricated They follow:

Bath Iron Works· Inspector, Commander E. H. De Lany, U S. Navy, retired; vice president and superintending engineer, Mr C P Wetherbee.

Bethlehem Shipbuilding Corporation: Inspectors, Rear Admiral George W McElroy, U S. Navy, at Quincy, Squantum, and Providence; Commander H. G. Leopold, U S. Navy, retired, at Union Iron Works, Lieut Commander E. C Oak, U S Naval Reserve Force, at Buffalo. Chief engineer, Mr. Robert Warriner.

Wm Cramp & Sons Ship & Engine Building Co . Inspectors, Rear Admiral R. T Hall, U S. Navy, at Philadelphia; Lieut Commander W. B Tardy U S Navy, at New York. Chief engineer, Mr. John F. Mettin

New York Shipbuilding Corporation. Inspector, Capt Gustav Kaemmerling, U S Navy. Chief engineer, Mr Philip Young.

Newport News Shipbuilding & Dry Dock Co · Inspector, Capt. Kenneth McAlpin, U. S Navy. Engineering director, Mr Charles F. Bailey

Mare Island Navy Yard: Engineer officer, Capt. C N. Offley, U S. Navy

Westinghouse Electric & Manufacturing Co : Lieut Commander C. A. Jones, U S Navy.

General Electric Co : Inspectors, Commodore John T. Newton, U S. Navy. retired, at Schenectady, N. Y ; Commander Goold H. Bull, U. S. Naval Reserve Force, at Erie, Pa

Allis-Chalmers Co., The Falk Co.. Inspector, Commander J. H. Rowen, U S Navy, retired

Babcock & Wilcox Co.. Inspector. Rear Admiral A. B Willits, U. S. Navy, retired.

The general inspector of machinery during this period was Rear Admiral W. M. Parks, U. S. Navy.

SUBMARINE CHASERS

Consideration had been given to the construction of patrol boats some time before our entry into the war, and as the design developed and inventory was taken of the building facilities and the demands that would be made on them for the production of other types of ships, it was decided that the adoption of gasoline engines would be most satisfactory for this type of boat as well as from the operating point of view. It was realized that the use of a gas-engine installation meant a large number of spare parts and replacements, and that in order to simplify supply and to avoid delay and confusion when repairs were needed there should be but one type of engine for all the boats.

The power required for the minimum permissible speed of these boats was 600 horsepower, and it was specially desirable that this power should be divided between two units. Here arose a serious question, there were no dependable gas engines of 300 horsepower on the market that could be put in quantity production and meet the dates of readiness contemplated for the hulls, which were to be constructed by builders of wooden boats. Many enthusiastic would-be contractors appeared ready to guarantee efficiency of engines of 300 and even of 400 horsepower, but when brief investigations were made it was found that their engine was either a mere idea, or that, at best, it existed on paper. Some of these enthusiasts were eager for the Bureau to embark upon a gigantic scheme of developing an engine in accordance with their ideas and it was with difficulty that they were made to understand that there was no time either for development or experiment, that what was wanted was an engine in being and one which had demonstrated its efficiency and reliability. This they were, of course, unable to produce.

The Bureau of Steam Engineering early in March, 1917, invited those builders of engines whose product was well known, and whose facilities for construction might be readily expanded, to send representatives to confer regarding the machinery equipment, and after careful consideration of all the features involved in the design, construction, and rapid production, decided to adopt the "Standard" engine of 220 horsepower. This meant the installation of three engines instead of two, with all the disadvantages attendant upon the multiplication of units. However, the advantages to be realized seemed so greatly to outweigh this one disadvantage that no hesitation was to be thought of. The engines had been well tried over several years of service and had also given satisfactory performance in the British 80-foot patrol boats, of which 550 had been built. The manufacturers were just completing the last British and a small Italian order, their shops and those of others upon whom they relied for important parts were equipped for quantity production; and they could proceed immediately with our work. Accordingly, contract was entered into April 2, 1917, with the Standard Motor Construction Co. for the construction of 150 sets of machinery, each set consisting of three engines and an auxiliary engine. This was soon followed by other orders until the total number of engines under contract rose to more than 1,400.

The engine is 6-cylinder, 4-cycle, air starting and reversing, with cylinders 10 inches diameter and 11 inches stroke, provided with an air compressor mounted on its after end whose piston is actuated by an eccentric on the engine shaft. The design contemplated the development of 220 horsepower with 350 revolutions of the engine.

The auxiliary engine, which is a very important part of the equipment, operates a fire and bilge pump, a circulating pump, a gasoline pump, an electric generator, and an emergency air compressor. It is a 2-cylinder engine, with cylinders $4\frac{1}{4}$ inches diameter and $5\frac{1}{2}$ inches stroke.

The propellers were designed by the Bureau of Steam Engineering and built by the Columbia Bronze Corporation and the American Manganese Bronze Corporation.

In preparing the general arrangement of machinery, it was thought that as these boats were to operate in the war zone heating apparatus might be dispensed with, as every pound added to the equipment would seriously affect the speed, which was none too high; but as many of them were retained on the Atlantic coast, it required only a short experience of winter conditions to show the necessity for heating them. As quickly as it could be obtained a hot-water heating system was installed in those in service and also in those whose construction had not been completed.

When the order originally placed was more than doubled, the contractors found it necessary to sublet more of the work with other firms than was at first contemplated. In the completion of these engines and in the endeavor to reach the expected production of 10 sets a week, much of the important work was done by the Lyons-Atlas Co., Indianapolis, Ind. The final assembly was, however, made by the Standard company, and the tests conducted at their works. These tests were for economy as well as power, and were of three hours' duration. Besides this, 1 set of engines in 20 was subjected to a continuous nonstop test of 24 hours' duration. By this procedure it was felt that there could be little question of the reliability of every engine shipped to a building yard.

SUB CHASER ENGINE. STANDARD MOTOR CONSTRUCTION COMPANY.

SUB CHASER ENGINES.

As work on the chasers progressed, it became apparent that the engines would not be ready as soon as the hulls, and although the contractor gave every assurance that the engines would not be delayed, subcontractors were so dilatory that eventually it became necessary for the Bureau to put its production section behind the orders for material and to insist upon prompt deliveries. This organization, supplemented by the work of the inspectors of engineering material, soon produced the desired results, and thereafter work progressed favorably and engines were supplied as required for installation in the hulls.

An idea of the speed of production may be had from a consideration of the fact that in May, 1917, the first set of three engines was tested, in June, 5 sets, in August, 9 sets; from which time it steadily increased, until in November 55 sets were tested, followed by 53 in December, notwithstanding the fact that the inspector reported many obstacles in the way of quantity production, such as delay in railroad transportation, the holiday season, accident to traveling crane, and delay in truck service on account of bad roads, and concluded with the statement that "the situation is not improving, but getting worse."

The Bureau of Navigation early established at Columbia University, New York City, a gas-engine school for the instruction of the engine personnel destined for these vessels, and this Bureau co-operated in the work by supplying two complete units for the purpose.

The *Hannibal* and the *Leonidas*, which were converted to tenders for these chasers, were fully equipped with machine tools, spare parts, and gas-engine supplies so that any repair or replacement might be undertaken. Minor modifications and improvements were made in the design from time to time, as experience seemed to dictate, but the performance of the machinery in general was very satisfactory, and its maintenance in operating efficiency was facilitated by reason of the fact that there was but one design for the entire flotilla.

The inspector of machinery at the works of the contractors was Rear Admiral William N. Little, U. S. Navy, and the conduct of the work on their part was under the direction of Mr. Eugene A. Riotte, the president of the company.

An idea of the reliability of the machinery of these little vessels may be obtained from a statement of the commanding officer of one of the three that were sent from Lisbon to Archangel, "that for 53 days they operated without repair ships or bases, and covered a distance of 6,950 miles," a truly remarkable performance for such craft. Regarding the last 5,600 miles he concludes by saying that

The performance of the boats during this period of running was excellent They averaged 3,400 miles per month until reaching Christiania, and during the entire period away from England there was not a single breakdown or delay for a chaser. They received no outside assistance for repair or overhaul

The latter part of this run, when unhampered by the tanker that had accompanied them, and which limited the speed of the chasers, was made at an average speed of 12 9 knots for 370 miles.

Another evidence of the reliability of the machinery was supplied by the experience of 12 that came all the way from Puget Sound to Charleston, S. C., a distance of about 5,600 miles on their own resources, without repair or mother ship, and for the greater part of the voyage without a supply vessel These boats upon reaching the Atlantic coast reported ready and were immediately assigned to duty with a convoy

The climax of the war service of the chasers came in a race from Bermuda to New York, participated in by six that had seen service in the Mediterranean, the time of the winner, *No. 131,* being 56 hours and 56 minutes, which was an excellent performance.

Other features in the engineering equipment of these boats are not less interesting than the main propulsion machinery. When originally projected they were regarded primarily as patrol craft. The defense nature of the antisubmarine warfare had led to the assignment of every available craft of every type able to keep the sea to the work of patrol, and large fleets of motor boats had been constructed by the Allies for this purpose.

By the time the earliest subchasers were approaching completion the development of submarine detection devices and antisubmarine weapons had reached such a stage that the long-sought means for direct and practicable offensive action against submarines appeared to be in sight. The first chasers to be completed were accordingly assigned to experimental work along this line, and progress was so rapid and promising that the mission of the whole class underwent a radical change As patrol vessels, their mission would have been to provide security in certain limited areas by virtue of their employment in such large numbers that no submarine could come to the surface without subjecting itself to attack, or having the news of its whereabouts immediately broadcasted. As they were finally sent into service they represented units of three boats each, equipped and trained to detect submerged submarines within a wide area, to follow them through all changes of course, gradually closing their distance until, finally, at close quarters an accurate determination of the submarine's location afforded the opportunity for effective depth-charge attack

The development of the detection devices was in itself one of the most satisfactory and notable achievements of the war; its story is told in another place. Possession of these devices would undoubtedly have multiplied the value of the chasers as simple patrol boats, but much more was necessary in order to transform them into real *hunting* groups. An intricate problem in tactics was involved, and its solution depended upon achieving a speed of communication between boats and a celerity in making certain navigational computations that had never before been approached in any other phase of naval activity. A satisfactory but difficult method of visual signaling for both day and night was finally devised, but it was the successful development by the Western Electric Co of a suitable wireless telephone that brought about the ideal solution

It is interesting in this connection to recall that the Navy Department had actively cooperated with the Western Electric Co in the development of the wireless telephone, and that the question of installing it on board large naval vessels had been discussed by the Navy Department several years previously The Bureau recommended against the project at that time, in view of the undeveloped nature of existing apparatus and the general conditions affecting radio communication, but suggested the necessity of continuing development work and pointed out that the most important field for its use would probably be found in connection with a concerted attack by destroyers or other small craft in close formation. It was exactly this necessity which brought forth the first satisfactory type of apparatus for naval use, and the chasers were the first naval vessels regularly equipped with this device. These little newcomers into the war zone had scarcely exhibited themselves to their somewhat patronizing colleagues, the destroyers and larger vessels, before the demand for similar equipment poured in upon the Bureau in a flood—from our Allies as well as from our own forces

It was extremely interesting to note the effect produced upon naval officers of all nationalities when inspecting these craft for the first time. As one feature after another was exhibited and explained—the very complete main-engine equipment with its auxiliaries; the three or four types of detection apparatus; the special signaling lights and other signaling equipment; the radio telegraph for distant communication and the radio telephone for tactical work; the novel armament and navigational devices, and the arrangement for messing, berthing, and heating—it became quickly apparent that these were no ordinary motor launches, but miniature ships, comparable in the intricacy and completeness of their equipment to imposing men-of-war of the line An expression that was frequently used by English-speaking visitors to sum up their admiration of this novel creation was "A perfect box of tricks " and its equivalent was heard in several f... ... W... admiration was the controlling sent'... ... ... it there were reservations of judgment with respect to the practicability in service of so elaborate a mechanical equipment. It is the more gratifying to the Bureau, therefore, that the war history of these vessels presents a record of mechanical performance, with respect to every feature under its cognizance, that would have been creditable to a project worked out under the most favorable conditions of peace-time development

THE EAGLES

As the war progressed it became apparent that a type of patrol vessel somewhat smaller than the present destroyers and larger than the submarine chasers, but without the speed of the destroyer would fill an important place in the destruction of enemy submarines. The development of new devices for detecting the presence of submarines and locating their position made it highly desirable that vessels specially adapted to the practical application of these devices be built. As in the case of the submarine chasers, the chief desiderata in connection with them were that they should be of such design as would admit of speedy construction and at places where their construction would not affect the labor engaged in destroyer work. This naturally pointed to the Gulf, the Mississippi River, or the Lakes, and to a firm that possessed a complete executive, engineering, and production organization, and preferably to one accustomed to "repeat" work

As a preliminary to placing the contract for such vessels, there had been in preparation the design of a vessel in which the following features were emphasized

(a) The design of a complete installation by the Department.

(b) The adoption of plans such as would permit of quick production by more or less inexperienced shipbuilders.

(c) Use of a type of machinery that would operate with little or no noise.

(d) Means for instantaneously stopping all machinery in order to listen for submarines

(e) Use of the facilities of the manufacturing plants of the middle west which had been engaged in the production of commercial materials

(f) Complete supervision of all details of design by the technical Bureaus concerned

While a design in conformity with this general plan was in course of preparation, the Ford Motor Co., in December, 1917, made a tentative proposition to the Department to build vessels of this general type. The Department acted promptly in the matter and requested the Ford company to send their experts to confer with the bureaus

The first conference was held December 27, 1917, followed by others on the 28th and 31st, and on January 12, 1918, at which the Ford representatives were given advice regarding the vessel and her machinery and were assured that the bureaus would furnish all information necessary and assist in every way in the preparation of the general and the detail plans. The result was a definite proposition from the Ford company on January 14, 1918, followed by an order from the Department January 17, 1918, for the construction of 100 such vessels, which was later increased to 112 in order to supply 12 to the Italian government.

The design contemplated a vessel 200 feet in length and of 500 tons trial displacement, under which condition the speed desired was 18 knots. To secure this speed, the following special machinery was developed:

An express type water-tube boiler of 1,500 square feet of heating surface, there being two of these for each vessel.

An impulse turbine of 2,500 S. H. P. driving a propeller through the medium of planetary reduction gear having a ratio of 4,000 to 475 revolutions per minute.

Rotary pumps for all purposes where experience had demonstrated that pumps of that type would be satisfactory.

The remainder of the machinery and the electrical equipment would be of the usual type.

Following the award of contract, work on the general and detail plans was prosecuted vigorously, often until late hours of the night, and as soon as they were ready were placed in the hands of the builders.

It should be borne in mind that the Ford Motor Co. had never built a turbine, nor for that matter any kind of floating craft, and the fact that the turbines constructed by them successfully passed every shop and service test is eloquent as to the excellent engineering organization of this company.

The turbines themselves and the reduction gear were from the design of the Poole Engineering Co., Baltimore, Md., which the Bureau had selected as being the combination best suited to the conditions under which these vessels were designed to operate. Having had no experience with turbines, it was but natural that the Ford company should be more or less solicitous as to the successful operation of this design, especially as it had been represented to them that there was danger of the rupture of the casing at high speed on account of the enormous stress due to centrifugal force. The shop test of the first turbine, however, served to set at rest these fears and to confirm the judgment of the Bureau, though the manner in which this was brought about would not have been desired. In shutting down the turbine, the operator neglected to shut off steam before releasing the load, with the result that the turbine "ran away" and completely wrecked the casing. The revolutions were estimated to have reached 8,000 per minute. The condition in which everything else was found was such as to set at rest the fears of the contractors and to inspire absolute confidence in the strength of the turbine as a whole.

Some of the boilers were built in the works of the Ford Motor Co., but the majority were constructed by the Brennan Boiler Works, Detroit, and the auxiliary machinery and equipment by the same firms that specialized in similar work for destroyers.

The trials of the first of these vessels were naturally watched with more than ordinary interest—an unusual design of hull and machinery, and built by a firm that hitherto had built nothing but automobile cars—would not ordinarily give expectation of a successful outcome without many modifications and tests. But so carefully had the details been worked out, and so well had the work been done, that *Eagle No 1* went through her official trial in a most satisfactory manner, realizing a speed of 18.3 knots for four hours in shallow water. The operation of the machinery was in every way satisfactory, the board reporting on the noiseless feature of operation in the following terms:

This machinery plant was especially designed for quiet running and freedom from vibration, and this has been obtained in a marked degree, by the substitution of direct turbine drive for geared and reciprocating drive in auxiliaries.

Inasmuch as comparatively few of these vessels had been delivered at the time of the armistice, it was desirable to discontinue the construction of those for which the fabrication of material had not proceeded too far. The survey which was made at the time showed that work on the machinery was far advanced; engines were completed for 71 boats, while those for 28 others were 50 per cent completed, and the material for the remaining 13 was on hand and 10 per cent fabricated. The boilers for 22 had been completed, and those for 20 more finished up to the point of assembly; material for the remainder was on hand and about 35 per cent fabricated. The auxiliary machinery, which forms a large part of the cost in small vessels, was ready for 67 boats, and the material for the remainder was on hand and about 75 per cent fabricated. Consideration of this condition and of the work on the hulls led to a decision to complete 60 boats and cancel the contract for the remaining 52.

That these vessels would have successfully filled the rôle assigned them in our campaign against the submarine is the judgment of all officers familiar with their design, their construction, and their performance under way.

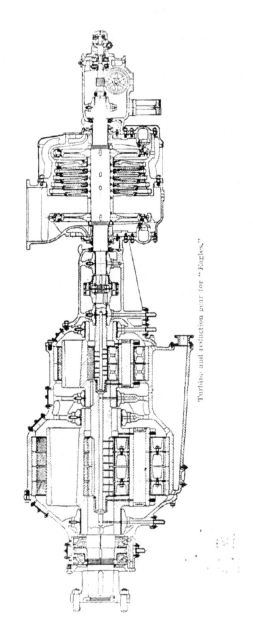

Turbine and reduction gear for "Eagles"

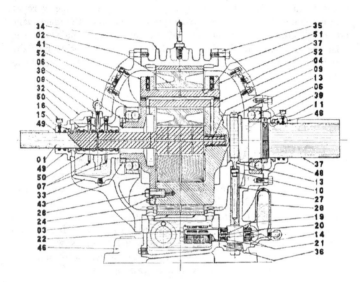

REDUCTION GEAR FOR EAGLE ENGINES.

The office of inspector of machinery was filled by Commander Carlos Bean, U. S. Navy, whose judgment and experience were of great assistance to the contractors in the production of the machinery and its installation. On the part of the contractors, the work was under the direction of Mr. William Mayo, the chief engineer of the company, whose broad engineering experience contributed greatly to the success of the undertaking.

MINE SWEEPERS AND TUGS

Our Navy was woefully lacking in mine sweepers and tugs when we entered the war, and reports from our representative abroad pointed to the necessity for building vessels of this type. Of mine sweepers we had none, and powerful seagoing tugs were often sadly needed in the war zone, where it was possible to save many a valuable torpedoed ship and cargo, which for lack of such auxiliaries would become a total loss.

To meet these requirements contracts were early let for 36 mine sweepers, which number was later increased to 54, and for 23 seagoing tugs. Their construction was intrusted to firms which had been engaged in building similar craft and which were not employed on other work for the Navy, as well as to two of our navy yards.

In each case the design of machinery followed the best commercial practice. The engine was one that had been well tried out in service, and the boilers were standard marine type, being of the Babcock & Wilcox type for the mine sweepers and of the Scotch type for the tugs. As the engine selected for the mine sweepers had been built by the Harlan & Hollingsworth branch of the Bethlehem Shipbuilding Corporation, arrangements were made with that firm for preparation of the detail plans and of the orders for material, as well as for the machining of a considerable part of the work and for its subsequent shipment to the several building yards. Much of the machining was also done at the navy yard, Philadelphia, not only for the mine sweepers built at that yard but also for those constructed elsewhere. The result was absolute standardization and duplication of equipment in each vessel.

Many of these vessels rendered excellent service in the arduous and dangerous work of sweeping up the mines of the North Sea barrage after the signing of the armistice, and in other activities incident to the war.

A similar method of construction was followed in the case of the tugs, except that each building yard was responsible for the production of its own material and for its machining.

The construction of the mine sweepers was intrusted to the following firms.

Alabama Dry Dock Co., Mobile, Ala
Baltimore Dry Dock & Shipbuilding Co., Baltimore, Md
Chester Shipbuilding Co., Chester, Pa.
Gas Engine & Power Co, Morris Heights, N. Y
New Jersey Dry Dock & Transportation Co, Elizabethport, N J
Pusey & Jones Co., Wilmington, Del.
Standard Shipbuilding Corporation, Port Richmond, N Y.
Staten Island Shipbuilding Co, New York
Sun Shipbuilding Co, Chester, Pa
Todd Shipyard Corporation, New York.
Navy yard, Philadelphia, Pa.
Navy yard, Puget Sound, Wash.

The inspector of machinery at the Harlan & Hollingsworth plant was Capt. W C Herbert U S Navy retired, who was also inspector at the following building yards: Chester Shipbuilding Co., Pusey & Jones Co, and the Sun Shipbuilding Co. The inspectors at the other building yards were

Commodore F H Eldridge, U S. Navy, retired, at Gas Engine & Power Co, New Jersey Dry Dock & Transportation Co, Standard Shipbuilding Corporation, Staten Island Shipbuilding Co., and Todd Shipyard Corporation

Commander C E. Rommel, U. S Navy, retired, at Baltimore Dry Dock Co

Lieut Commander H. S. Burdick, U S Navy, and Lieut. (T) Chauncey R Doll, U. S. Navy, at the Alabama Dry Dock Co.

At the Philadelphia and Puget Sound Navy Yards, by the engineer officers Capt. C A. Carr, U S. Navy, and Commanders W B Wells and M E Reed, U S Navy.

The seagoing tugs were built by:
American Shipbuilding Co, Buffalo, N. Y.
Ferguson Iron & Steel Co, Buffalo, N Y
Seattle Construction & Dry Dock Co, Seattle, Wash.
Staten Island Shipbuilding Co, New York
Navy yard, Puget Sound

The inspection at Buffalo was under the direction of Commodore George R. Salisbury, U S Navy, retired, that at Seattle under Commander W W Bush, U S Navy, retired, and that at Puget Sound under the engineer officer of the yard, Commander M E. Reed, U S Navy

In addition to the seagoing tugs, there were also constructed 40 wooden harbor tugs of standard design, the necessity for whose construction was daily growing on account of congested conditions in our principal ports. They were built by a number of small-boat builders, some of whom had built submarine chasers, and by the navy yards, Charleston, S. C., and New Orleans, La.

SUBMARINES.

The insufficiency in numbers of our submarines was keenly felt even before we declared war, and many of the 37 boats in service were of such an obsolete type as to reduce the number of effectives to less than one-half that number. Nearly all of these were equipped with 2-cycle engines, which had proved unreliable in service and, therefore, could not be depended upon for an active campaign. There were, however, 25 others under construction, some of them nearing completion, the reliability of whose machinery was unquestioned; but in order adequately to strengthen this arm of the service, Congress, in the act of August 29, 1916, authorized the immediate construction of 27 coastal submarines and 3 seagoing ones. Contracts for these were awarded in December, 1916, and January, 1917, and for 48 others a few months thereafter. Clauses were inserted in the contracts which authorized the payment of a bonus for speedy construction; and although none of this program was actually delivered during the war, the completion of the first lot followed rapidly thereafter.

In addition to these submarines of the R and S types, there were completed at the navy yard, Puget Sound, and delivered before the signing of the armistice four submarines of the H type, with two more following within two weeks. These were purchased in "knocked down" condition, having been originally intended for the Russian Government, and were assembled at Puget Sound.

The engines in all the boats delivered during the war are of a thoroughly reliable type, in which no experimental features were introduced, and they measured up to every expectation.

The total horsepower of the 84 submarines of the new program that were under construction in 1917 and 1918 is 115,480, which is nearly twice as great as the horsepower of those that were in commission at the time of the armistice.

The sources of supply of the engines installed in these boats were the New London Ship & Engine Co., New London, Conn., and the Busch Sulzer Diesel Engine Co., St. Louis, Mo. The inspector of machinery at the former was Lieut. Holbrook Gibson, U. S. Navy, and at the latter, Commander Louis Shane, U. S. Navy. The installation of machinery at the building yards was under the direction of the inspector of machinery, Rear Admiral George W. McElroy, U. S. Navy, with Lieut. C. M. Cooke, jr., U. S. Navy, specially detailed for this work, at Fore River, Lieut D. C Laizure, U. S. Navy, at the Lake Torpedo Boat Co.; Lieut Commander I H. Mayfield, U. S. Navy, at the California Shipbuilding Co.; and the engineer officer of the yard, Commander M E. Reed, at the Puget Sound Navy Yard.

The storage batteries were supplied by the Electric Storage Battery Co and the Gould Storage Battery Co, and the inspection was carried out under the direct supervision of Lieut L C. Dunn, of the Philadelphia inspection office

Because of the unsatisfactory operation of the engines installed in the early submarines, all of which were of a different design, and each more or less experimental, contracts were entered into before the war for new engines of a standard design for the boats of the F class and during the war new engines, also of a standard design, were provided for those of the H and K classes Some of these engines were obtained by purchase, but most of them were built in navy yards under license from the New London Ship & Engine Co Owing, however, to the fact that the boats could not be spared from the duty upon which they were engaged, installation of these new engines was not made until after the armistice The net result has been to transform 10 unreliable boats into serviceable submarines that can be depended upon to perform any service required, although the transformation was accompanied by a slight reduction in maximum speed This is, however, of little consequence compared with the reliability that has been secured

New batteries were ordered in sufficient quantity to meet any demand, and thin plate batteries installed in some cases Equipment was also supplied for the bases established at San Pedro, Calif, and to Coco Solo, Canal Zone, as also a large supply for the boats stationed at the Azores and in British waters.

ELECTRICAL.

The electrical work of the Bureau that was not associated with the design of new ships comprehended as great a volume of work relatively as did that of the corresponding mechanical engineering division, and this work was also equally as diversified. In searchlights, it involved mechanical control, the introduction of high-power lights, the substitution of incandescent signaling lights for the old Ardois system, and the equipment of submarines, patrol boats, and other auxiliary vessels.

By far the most important work done was that in connection with fire control, which was, of course carried out in cooperation with the Bureau of Ordnance, and involved all circuits, telephones, call bells, and voice-tube leads. Not only had new ships to be equipped with the latest system, but systems had to be developed for the older ships and for all vessels of the Coast Guard and other Government departments, as well as for the auxiliary and patrol vessels. The changes required in fire-control systems resulting from the information that was acquired after we entered the war, and also in conformity with the recommendations of the Turret Board, were of such extent as to make necessary the sending to the battleships at Base 2 of working details from navy yards in order to prevent congestion at the yards, and also that the services of the mechanics of the ships might be utilized in expediting the work of alteration.

Auxiliary lighting systems were developed, as were also signal and recognition lights, and cruising lights for vessels in convoy.

Loud-speaking telephones were supplied to capital ships and telephones developed for aircraft use.

Six months or more before we became a belligerent, a survey was made of our probable requirements and of the sources of supply, as stated elsewhere, and we were, therefore, ready to act promptly and effectively when war was declared. One of the greatest problems that confronted us was that of obtaining an adequate supply of wire and cable, and it was only after a conference with 15 of the largest manufacturers, in which the Bureau of Supplies and Accounts also participated, that a satisfactory solution of the difficulty was effected. Thereafter the supply was apportioned in such a way that no delay was experienced in obtaining wire as it was needed.

Other matters which came under the direct supervision of the Electrical Division were storage batteries and electric motors for submarines, and submarine detection, both of which are treated separately.

The officers of the Electrical Division were:
Commander G W. S. Castle, U. S. Navy, in charge
Commander L S. Thompson, U S. Navy, retired.[4]

Fire-control section: Lieut. Commander Alex. Sharp, U. S. Navy; Lieut Commander A. M Charlton, U S. Navy; Lieut. (T) W A Mason, U. S Navy; Lieut T. P. Lovelace, U. S. Naval Reserve Force; Lieut. W H Smith, U. S Naval Reserve Force; Ensign H R. Adams, U. S. Naval Reserve Force

Searchlight section: Lieut Commander C S Bookwalter, U. S Naval Reserve Force[5]; Lieut Commander Gerald Howze, U S Navy, retired, Lieut R. Kelly, U. S. Naval Reserve Force; Lieut. R M. Knight, U. S. Naval Reserve Force; Ensign J. C. Small. U S Naval Reserve Force.

Submarine section: Lieut. Commander F. A Daubin, U S. Navy[6]; Lieut. Commander A. H. Gray, U. S. Navy; Lieut Commander G. A Rood, U. S. Navy.

Submarine detection: Lieut. Commander G K. Calhoun (M C), U S. Navy; Lieut. A Davis, U S. Naval Reserve Force.

Repair section: Capt. C. H Johnson. U. S. Coast Guard; Lieut H. A. Gosnell, U. S. Naval Reserve Force.

Supply section: Lieut Commander H H J. Benson, U S Navy[7]; Lieut. (T) W. A. Vick, U. S. Navy; Lieut. H. T. Benzing, U S Naval Reserve Force; Lieut E. J. Carroll, U. S. Naval Reserve Force, Lieut Darrow Sage, U S. Naval Reserve Force Lieut H. H Stirling, U. S. Naval Reserve Force; Lieut L S Webster, U S. Naval Reserve Force Lieut. B. J. Caldwell. U. S Naval Reserve Force; Ensign E. B Janvrin, U S. Naval Reserve Force; Gunner W M. Evans, U. S. Naval Reserve Force.

---

[4] Until May 17, 1917
[5] Until Sept. 27, 1917.
[6] Until Dec 7, 1917
[7] Until Aug 18, 1917.

SUBMARINE DETECTION.

No work undertaken during the war was attended by greater interest than that conducted under the general direction of the Bureau on the development of devices for the detection of submarines. The one subject that transcended all others in public interest and in the magnitude of the financial consideration involved was the destruction of allied merchant tonnage, which at the time we entered the war had reached such a figure as to cause the greatest apprehension regarding the ability of the Allies to maintain a supply of munitions for the troops in France.

Even before we declared war on Germany, the Bureau had investigated some detection devices which appeared to possess merit, and even some which were not in this category, but whose promoters had made such statements as to what had been accomplished with them as to leave no course open except to test them under the conditions that prevail in service. The results were almost without exception such as to stamp the particular device as unsuited to the special purpose of detecting submarines.

Our submarine force operating off Pensacola, Fla., during January, February, and March, 1917, carried out tests and investigations of all available listening devices, which were those of the Submarine Signal Co. These tests were conducted to determine the range of these devices under different service conditions. Submerged submarines listened to surface vessels of different types as well as to other submarines, and tests were carried out from surface craft listening to submerged submarines. It was determined from these tests that the submarine offered a better listening station than the surface craft, and that with the devices then available the probability of successfully detecting submerged submarines was rather remote.

On March 5, 1917, the National Research Council, through the chairman of its Anti-submarine Committee, Dr. R. A. Millikan (later lieutenant colonel in the Signal Corps) proposed to the Bureau a plan for the further development of a detecting device which the Bureau had previously tested with negative results, and acting on the suggestion of Dr. Millikan the chief of bureau authorized him to express to the Western Electric Co. the desire of the Bureau that they assist in its development. The interest of the Western Electric Co. was immediately enlisted and continued.

About the same time conferences were held between the Submarine Signal Co. and the Western Electric Co on the general subject of submarine detection and its bearing on certain experimental work which the latter was carrying on in the vicinity of Fortress Monroe for the Coast Artillery In this work, the Western Electric Co. had planned a fundamental study of the disturbances actually given off by a submarine and an analysis of other disturbances of a like nature that might be encountered.

Magnetic detection had been proposed from many quarters; and in order to set at rest the value of this method, the Bureau, in May, 1917, assembled in Washington a group of scientists to consider the question The members of this group, who served without remuneration other than actual expenses, were suggested by Dr Millikan, of the National Research Council, and were: Prof Ernest Merritt, of Cornell University, Prof. A. C. Lunn, of the University of Chicago; Prof. H. A. Bumstead, of Yale University; Dr. L. A Bauer, of the Carnegie Institution, Washington, D. C ; and Mr. W. H. Nichols, of the Western Electric Co. After a theoretical investigation of the various projects that might appear to offer some success in locating submarines, this committee submitted nine methods which might be employed, a few of which they considered of enough importance to justify practical investigation and development. The general tenor of their conclusions, unanimously reached, was that magnetic detection has a very limited range, and it was, therefore, decided that this method of detection was not the one to pursue in attempting to overcome the submarine menace.

Amongst other problems that had been presented to the Naval Consulting Board was that of finding a practical submarine detection device, and in their efforts to accomplish this they appealed to the Submarine Signal Co., who expressed a willingness to proceed with the construction of a station for the development of devices for detecting submarines from fixed stations along the coast The Naval Consulting Board, by resolution of March 10, 1917, expressed appreciation of this action

The Submarine Signal Co. proceeded immediately with the construction of a station at Nahant, Mass , which was completed April 7, 1917, when that company and representatives of the General Electric Co began active work.

Upon the recommendation of the Chief of Bureau of Steam Engineering the Secretary of the Navy invited the General Electric Co., the Western Electric Co , and the Submarine Signal Co., to send representatives to Washington on May 8, 1917, for a conference on the subject, with a view to securing the active cooperation of the three companies. Following this conference, representatives of the Western Electric Co joined the representatives of the other companies at Nahant and proceeded with the work of developing detection devices.

Another result of this conference was the creation, on May 11, 1917, of the Special Board on Antisubmarine Devices The board, of which Rear Admiral A W. Grant, the submarine force commander, was senior member, was appointed for the purpose of procuring, either through original research, experiment, and manufacture, or through the development of ideas and devices submitted by inventors at large, suitable apparatus for both offensive and defensive operations against submarines The other members of the board were Commanders C S McDowell and M. A Libbey To Commander McDowell, who acted in the capacity of secretary to the board, the Bureau is indebted for nearly all the material relating to its work

The board was directed to cooperate actively with all companies whose resources offered anything of promise in the work in view, and specifically with the General Electric Co, the Western Electric Co, and the Submarine Signal Co, whose experience, equipment, and research facilities gave promise of being especially valuable along the lines indicated A representative from each of these companies and one from the National Research Council were appointed as advisory members of the board These advisory members were Dr. R A Millikan; Dr. W. R Whitney, of the General Electric Co; Dr. F B Jewett, of the Western Electric Co (later lieutenant colonel in the Signal Corps); and Mr. H. J. W. Fay of the Submarine Signal Co

In June, 1917, the special board met at Boston, Mass, and a definite organization for it, including its advisory members and groups, was drawn up to facilitate close coordination of the various groups, the Naval Consulting Board, and the National Research Council Arrangements were made to procure two patrol vessels, one for the Nahant group and one for the New London group, to be devoted entirely to experimental work At this time also the British Mission, consisting of Sir Ernest Rutherford and Commander Cyprian Bridge, R. N., and the French Mission, composed of Major Fabry, Major Abraham, and Captain Dupray, of the French Embassy, were taken to New London and Nahant to witness tests upon the apparatus under development at those stations

In July, 1917, the British Admiralty sent to the United States as liaison officer for the work carried on in this country and in England, Lieut. (later lieutenant commander) S. C Houghton, R N V. R, who continued in this capacity until the end of the war He was of great assistance to the board

July 26, 1917, Capt S. S. Robinson succeeded Rear Admiral Grant as senior member of the board, and he in turn was succeeded by Rear Admiral B. C. Decker, who continued in that capacity for the remainder of the war.

A large number of antisubmarine devices, submitted by naval officers and inventors from all over the United States, were examined and tests witnessed by members of the board. Several designs of submarine nets were submitted, one of the earliest being the Elia-Sperry antisubmarine net, invented by Commander G. E. Elia, retired, of the Italian Navy, and Mr. E. A. Sperry, of the Sperry Gyroscope Co. On June 9, 1917, very extensive tests were carried out on the Elia-Sperry net with two submarines. These tests were witnessed by the members of the special board as well as by the officers of the mine force; and although the results were not entirely successful, valuable information was obtained as to the developments necessary

The above is only one of a large number of similar tests witnessed by the special board during the Summer of 1917

A meeting called by the National Research Council was held in Washington on June 1, 1917, with scientific representatives from England and France, members from the naval bureaus at Washington, representatives from the Western Electric Co, General Electric Co and Submarine Signal Co, and several professors and individual investigators who had shown interest in this problem at various universities in the United States At this meeting the foreign representatives explained fully the program which had been followed abroad and suggested various problems to be considered and developed by the investigators in this country for the improvement of antisubmarine devices.

Sir Ernest Rutherford described the striking results which he and other experimenters had obtained by using the binaural effect with so-called Broca tubes, and those in attendance were urged to begin their underwater sound work by repeating these experiments and thus become familiar with the precision obtainable with nothing more than two separate receivers supported about a meter apart in the water and connected by separate rubber tubes, one to each ear of the observer.

It may be noted that, although this utilization of the binaural effect for the detection and orientation of submarine sounds had been known in England, it had not been developed satisfactorily for application, and that this effect became the basic principle on which acoustical apparatus was devised in this country and supplied to our own Navy and the British as well.

At this same conference the supersonic work which had been begun in France by Prof. Langevin was presented in full by Majs.

Fabry and Abraham The New York group, under the direction of Dr. M. I Pupin, of Columbia University, selected at this time supersonic work as its major activity and continued work on this problem at New York, Key West, and New London, under the direction of the special board, during the continuation of the war The San Pedro group, under Mr. Harris J. Ryan, also started work about this time on supersonic and kindred lines of research Maj Abraham also at this conference made a full presentation of the Walzer apparatus as developed in France, and from which Prof Mason obtained his original ideas which led to the production of our best forms of acoustical devices

Following the conference the various individual experimenters and professors returned to their universities and laboratories and continued to work under the guidance and supervision of the special board. At the suggestion of the National Research Council certain scientists were brought together at New London to work on some special problems which were developed at the Washington conference This was the foundation of the New London group, which later came directly under the Navy and was the foundation of the naval experimental station. The original group consisted of: A. A. Michelson, chairman; E. Merritt, vice chairman and secretary, H. S. Bumstead. M. Mason, G. W. Pierce, E. F. Nichols, J. A. Wilson, and J Zeleny.

A portable house was erected for a laboratory and the converted steam yachts *Thetis* and *Varada* were provided for the use of the experimenters During the early part of the summer the only members of the group working at New London were Profs. Pierce, Mason, Merritt, and their assistants, the other members being at New Haven and reporting occasionally at New London for tests At the meeting held in New London on July 3 1917, Prof. Mason proposed the construction of apparatus which later became known as the M. V. apparatus. The first device of this type was constructed at the University of Wisconsin, and was installed on the *Thetis* at New London about July 15, 1917.

With the creation of the special board, all scattered activities were brought into fruitful cooperation. Through its affiliation with the civilian organizations mentioned, a selected group of highly qualified scientific men was obtained to begin work at New London, and this station immediately became a central headquarters The groups already established at Nahant, New York, San Pedro, and elsewhere, and the individuals working in the laboratories of colleges and universities throughout the country, continued their investigations along the more or less specialized lines in which they had started, but the effective of de   vell as its value in promoting the common aim, was tremendously increased by the system of information and the supervision of the central organization Also, by virtue of the official character of the board, it was possible to keep in close touch with progress along similar lines in foreign countries

At first the work naturally took the form of testing out abstract ideas evolved from the whole range of possibilities presented by the fields of sound, light, heat, and electricity. Each such test necessitated, first, some mathematical consideration of the subject and, second, the construction of elementary apparatus The apparatus desired had to be constructed either by the scientists themselves or by such facilities as the station and neighboring manufacturing plants afforded The first practical test of any idea was more likely to develop difficulties and unsuspected collateral phenomena than to afford a definite answer to the immediate question under investigation, leading to further study, computations, and manufacture of new apparatus even further removed from the conception of a practical design. It was an entirely new field, and the first steps had to be, in a sense, backwards into the unexplored regions where fundamental physical truths and engineering data were concealed.

Governing all activity was the insistent demand for haste. Whenever it appeared that there were several alternate lines of promising development it was necessary to undertake them all, or as many as could be handled, simultaneously, rather than to risk the chance of a single successful solution, and at the same time to exercise a broad judgment that would insure actual progress and prevent the frittering away of time, money, and intelligence in the investigations of unessential minutiæ.

With the association of men of such ability as those gathered at New London and Nahant, it was inevitable that the number of projects and demands for experimental work should multiply much more rapidly than material, facilities, and personnel could be provided for their execution Investigations along special lines were "farmed out," either to subsidiary groups or to the research departments of the associated commercial companies, or to individuals working in their own laboratories throughout the country. Additional personnel was secured by the direct employment of men specially qualified as investigators and designers, and through enrollment in the Naval Reserve of others of the same type and of skilled artisans in many trades.

During the early period of the war several destroyers were equipped with standard apparatus for underwater signaling, manufactured by the Submarine Signal Co This apparatus was proposed for use in the detection of submarines and, at the time of installation, was the only apparatus available which had possibilities for detecting the sounds given off by these boats. Later, Prof R A. Fessenden, of the Submarine Signal Co , developed other improved methods and devices which were installed in the destroyers *Aylwin* and *Colhoun*. These vessels were immediately dispatched to the war zone in order that practical demonstration might be made of their suitability for detecting submarines No instruments that had been developed up to this time and installed in destroyers had given results superior to those obtained from these devices, but as development work at New London proceeded—in which it will be remembered that the Submarine Signal Co was cooperating—other devices were produced which were considered better suited for use in destroyers, and further installation of the Fessenden devices was suspended. The original research and experimental work conducted by Prof. Fessenden in connection with the methods and apparatus which he proposed resulted in making available to other investigators knowledge and data the value of which should be fully recognized in the history of submarine detection.

Soon after its formation, the special board requested Maj. R D Mershon to take general charge under the board's direction of the magnetic schemes, and to follow them in their preliminary development. It was realized by all concerned that all magnetic means of detection must of necessity be of very short range, and be more or less of an adjunct to other methods of detection or location of submarines. A great deal of praise is due to those who devoted their time and energy unceasingly on various magnetic devices with the realization, always, of the exceedingly difficult problem which confronted them It will be seen later that real results were obtained by these investigators, and that short-range magnetic and electric devices were developed which could be utilized both on shipboard and from shore stations.

The board similarly requested Dr. H. E. Ives to supervise and advise in general on all work connected with "light" Under Dr Ives's supervision a number of tests were carried out to develop a goggle for use by lookouts on ships and on airplanes, which would remove glare and make the submarine's periscope and its wake stand out in greater relief As a result of these tests a standard goggle was developed and adopted by the Navy Department for the use of lookouts.

Another of the early experiments with "light" was to determine the extent to which light rays from a high-powered searchlight could be transmitted through water. These tests were carried out at sea in deep water with a 36-inch high-power searchlight lowered about 20 feet beneath the surface The result proved conclusively that practically all of the light was diffused forming a ball, with no beam, so that a low-power light was as effective as a high-power one, and that, therefore, no effective results could be obtained in locating submarines by the use of light beams.

COOPERATION OF MANUFACTURING COMPANIES.

During the summer of 1917, the investigations progressed very rapidly, and the board extended its activities to include the advice and cooperation of several of the leading physicists and engineers of the various universities and organizations of the country. In accordance with the orders from the Secretary of the Navy, instituting the special board, which stated that cooperation should be maintained with all industrial companies which gave promise of offering material and advice of a character which would prove of value to the board, several leading manufacturing companies were invited to become affiliated with the work of the board, in addition to the three already mentioned. These companies gave very valuable assistance through their hearty cooperation and willingness to supply overtime work and deliver material which was urgently needed. In addition to the three companies already mentioned, the following companies cooperated United Wire & Supply Co., of Providence; Westinghouse Electric & Manufacturing Co; Victor Talking Machine Co, Locomobile Co of America; Ford Motor Co.; Willys Overland Co; Standard Parts Co of Cleveland; Bryant Electric Co.; Worcester Polytechnic Shops, and Pittsfield Machine & Tool Co

ESTABLISHMENT OF LISTENING SCHOOLS.

As the development of the antisubmarine apparatus progressed it was realized that the Navy personnel who were to operate the devices on the ships should have a special training, and a listeners' school was therefore authorized by the Bureau of Navigation in August, 1917 The first class was started in September at the submarine base, but in July, 1918, the school was moved to the State Pier, New London. At each place a complete equipment of apparatus was provided, which enabled an extensive program of training to be instituted Over 1,500 qualified listeners were graduated up to the time of the signing of the armistice

ESTABLISHMENT OF THE NAVAL EXPERIMENTAL STATION.

By September, 1917, the activities of the various groups, especially of the New London group at the submarine base, had increased to such an extent that it was decided to start an experimental station with sufficient accommodations to allow for the growth of the activities of the special board

An abandoned machine-shop building, which stood on the property adjoining the Fort Trumbull Reservation, was leased and, after extensive repairs and remodeling, was converted into an experimental laboratory. An intensive reconstruction program was started, and in the early spring of 1918 a fairly complete and efficient plant had been developed. A machine shop, very completely equipped, was organized, and a personnel of Navy machinists, carpenters, etc., assigned to the station. A marine railway was rebuilt and put in condition to haul out the experimental boats for installations and repair. Several additional wooden buildings were erected to accommodate the increasing personnel of the station, and offices and experimental booths assigned to the technical staff in order to facilitate this development work as much as possible.

As indicating the growth of work at the experimental station, it is of interest to state that at the time it was officially taken over in October, 1917, there were about 10 enlisted men attached to the station, 4 of whom were doing guard duty. The number was rapidly increased to about 200 at the beginning of 1918, and at the time of the signing of the armistice over 700 enlisted men were on duty there.

To enlist the interest and cooperation of additional companies, the special board asked the Westinghouse Electric & Manufacturing Co to lend the services of an experimental engineer. The board was fortunate in thus obtaining Mr S W Farnsworth, whose services were invaluable in starting the experimental station. Later, Mr Farnsworth went to London as one of the scientific attachés at the American Embassy.

EARLY PRACTICAL DEVELOPMENTS.

By the fall of 1917, the Nahant group had developed a type of listening device known as the C-tube. Later, adapting to use with microphones, the rotary compensator that was developed at New London for acoustical work, this group developed the apparatus known as the K-tube.

On the 21st of August, 1917, a very interesting practical demonstration of the use of the C-tube was given in Boston Harbor. The test was arranged to duplicate as nearly as possible an actual offensive attack upon an enemy submarine, with three chasers equipped with C-tubes and various signaling apparatus to intercommunicate the bearings obtained on the submarine.

Miniature depth bombs, consisting of electric light bulbs designed to explode 50 feet below the surface, were dropped near the submarine to indicate that it had been located and could actually have been destroyed. The most interesting feature of this test, aside from the data obtained, was the fact that

veloped in less than four months from the time investigations had been started. While this apparatus was naturally rather crude in many details and was capable of improvement, it embodied important and necessary features of a successful device.

In October, 1917, progress had been made to such a point that the successful completion of several useful devices was practically assured. The questions of mechanical design and quantity production then presented themselves as of the same order of magnitude and complexity as the original research work. Laboratory apparatus had to be redesigned with reference to the installation upon seagoing craft, and intricacies of operation simplified for use by seagoing personnel. In order to preserve secrecy, it was necessary in some cases to distribute the manufacture of parts among several manufacturers. Special raw material had to be obtained and special manufacturing processes developed. The manufacturing firms equipped to do work of the novel character and nicety required were few at best, and at this time all the industries of the country were crowded with other war work.

In December, 1917, Capt. R. H. Leigh, U. S. Navy (then Assistant Chief of the Bureau of Steam Engineering) was detailed to take to England sample sets of all of the latest apparatus that had been developed. This was installed in British craft as well as in our own destroyers abroad, and demonstrations of its capabilities were given. As a result of these demonstrations a large number of K-tubes and of MF-tubes were requested by the British Admiralty and supplied from this country, and later other forms of detection devices, including tripod listening equipments, were supplied to it. Capt. Leigh remained at the United States naval headquarters in England on Admiral Sims's staff for the rest of the war, having charge of our antisubmarine work abroad.

In the development of our special devices it was, of course, necessary to keep constantly in mind the practical procedure that would be demanded of the seagoing personnel in order to make effective use of them. It was in this connection that the organization of the special board, composed of experienced naval officers working in close relation with physicists of the highest attainments, proved of the greatest value. The question of practicability from a naval standpoint was kept always in the foreground, and must constantly have worked insensibly, as it often did directly, to prevent development along impracticable lines, however promising the outlook from the point of abstract theory. Incidentally, it was this feature as much as any other that accounted for the superiority of American devices and the completeness of American plans and equipment, as compared with those of the corresponding antisubmarine forces of our European allies.

Consideration of the practicability of apparatus and of the methods necessary to employ it most effectively, led directly into two developments of the utmost importance, viz:
(1) Types of vessels to which adapted
(2) Tactics to be employed and training of personnel.
Both of these subjects need special comment

TYPES OF VESSELS

The special point that had to be kept in mind was to produce apparatus that would be effective against submarines, and there was no limitation upon design on account of the type of vessel that would be required to make effective use of it. Nevertheless, the critical nature of the situation when this country entered the war practically restricted the design of apparatus to something that could be utilized by existing types. It was not possible, for instance, to consider in the beginning the construction of vessels in which all other considerations were subordinated to a single specialized operation, as was done by the British in several instances, although later, the Eagles were projected more or less in accordance with this principle

The destroyers were generally regarded as the ideal antisubmarine craft, and the destroyer building program had been assigned priority over all other activities. It was natural, therefore, that the special necessities of these vessels should receive primary consideration in the design of apparatus. However, the destroyers did not offer so promising an outlook in every respect as that presented by the subchasers. These vessels had been provided for at the very outbreak of war, before "listening gear" had been conceived, and they were rapidly approaching completion about the time the first practical devices took definite shape. Although the chasers had been designed primarily as patrol boats and without any idea as to the very specialized operation that was to be evolved for submarine chasing, it was a fortunate circumstance that the early detection devices lent themselves to easy installation in these vessels, while the general design of the latter, although not ideal in some important respects, was far more favorable for the purpose than any other type. In this way the chaser project became intimately associated with the work of the board. It would be difficult to say to what extent the development of apparatus was influenced by the special needs of the destroyers and chasers, but the field represented by vessels of other types, including aircraft, and by shore installations, was never lost sight of

TACTICS AND PERSONNEL.

The earliest forms of practicable apparatus had limitations which made the whole question of success or failure depend upon skill of personnel and an adequate plan of procedure, that is to say, the tactics of the antisubmarine craft. The same thing is generally true as regards any sort of naval equipment, but in the present case the degree of skill required and the special character of the tactics that had to be elaborated and made practicable introduced problems the solution of which might have been regarded as impossible except under the spur of absolute necessity. For example, all varieties of detecting gear gave only the direction and not the distance of the submarine. To determine with necessary accuracy the submarine's position, or, in technical language, to obtain a "fix," triangulation was required, and this at once made it plain that hunting craft must work in groups. Again, the detecting apparatus could be used only when the hunting vessels were dead in the water, which enormously decreased the effective speed of hunting units. Also, to attack with the depth charge was a much more intricate problem than to open fire with a battery of guns: it was necessary to fire a whole group of ships accurately at a given "fix."

The procedure of conducting a successful chase and attack thus involved details of ship handling, navigational plotting, and communication between ships with a degree of speed unheard of before in any kind of naval craft. The special equipment to make this possible was devised and provided, but manifestly the question of training was as important as anything in the line of equipment. Since the chasers were to be manned by an untrained personnel and a certain period of training would be necessary in any case, the opportunity was presented to equip and train these vessels along the specialized lines indicated. In the case of the destroyers, the demand for whose services in connection with the convoy system outweighed all other considerations, the best that could be done was to furnish them with the apparatus, leaving them to work out the necessary procedure for concerted action while in active service.

NEW MEMBERS OF THE SPECIAL BOARD.

The addition to the special board of Capt. J. T Tompkins, U. S. Navy, of Naval Operations. Capt A. J. Hepburn, U S Navy, in command of naval district base, New London; and of Commander E. C. S Parker, U S Navy, in charge of the tactical group at New London, in January, 1918, increased the activities of the board's work. Capt. Tompkins followed the antisubmarine work in the Navy Department. Capt. Hep[burn] ... equipment and training of submarine chasers ... Parker, through the tactical group, cooperated in developing the tactics and methods of operation of the chasers which were equipped with detection apparatus.

In May, 1918, Commander Parker was detached from duty with the special board and was succeeded by Capt W P. Cronan, and in July, 1918, Capt Hepburn was ordered to command the submarine chasers based on Queenstown, Ireland. He was relieved by Capt W. T. Tarrant. In September, 1918, Commander McDowell was ordered to naval headquarters, London, for antisubmarine duty, and was succeeded as member and Secretary by Capt J. R Defrees

In order to secure close cooperation between the board and the Department, the following named officers were appointed members of the board in May, 1918· Lieut. Commander G K Calhoun (Math) U. S. Navy, of the Bureau of Steam Engineering; Lieut. Commander P. S Wilkinson, jr, U. S Navy, of the Bureau of Ordnance; and Lieut Commander H R. Bogusch, U. S. Navy, of the Bureau of Construction and Repair.

EXPANSION OF ACTIVITIES AT EXPERIMENTAL STATION

During the spring and summer of 1918 the scope of the special board's activities caused the experimental station to expand greatly New buildings were erected and civilian experts were obtained from all parts of the country to assist in the design and development of the apparatus, both from technical and engineering standpoints. A test department was formed to compare the various devices at sea, and this department also investigated the ability and comparative merits of the devices submitted by the various groups and individual experimenters of the other stations. Exceptional facilities for extensive tests at sea were afforded through the assignment of the destroyer *Jouett*, three converted steam yachts, and three submarine chasers to the exclusive use of the experimenters and the test department The submarine base assigned submarines as required, thus allowing extensive tests to be carried out, using submarines as noise makers and as listening craft Installations of nearly every type of submarine detector developed at this time were made on the *Jouett*, and valuable data were obtained relative to the applications of the devices for service conditions These preliminary installations led to the practical development of the MV-tube and its quantity production and installation

HYDROPHONE SCHOOL AT NEW LONDON

A hydrophone school was authorized by the Bureau of Navigation on September 9, 1918 for the training of hydrophone officers The listening school which had been in operation since July, 1917, had great success in training the enlisted men to do the actual listening on the various devices installed on board ship and at shore stations As the installations increased it was realized that a force of officers was needed to supervise the installation, care, upkeep, and repair of the devices Accordingly, a trial school was formed in July, 1918, which graduated about 50 officers. The results were so favorable that the school was officially approved by the Bureau of Navigation, and the first official class was started in September, 1918, and continued for three months, during which time about 150 hydrophone officers were trained

The school was equipped very completely with models of the latest antisubmarine devices, and several boats were assigned to its use for practical training at sea

PUBLICATION DEPARTMENT.

As the number of antisubmarine devices increased and their extensive application was made to boats and stations in this country and abroad, it was found necessary to supply pamphlets and bulletins describing the operation of the apparatus It was also desired to keep the British and French antisubmarine divisions informed of the progress being made in this country. The first publications were principally in the nature of instruction books, covering the general principles, descriptions, operation installations, and care of the different apparatus, but in the latter part of the summer of 1918 a regular publication department was established, with Mr J. R. Hewett, editor of the General Electric Review, as head of the department, and with Mr G S De Reemer, formerly secretary of the Ship Protection Committee of the Shipping Board, as assistant Monthly publications were issued from this time until after the armistice was signed, giving in considerable detail the various developments under way and results obtained on the different problems

SCOPE OF ACTIVITIES OF SPECIAL BOARD.

The primary object of the special board was to further the development of any apparatus or device which would assist in the detection of enemy submarines and aid in their ultimate destruction. Most of the devices developed through the agency of the special board were based on the principle of detection through the water of the noises given off from the submarine These devices were extremely varied in principle and form, but their objective was maximum range combined with directional accuracy and freedom from extraneous noises.

A second fundamental problem was that of detecting a "silent" submarine. either lying on the bottom or operating at its most silent speed, which rendered detection by sound almost impossible.

The experiments undertaken were practically centered about these two problems, with the idea of installing suitable devices on various types of surface craft, submarines, aircraft, and shore stations, which would reveal the presence and location of the enemy

In addition to the above problems a large number of closely allied investigations were necessary for systematic hunting, chasing, and attacking the submarine This led to the development of secret signaling, plotting apparatus, intercommunication systems for operations between the elements of a chasing patrol group, silencing of machinery noises, and a large number of similar devices.

An idea of the magnitude of the research work undertaken by the various groups under the supervision of the special board is shown by the following data:

The six groups, namely, New London, Nahant, San Pedro, Chicago, Wisconsin, and Key West had undertaken, up to the close of the year 1918, 230 separate problems, over half of which had been completed and a final report submitted. A considerable number of the completed problems resulted in the development of apparatus ready for standardized quantity production and installation In practically every case the reports led to important results in connection with other problems, or to the elimination of methods and devices which were found impracticable

The diversified nature of the various investigations being undertaken, together with the large number of investigators who were often simultaneously studying the problems, makes it difficult to outline the progress of these activities in a chronological order In order to touch upon the contributions of the various experimenters and to maintain a logical sequence of development it seems advisable to subdivide the work into several classes and to follow the growth of each separately.

A broad subdivision of the work may be stated as follows:
1 Development of sound-detection apparatus.
2 Detection of submarines at rest
3. Application of detection apparatus to aircraft
4. Installation of shore station anti-submarine apparatus
5. Miscellaneous apparatus

DEVELOPMENT OF SOUND DETECTION APPARATUS

A majority of the problems investigated by the various groups depended on the existence of audible submarine sounds The efforts of the Nahant group resulted in the production of the C-tube, the K-tube and of several types of towing devices known as OS, OK, and OV tubes, as a result, principally, of the work of Dr Irving Langmuir, Dr. W D. Coolidge, and Mr C E. Lveleth.

At the experimental station, New London, Conn., the early work on this problem was carried out by Profs. Bridgeman, Mason, Merritt, and Pierce, who had started preliminary investigations at the submarine base.

The efforts of the New London group resulted in the practical development of several types of devices known as the MB-tube, the MF-tube, and the MV-tube, which were installed very extensively on submarine chasers and destroyers.

The methods used for detecting the sound waves sent out from the submarine may be divided into two general classes, electrical and mechanical.

In general, the efforts of the experiments were concentrated on one or the other of these two methods. However, it would be difficult definitely to separate the activities of the several men. Very frequent technical council meetings were held by Commander McDowell, secretary of the board, at which all the experimenters discussed in detail the work of each as well as the numerous schemes and contributions from the outside groups which were working on similar problems.

GENERAL DISCUSSION OF ACOUSTICAL DETECTING APPARATUS.

The general requirements of a listening apparatus which embodies all that could be desired are as follows. It must be adapted to detect a submarine at a considerable distance without interference from noise produced by other shipping, by water noise, or by noise due to motion of the vessel on which it is installed; it should be able to give the direction and distance of the submarine accurately; it should be seaworthy, of robust mechanical construction, convenient, and rapid in operation.

No instrument has as yet been devised which satisfied all these requirements. In fact, no single instrument can yet give the distance of the submarine. Instruments were developed, however, for successful use with the listening boat underway, at speeds up to 14 knots, and with which directions could be obtained within 2 or 3 degrees.

Listening apparatus may be divided into several groups as follows:
> Directional
> Nondirectional.
> Mechanical.
> Electrical.
> Resonant.
> Nonresonant.
> Single.
> Multiunit.
> Instruments mounted directly in the vessel.
> Instruments mounted outside the vessel.

DIRECTIONAL AND NONDIRECTIONAL INSTRUMENTS.

In the early days of the war, before the possibilities of detection were understood, and when any instrument of any use whatever was urgently needed, a large number of nondirectional instruments were manufactured in England and supplied to patrol vessels for the purpose of determining whether there was a submarine in the vicinity. These instruments, of course, were of little value in the pursuit of submarines, because the only practicable method of use was to listen to the submarine, then move on and listen again, judging by the change of intensity of sound whether the course was in the correct direction or not. This method of procedure was very slow and few submarines were destroyed by it.

The simplest nondirectional instrument consists of a microphone mounted inside a cavity, closed by a flexible membrane. The membrane is moved by the pressure produced when a sound wave passes over it and this actuates the microphone. Since the pressure in a sound wave is purely hydrostatic, that is, the pressure is the same in every direction, it is impossible to tell with an instrument of this kind from what direction the sound comes.

Very shortly, however, after the beginning of the war directional instruments began to make their appearance. One of the simplest of these, which was developed by the British, consists of a diaphragm in a rigid ring with a microphone mounted at the center of the diaphragm. If sound strikes the diaphragm from the left or from the right, the diaphragm will move and the microphone will respond, but if sound approaches the instrument from above or below, it will divide on the heavy metal ring, giving two impulses to the diaphragm of equal intensity from opposite sides. These two impulses in opposite directions will neutralize each other, and the diaphragm will remain stationary and the microphone will not respond. As this instrument is turned around in the water, the sound given by it will be the loudest, therefore, when the plane of the face of the diaphragm is at right angles to the direction of the sound, and faintest when the plane of the diaphragm has the same direction as the sound. In this way some idea may be obtained of the direction of the sound, but it will be noticed that the indications of the instrument are not positive, because it is impossible to tell with it whether the sound is coming from one direction or from another diametrically opposite. There are several of these bidirectional instruments.

The simple English bidirectional microphone above described may be made unidirectional; that is, to give unambiguous indications of the direction of sound if a simple sound screen, or "baffle," as the English call it, is combined with it. This sound screen consists of a hollow box of xylonite mounted several inches to the left of the diaphragm This sound screen absorbs sound coming from the left, so that it is easy to tell by comparing the intensity in different positions from which direction the sound comes. When the sound is an absolute maximum, it is coming from the side of the diaphragm away from the sound screen, and the plane of the diaphragm is at right angles to its direction.

Most directional instruments developed by the British use the principle of the sound screen. The directional instruments devised on this side of the Atlantic, however, nearly all depend on another principle, and the extensive application of this principle in determining direction constitutes one of the most important original contributions of this country to the problem of submarine detection These American instruments use the principle of binaural determination of direction. When sound from an object takes the same time to reach both ears it will appear to be neither to the right nor to the left. The principles of binaural determination of direction were known for a long time before the war, but most of the early efforts in England were devoted to developments of the sound screen as likely to be simpler and yield more immediate results. The discoveries that microphones with properly constructed receivers may be used binaurally, and that a nonresonant and relatively insensitive receiver is better for binaural use, materially extended the practical use of the binaural principle

The directional instruments which use the binaural principle are either rotatable or else are connected with a device for changing the length of air paths, or electric paths, to the different receivers in such a way that the sound seems to be centered Such instruments are called compensators.

RESONANT AND NONRESONANT INSTRUMENTS

Whether an instrument should be resonant or nonresonant is a question about which there is still divergence of opinion and practice At the beginning of the war, when the conditions of operation were not so clearly understood as they are now, it was assumed universally that the first requirement of a detecting instrument was great range and, therefore, great sensitiveness There is no question that the most sensitive receiver is a resonant receiver. Everyone is familiar with the fact that a pendulum may be thrown into violent oscillation by a succession of very weak impulses so timed as to coincide with the natural period of the pendulum. In the same way, a diaphragm in water may be thrown into violent agitation by a comparatively feeble source of sound if the frequency of the sound waves is the same as the natural frequency of the diaphragm.

Calculations made on this point shortly after the war began showed that it is possible in this way to throw a diaphragm into a motion of 1,000 times the natural amplitude of the sound waves. If the amplitude is multiplied by 1,000 this means that the intensity is multiplied by 1,000,000, since the intensity varies as the square of the amplitude. Such a possibility offered much promise, and much early work of the British consisted in applying microphones to tuned diaphragms and in this way getting very great sensitiveness. But it soon appeared that mere sensitiveness, with nothing else, is one of the last requirements in a listening apparatus. When listening for a submarine there are all kinds of noise besides the submarine to listen to, and the problem is to pick out a submarine from the mass of other noise. If the instrument is sensitive to all kinds of noise, there is no advantage in making it sensitive beyond a certain point.

Another disadvantage is that a resonant instrument is most sensitive to only one pitch—the natural pitch of the instrument itself. A submarine or any other boat heard on such a resonant instrument is almost devoid of quality, the only means of distinction being the rhythm. A trained listener is able to separate and identify boats by the quality of the sound given by them, but this advantage is entirely lost in a resonant instrument. In order to overcome this disadvantage, there were many attempts in the early days of the war to find what the characteristic frequency of a submarine was and to tune the diaphragm to this frequency. It was found, however, that the submarine emits no characteristic frequency, but gives out sound covering most of the range of the audible. Another disadvantage of resonant instruments is that they can not be used binaurally, because they do not faithfully reproduce phase.

In this country, on the other hand, emphasis was laid on the development of nonresonant instruments. These instruments are not so sensitive and can not have so great a range when entirely free from disturbance, but they do give faithful reproduction of sound and make it possible for a trained listener to distinguish, by the quality of sound, the submarine from other boats or water noise, or from noise of his own engines. Such instruments are also particularly adapted to the determination of direction by the binaural method.

MECHANICAL AND ELECTRICAL INSTRUMENTS

The method of reception of sound from water may be either mechanical or electrical. There are two principal methods of electrical reception. One is with the microphone. The microphone is mounted on a diaphragm which is set in motion to the microphone, which latter responds and reproduces the sound in a telephone by ordinary methods Another electrical method of reception is the magnetophone. A coil of wire is placed in a magnetic field, mounted on a diaphragm which is actuated by the sound waves in the water Transient currents are generated in the coil when it is moved in the magnetic field by the sound waves. Those transient currents are led to the telephone in the ordinary way The microphone has the advantage of greater simplicity and convenience, and it has been used almost exclusively

The best-known example of such an instrument developed in this country is the K-tube A magnetophone gives more faithful reproduction of sound than the microphone, and is freer from disturbance, but its sensitiveness is so low that it must be used in connection with an amplifier, and this additional complication was sufficient to prevent its general adoption

Another method of electrical reception of sound waves from water which showed considerable promise was the electrical condenser If a condenser is put into water and subjected to sound waves, its dimensions change in virtue of the changes of pressure in the water, and consequently its capacity changes also. If the condenser is charged, changes of potential are produced by these changes of capacity. These changes of potential in the proper electrical circuit produce fluctuating currents which may be led to a telephone and converted into sound. The chief disadvantage of the condenser is that it must be used with an amplifier, thus introducing electrical complications If the condenser is made up in a long narrow form it has the advantage of being automatically more sensitive to sound from one direction only, thus giving a simple directional instrument.

The receivers of mechanical instruments consist usually of a flexible chamber of metal or rubber placed in the water and exposed to sound waves, connecting through pipes with the ears of the observer These receivers were called Broca receivers in this country, this name being taken from the French In England, such receivers are frequently called "stethoscopes." In this country, the term "stethoscope" has been applied only to the tubes entering the ears. Broca receivers do not in general have the sensitiveness of the microphone, but a good Broca gives a very much more faithful reproduction of sound and, for that reason, is much preferred by many in submarine detection. Besides superior quality, an advantage of the mechanical instruments is simplicity A disadvantage is that it is impossible to use long leads, thus making it necessary to place the observer and the compensator near the receiver. This often results in inconvenience in operation

In this country, the best known examples of mechanical instruments, are the C-tubes and all the multiple-unit devices. In France, the Walzer plate is the best known example.

SINGLE AND MULTIUNIT RECEIVERS

Most of the instruments developed abroad were of the single-unit type. The multiunit instrument was most extensively developed in this country, although suggestions were made for such instruments in England before this country entered the war, and the French Walzer plate is a multiunit device. As the term is used here, multiunit instruments embrace those instruments in which a number of receivers are so connected as to bring the sound in phase within the instrument itself, when the instrument is correctly adjusted. According to this use of the word, the C-tube, which consists of two single receivers, one connected to each ear, would not be termed a multiunit instrument, but a "single-unit instrument used binaurally." A distinctive property of multiunit instruments is that they may be focused in a definite direction, just as a telescope may be similarly focused, and in this way the sound of a submarine may be magnified at the expense of other sounds, such as water noise, or the noise of other vessels which do not have the same direction as the submarine. Practically all results obtained from boats in motion with apparatus mounted directly in the boat have been obtained with instruments of this class, and it is along the line of multiunit instruments that probably most of the important future developments will take place.

APPARATUS MOUNTED DIRECTLY IN THE BOAT AND APPARATUS MOUNTED OUTSIDE THE BOAT.

The most convenient location, of course, for listening apparatus is on the same boat with the observer, but because of the difficulty of using such apparatus with the boat under way, a great deal of effort was devoted to developing apparatus which could be towed behind the boat, in this way getting rid of the noise of one's own engines and a large part of the water noise. Successful development of the MV apparatus, mounted on the vessel itself, eliminated to a great extent the necessity for towed devices. The Nash fish is a towed listening apparatus developed in England. The OS-tube, the OK-tube, and the microphone eel are successful developments in this country.

DETECTION OF SUBMARINES AT REST.

This problem was studied very extensively by a large number of individual investigators and groups.

Prof. Merritt, at the experimental station, was at work on this problem at the time the special board was appointed in May, 1917, and actively followed the progress of the various schemes proposed until the close of the war. By the middle of the summer of 1918, he had developed a device known as the AD-tube, which gave very satisfactory operation for short-range work.

Of the various schemes proposed and studied, by groups not working at New London, there were two devices which showed special merit, and extensive tests were made upon each at the experimental station.

Prof. V. Bush, of the American Radio & Research Corporation, started investigations upon a magnetic method of detection of a quiet submarine early in 1917, and went to New London with the apparatus where a number of tests were conducted. The apparatus known as the audio telegraph was developed up to the point of being ready for quantity production, but it was not put into general use.

Mr. B. G. Lamme, chief engineer of the Westinghouse Electric & Manufacturing Co., and a member of the Naval Consulting Board, undertook investigations upon the detection of submarines at rest, shortly before the United States declared war, and developed an experimental device at Pittsburgh, Pa. After exhaustive tests over a period of several months, the final product was brought to New London for further development and tests under actual sea conditions.

At the time of the armistice, the status of the four principal devices was such that they could be readily built in quantity production and installed on submarine chasers with assurance of fairly consistent operation over short ranges.

A second method of detecting a submarine at rest was investigated very thoroughly in this country by a great many experimenters under the supervision of the special board. The confidential nature of the work prevents a detailed account of the progress made, but mention should be made of the following men who contributed largely to the success of the work: Profs M. I. Pupin, A. P. Wills, J. H Morecroft, G. B. Pegram, and Mr. E H Armstrong, of Columbia University; Lieut. Col. R A. Millikan, of the National Research Council; Prof. W G. Cady, of Wesleyan University, Dr. Irving Langmuir, Dr A. W. Hull, Mr C E Eveleth, and Mr. A. L. Ellis, of the General Electric Co.: and members of the San Pedro group, including Messrs H. J. Ryan, L F. Fuller, H D Babcock, and R A. Anderson.

APPLICATION OF DETECTION DEVICES TO AIRCRAFT.

Aircraft, both seaplanes and dirigibles, possess certain advantages for detection of submarines over surface craft. On account of the height of the observer from the surface, a very large area may be observed; in addition, the wake of a periscope appears as a white ribbon against the dark background of the sea, and the superior speed of aircraft permits them to reach quickly any supposed location of a submarine. To be able to detect a submarine totally submerged, aircraft must be able to drop some form of listening device under water, because a submarine, save in exceptionally clear water with sandy bottom, becomes invisible from the air as soon as the periscope is entirely under. On account of its ability to stay practically stationary in the air, the dirigible can utilize a form of listening device which can be lowered from the craft and towed under water. Several towed listening devices were developed to accomplish this, the most satisfactory being the "electric eel" and the OK-tube, compensators being used by the listener in each case. Dirigibles, when equipped in this manner, should prove very effective offensive craft for use against submarines in the daytime and in ordinary weather. It would usually be necessary to have cooperation between aircraft and surface craft maintained by means of radio telephone communication so that surface craft may be called in to assist in destroying a submarine which had been located. During the last few months of the war there were a number of cases of such cooperation between aircraft and submarines, although none of the aircraft in the war zone was fitted with listening devices, except for experimental trials.

On account of their speed seaplanes can cover greater areas visually than dirigibles, but to hear a submarine they must land on the water. To afford means of listening on seaplanes, there were developed devices for listening when the seaplane had landed on the water and was drifting, the most satisfactory being the PB-tube, consisting of three microphone units suspended separately from three rings on the bow of the plane, so as to form a triangle; and the electric eel, a multiple-unit microphone device encased in a long rubber tube. Both of these devices were used with a compensator, and a number of them had been supplied to aircraft in this country before the armistice, and some had been sent abroad.

SHORE STATION ANTISUBMARINE APPARATUS.

For the detection of submarines at certain congested lanes near the coast, and at entrances of harbors and bays, the British rather early in the war developed a tripod, with a microphone mounted upon it, which was lowered to the bottom and a listening station established on shore with connection by cable to the tripod. This apparatus was nondirectional, so that the only way a submarine could be located approximately was by judging its nearness to one of several such tripods by the intensity of the sound received. The first apparatus developed in this country was, in general, similar to that used in England, except that, instead of using a separate cable to each microphone, one cable was used for twenty microphones with a selective switching system, allowing the operator to connect to any one of the detectors.

Later it was seen that the binaural principle could be more effectively used, and tripods were equipped with three microphones in the form of a triangle, giving, in effect, the same results as a K-tube supported from the bottom of the sea, the compensator being located at the listening station on shore. The switching arrangement for this apparatus required considerable study and experiment, but eventually they proved very satisfactory. The submarine cable used in this installation had to be specially designed so as to keep both circuits of the binaural system as near alike in their electrical characteristics as possible, and also to prevent interference between the two circuits, in other words, they had to be electrically equal and electrically balanced. There were many details of this apparatus which required long and careful tests and experiments, but finally satisfactory stations were installed at the entrance to Long Island Sound and Chesapeake Bay. In addition, orders had been placed for a number of additional installations at other locations along the coast, and equipment consisting of six tripods with necessary cable and shore apparatus had been sent abroad at the request of the British Admiralty, and was in course of being planted when the armistice was signed. This tripod shore station installation required the development of means of plotting the submarines located, and means of communicating to shore fortifications, searchlight stations, and hunting craft, which were cooperating with shore stations. This shore station tripod development was carried out principally by engineers of the Western Electric Co. working with certain officers under the special board, and was in direct charge of Mr. E. H. Colpitts, of the Western Electric Co.

In addition to listening devices with shore connections, there was developed a system of magnetic loops for detecting by means of a galvanometer on shore when a submarine passed over a loop. These loops were laid in a number of different forms, the principal purpose being to determine by the sequence of deflections received from the different leads the exact position of the submarine. The magnetic loop, similar to all other magnetic devices, had a very short range, but would indicate when a submarine crossed a cable laid across a channel or entrance; and as it was of short range, no confusion would be experienced by a large number of vessels in the same general vicinity as would be the case when using tripod listening devices. Thus the magnetic loop was an adjunct to the tripod stations to a certain extent. The magnetic loop was originally developed abroad, and was used rather extensively by both the British and the French. The developments in this country consisted principally in the form of loops, the method of recording the galvanometer deflections or indications, and the method of eliminating shore disturbances, such as those caused by trolley systems. This apparatus had been satisfactorily installed at the entrance to Chesapeake Bay and was in operation when the armistice was signed. The development of the magnetic loop in this country was carried out by certain officers and others from New London in cooperation with the engineers of the Western Electric Co and was in general charge of Mr. E H Colpitts.

MISCELLANEOUS APPARATUS.

The application of listening devices and other detection apparatus to various types of craft and to shore stations showed the need of other apparatus for the proper working out of the tactics of approach and attack.

The early study of the tactics required for successful location, approach, and attack on submarines developed the three-ship unit as standard for hunting. Each vessel of the unit would obtain a bearing of the submarine, which was then transmitted to the unit leader, where the three bearings were plotted on the plotting instrument and the true bearing and distance of the submarine obtained The course and distance to be run was then transmitted to the vessels of the unit, and orders given as to speed, dropping of depth charges, etc This required very quick methods of communication which must be dependable at all times. For this purpose a short-range radiotelephone was developed by the Western Electric engineers in general charge of Mr. E. B Craft. This radiotelephone was similar, in general, to that developed for aircraft, and the development of the two was carried on at the same time, but the radiotelephone was in satisfactory operation on submarine chasers before it was adopted for aircraft

As an auxiliary method of communication on subchasers there was developed a visual indicator to show the direction of a submarine heard and the course to be run, which consisted of a large vertical arrow which could be rotated in the vertical plane like the hand of a clock to show angles, and could be rotated in azimuth so as to face the ship to which information was to be transmitted Other instructions, such as speed stopping, and getting under way, and distance to be run, could be transmitted visually by means of shapes and balls.

The plotting instrument referred to consisted of a reverse three-arm protractor developed for this particular purpose by means of which the bearings from the three vessels could be quickly utilized to obtain a "cut" or intersection, and thus the bearing and distance of the submarine from the center ship.

Another problem which presented itself was the provision of means for signaling at night between vessels of a hunting group and between different vessels in convoy, without any possibility of detection by an enemy. To accomplish this, there was developed transmitting and receiving apparatus utilizing invisible light rays which had a range of about 5 miles in the type adopted for smaller-sized vessels. This research was the original work of Mr. Theodore W. Case, the practical development being carried out by him at the experimental station, New London.

There was a large number of other developments successfully undertaken which are not covered here, but it is believed that the scope of the antisubmarine work has been indicated and that a realization can be obtained of the effective cooperation which was maintained by all concerned in this work. It seems clear also that this country was very well prepared to meet effectively and to overcome the submarine menace if the war had continued.

PRACTICAL DEMONSTRATION IN THE WAR ZONE.

A review of the antisubmarine activities would not be complete without a brief summary of the practical results accomplished in the war zone, by the hunting crafts of the allied navies, which were equipped with various detection devices.

The prime object of the antisubmarine campaign, and the one which first comes to the mind of the average reader, is that of providing means to actually destroy the enemy submarines. This is, undoubtedly, the most important and effective factor in the solution of the problem of making the seas safe from enemy submarine attacks. However, the numerous antisubmarine methods and apparatus developed and brought into use in this country accomplished most important results in various ways, a few of which are enumerated below:

(*a*) Detection and location of the submarine, to allow its ultimate destruction by torpedoes, depth bombs, or gunfire.

(*b*) Improvement of equipment of patrols and shore stations, which resulted in certain areas being practically freed of enemy submarines.

(*c*) Addition of listening devices to allied submarines to act as "ears" while totally submerged, thereby increasing their underwater operations.

(*d*) Demoralizing effect on enemy submarines, due to their knowledge of the existence of improved detection apparatus on allied craft.

(e) Use in convoys in locating the position of several units

(f) Avoiding collisions between allied craft in thick weather

It is not necessary to discuss in detail the advantages of the antisubmarine devices as outlined in the foregoing list, as the points are self-evident. However, it might be well to speak briefly of the advantages given the allied submarines by the installation of sound detectors. Previous to their use, a submarine which was submerged below periscope depth was completely ignorant of the activities of surface craft and other submarines.

Almost without exception, the commanding officers of submarines welcomed the addition of sound-detection apparatus with great enthusiasm. It supplemented the use of the periscope while on the surface and enabled them, while submerged, to detect the presence of any near-by surface craft or other submarines when making sufficient noise to be heard. This naturally led to the avoidance of collisions as well as to the detection and hunting of enemy submarines.

There are several cases on record of destroyers and chasers being saved from collision in foggy weather and at night by virtue of the sound being picked up on the listening devices in time to change the course and avert a collision.

It is very difficult to determine the exact number of enemy submarines which were destroyed through the use of the detection apparatus, in recognizing the presence of the submarine and giving the bearings which allowed a successful pursuit to the spot, when torpedoes or depth bomb could effect a sinking. In many cases, the submarine was sighted on the surface and pursued until it submerged, when the listening gear took up the chase and located it.

It has been unofficially estimated by those in a position to form such an estimate that the destruction of six, and possibly seven, enemy submarines was due to the use of American antisubmarine devices. The economic value of the sinking of six or seven submarines can best be realized by referring to an estimate made of the amount of shipping sunk in a year by one submarine. It is estimated that for each enemy submarine destroyed there was saved annually to the allied powers 40,000 tons of shipping, representing an annual saving of approximately $150,000,000. The sinking of six or seven submarines would, therefore, represent an annual saving of, roughly, $1,000,000,000.

Viewing these results from a purely economic standpoint, this annual saving of $1,000,000,000, in contrast with approximately $2,000,000, or two-tenths of 1 per cent, expended for research and development work upon the problem, gave considerable satisfaction to those contributing to the activities of submarine detection.

REPAIRS AND CONVERSIONS.

It will be appreciated that the maintenance in efficient operating condition of the machinery of such a large fleet as was assembled, both on our coasts and in European waters, composed as it was of "all sorts and conditions" of machinery, was a task of no small magnitude. For successful accomplishment, it demanded the most intimate knowledge of the principal details of design, so that if any weakness or casualty occurred the means for promptly meeting the situation would be at hand For instance, it meant that there should be available propellers or propeller blades to replace those damaged or lost, boiler tubes, condenser tubes, and shafting to fit any ship; steam pumps, forced-draft fans, electric generators, radio apparatus, and storage batteries for every auxiliary service and for submarines When the number and the size of the various installations are considered, it will be seen that the work of so organizing the divisions of the Bureau as to insure that provision would be made for meeting all these demands was a matter of much painstaking labor and perseverance Of slightly less importance was the provision of a suitable stock of these engineering supplies which were peculiar to one ship or to a particular class of ships.

When the war began, we had a Navy of about 350 vessels of all classes—in commission, in reserve, or building So rapidly did the fleet grow that on June 30, 1918, there were either in service or soon to be commissioned 1,959 vessels This total comprised 570 of the regular Navy, 93 drawn from the service of other Government departments, 937 merchant ships converted to use as troop transports, naval auxiliaries, or patrol vessels, and 359 built by the Emergency Fleet Corporation for the Naval Overseas Transportation Service.

The preparation of the existing fleet called for comparatively little work, for it has always been our pride that our ships were ready. The battleships of the active fleet needed little work. Fortunately, those of the reserve fleet had been kept in good condition and few repairs were needed to put the machinery in the best condition that was possible considering the age and previous service of the individual ships. A fire-control system for them was developed and installed Two battleships, the *Virginia* and the *Georgia* were having new boilers fitted, as was also the monitor *Tonopah*, and this work was rushed to completion as quickly as possible. The machincy of the armored cruisers was in fairly good condition, but the ships were deficient in operating personnel which militated against their instant readiness. New engines were under construction for the scout cruiser *Salem*, but as rapid prosecution of work on them would have interfered with the destroyer program, which work was given priority, the completion of the *Salem's* engines was delayed longer than otherwise would have been the case.

The machinery of the destroyers was in very good condition. As is usual with them, a few were under overhaul and others had repairs in prospective. Those that had been assigned to service abroad were sent to their home yards immediately upon the declaration of war and given the finishing touches necessary to fit them for the arduous campaign ahead of them. The condition in which they arrived in the war zone is a source of pride to the Bureau and reflects credit upon their engineering personnel. The way in which their machinery withstood the long and continuous service which it had to perform bespeaks the excellence of its construction, as it also justifies the care that was given to its inspection.

To keep these vessels in the condition they were upon arrival required that there should be an ample supply of consumable stores and of spare parts. To accomplish this the greatest care was given to the preparation of lists of the necessary material and supplies before the sailing of the tenders *Melville* and *Dixie*. The British Admiralty had informed us that casualties to propellers were numerous, and we accordingly sent to Queenstown a large number of propellers in the *Dixie*. So also with boiler and condenser tubes and pumps—enough tubes to completely retube the boilers or condensers of any single destroyer.

Large orders were placed for shaft forgings, which for lack of storage facilities at Queenstown, and also on account of the value of eastbound cargo space, were retained at east coast navy yards until the necessity for using them arose. In only two cases was this required, and in each case the shafting, ready for installation, was delivered before the hull repairs were far enough advanced to permit its installation.

Another important undertaking that was entered into for the purpose of reducing the time that a destroyer might possibly be out of service was the construction of a set of boilers (4) of each of the four types in use in destroyers operating in the war zone. The work was assigned to four navy yards, and the value of it was shown when the boilers of one of the Queenstown destroyers needed retubing. As soon as the boilers were ready the vessels was ordered home, the old boilers renewed and the new ones installed in seven weeks, and the destroyer returned to service. A side light on this illustrating the desire of officers to remain near the scene of operations, was the insistence of the commanding officer upon keeping his vessel abroad and having the boilers shipped over for installation, but as they would occupy valuable cargo space, and would be subject to loss by submarine attack, it was decided to withdraw her temporarily and substitute another destroyer

The one thing that more than anything else contributed to the "ever ready" condition of our destroyers in the war zone was the presence at Queenstown of the tenders *Melville* and *Dixie*. It seems fitting that the *Melville* should have played such a conspicuous part, as it was to the vision of one of my distinguished predecessors, Rear Admiral George W. Melville, for whom she was named, that our repair ship—and the first of any Navy—the *Vulcan* was equipped for similar service during the Spanish war. No job was too big for the *Melville* and the *Dixie* to undertake, and it was on account of their capability and the excellence of their work that our destroyers based at Queenstown spent so little time at a dockyard. Perhaps the best appreciation of their work is contained in the following encomium from Admiral Sir Lewis Bayly, R. N., who was in command at Queenstown:

> Without these repair ships, the work could never have been done Working full 24 hours, in three shifts of 8 hours each; sleeping among the noises of the machinery, always ready for extra work when an unexpected accident happened or an unforeseen call was made on a destroyer that was being dealt with, they never failed nre Capt J R F Pringle, of the *Melville*, and Capt. H B. Price, of the *Dixie*, were not only always ready to do the expected, but used their utmost endeavors to be prepared for the unforeseen, and the result was such as their country has reason to be proud of.

The organization at Queenstown was such as lent itself admirably to expeditious accomplishment of work, and this is exemplified by the fact that the boilers of a destroyer were completely retubed in place without interfering with her regular patrol and convoy duty. This was accomplished by working on one side of the boiler during the 5-day overhaul period, and allowing the vessel to operate between periods on three boilers until retubing was completed. Meanwhile, she was capable of making upward of 25 knots

One excellent rule that prevailed was that as soon as a destroyer entered harbor and tied up to a buoy she was not to be called upon for any work that involved the use of her boilers or engines As a result of this, the customary overhaul by the ship's force could proceed without interruption, and with assurance that if it should be necessary to change berth the service of a tug would be available.

The repair ships handled all work that was beyond the capacity of the destroyers themselves, but the repair officers were insistent that the latter do everything within their resources. It was in this way that the destroyers were always ready and that the repair ships were also able to care for the work on shore which such an important base entailed.

Other repair ships, the *Prometheus*, the *Panther*, and the *Bridgeport*, were stationed at Brest, and the *Buffalo* at Gibraltar, and performed like service for the patrol vessels and destroyers operating from those ports. The *Bridgeport* did not arrive until late in the war, but did admirable work, especially in connection with the repair of transports and auxiliaries after the armistice. She was splendidly equipped.

Small repair shops were established at Brest, at Pauillac, and at Gibraltar, which assisted materially in keeping the small patrol vessels ready for operation.

As is stated in the chapter on repair of the damage to the ex-German ships, the repairs to the machinery of those that were used as troop transports were of quite as extensive character as was the actual work of remedying the damage caused by vandalism, this on account of the long period of idleness and lack of care of the machinery during that time. In many cases entire renewal of boiler tubes had to be undertaken, and in some material increase made in the distilling capacity. Besides this, all had to be provided with such electrical equipment as truck lights and controllers, blinker signal sets, man-overboard and breakdown lights, loud-speaking telephones, fire-control voice-tube and telephone systems, general-alarm gongs, revolution telegraphs, revolution indicators, and increased lighting equipment to suit the rearrangement for troop transport, as well as an auxiliary lighting system. All were provided with a suitable equipment of machine tools, for although their runs were, as before, between fixed ports, the demands on the repair facilities at Brest—which at best were none too good—were so great that reliance could not be placed on Brest for such work. In fact it not infrequently happened that these transports, by reason of their equipment, were able to assist in making repairs to other vessels.

For maintenance of the engines of submarine chasers a liberal supply of spare parts and of consumable material was made to the bases from which they operated abroad, as well as to the *Hannibal* and *Leonidas*, which were equipped as tender for them. The latter was stationed at Corfu and served the chasers which did such effective service in the Adriatic.

Many additions and alterations were required in all the merchant auxiliaries. Few of them were adequately provided with distilling apparatus, the service on which they were previously employed either not requiring it or only to a capacity sufficient to satisfy the marine insurance companies. Even before war was declared we had begun the installation of fire-control voice tubes and telephones on merchant ships that carried armed guards, and this was continued with all auxiliary vessels as rapidly as they were taken over. All had to be provided with screened speed lights, and the patrol vessels generally with searchlights

The vessels of the Coast Guard, the Lighthouse Service, the Coast and Geodetic Survey, and the Fish Commission required the usual repairs and, in addition, special equipment and fittings to make them suited to the duty to which they were assigned.

With the increase in the number of destroyers and submarines, it became necessary to prepare other vessels to serve as tenders The work on the *Bridgeport* and *Buffalo*, which were designated destroyer tenders, was completed in time for them to render efficient service, but work on the *Beaver*, *Camden*, *Prairie*, and *Rainbow* was not completed before the signing of the armistice

The navy yards, of course, could not handle all the work of this character and also routine repair and upkeep It therefore became necessary to utilize to the fullest the repair facilities of the several ports from which vessels operated. As New York was the principal port of embarkation of troops, as well as of shipment of supplies, a large portion of the work was accomplished by the private repair yards of that port The facilities of Boston, Philadelphia, Norfolk, Newport News, and Charleston were also utilized as required Commandants of navy yards and naval districts were authorized to make local contracts for the repair of patrol vessels These were generally with firms whose facilities could not be utilized for the more important ships.

The following named officers were on duty in the Repair Division of the Bureau:

Commander W A Smead, U S Navy, in charge
Lieut Commander B Bruce U S. Navy
Lieut Commander F. W. Osburn, U S. Navy, retired.
Lieut. Commander H F. D. Davis, U. S. Navy.
Capt of Engineers F E. Gagger U. S Coast Guard
Capt of Engineers F. E. Fitch, U S Coast Guard
Capt of Engineers C. J Oden'dhal, U. S. Coast Guard.
Capt of Engineers M. W. Torbet, U. S. Coast Guard
Lieut. (T) A C Byrne, U. S Navy.
Lieut. (T) J. P Millon, U. S Navy
Lieut. (T) C E. Veth. U S Navy.
Lieut. E. R. Fitch, U. S. Naval Reserve Force
Lieut F S. M. Harris, U. S Naval Reserve Force.
Lieut. W E. Hubbard, U S. Naval Reserve Force.
Lieut (j g.) R T Hass, U. S. Naval Reserve Force
Lieut (j. g.) H B. Phillipps, U. S Naval Reserve Force

REPAIRS OF THE EX-GERMAN SHIPS DAMAGED BY THE VANDALISM OF THEIR CREWS.

There was probably no other work undertaken by the Navy, unless it were the destroyer program, that compared in importance with the repair of the machinery of the German ships that were interned in our harbors at the outbreak of war. Many of them were first-class passenger steamers of large carrying capacity whose services would be invaluable as troop transports, while many others would be of incalculable value in the shipment of supplies But when they were taken possession of on April 6, 1917, it was discovered that their machinery had been so badly damaged as to preclude the possibility of utilizing their services for a year or 18 months, if the usual method of repair were resorted to This, of course, could not be seriously considered. The tonnage of allied shipping had been greatly reduced through German submarine attack, and to win success in the war it was vital that these ships be put in condition for service with the least possible delay

It will be recalled that the German Government had notified the United States Government that unrestricted submarine warfare would begin on February 1, 1917, and it is significant that documentary evidence secured on board one of these ships at New York in the shape of a memorandum by her chief engineer shows that the wrecking of her machinery had actually started January 31

When first taken over, the ships were placed in the custody of the collectors of customs until such time as they could be transferred to the Shipping Board In the case of the vessels at New York, the commandant detailed the engineer officer of the yard, Commander E. P. Jessop, to give technical advice to the collector until all the vessels were so transferred

Commander Jessop states, in the Journal of the American Society of Naval Engineers, that two boards were appointed to examine the machinery, one appointed by the collector, composed of engineers of the Erie and New York Central Railroads, and the other by the Shipping Board The latter board recommended renewal of all cylinders that were seriously damaged, which was in accord with prevailing practice and with the requirements of the marine underwriters, while the former, composed of engineers experienced in the

79

application of electric welding to iron castings, were convinced that renewal was not necessary and that all broken castings could be reclaimed. Great opposition was, however, shown to the use of electric welding by the representatives of the Shipping Board, and it was not until the larger vessels were transferred to the Navy Department in July, 1917, for conversion to troop transports that authority for the use of electric welding was given by that Department.

Previously to this, realizing that the operation of these particular ships would necessarily have to be placed in the hands of the Navy, the Bureau had kept in touch with the work that was proceeding on all the interned German ships at all navy yards and in the port of New York. Commander Jessop had, as early as May 12, 1917, informed the Bureau, in telephone conversation, that in his judgment nearly all the damaged cylinders could be saved by welding, and when in June it was practically settled that the passenger-carrying vessels would be transferred to the Navy, the Bureau detailed Capt. O. W. Koester to visit New York, confer with Rear Admiral Burd, industrial manager of the navy yard there, and with Commander Jessop, and make an inspection of the ships, in order that it might be in a position to estimate the extent of the damage and the time necessary to make the repairs. Upon his return Capt. Koester reported his concurrence in the judgment of the board of railway engineers and of Commander Jessop that electric welding would save all the broken cylinders. The Chief of Bureau then conferred with Rear Admiral Burd, who also expressed confidence in the ability of experienced welders to make successful repairs and thus avoid the great delay that would result if new cylinders were made. Instructions were then given to proceed with electric welding and to resort to mechanical patching only when welding was impracticable. The subsequent work on the part of the Bureau was placed under the immediate supervision of Capt. Koester, who cooperated in every way with the engineer officers of the several navy yards in the successful completion of this undertaking.

The order for the Navy to take over these ships was received in the Bureau July 11, 1917, and the industrial manager of the New York Navy Yard was immediately notified by telephone and directed to return yard workmen to the *Vaterland*, from which they had been withdrawn on account of friction with representatives of the Shipping Board. Similar instructions were sent to the Boston and to the Norfolk Navy Yards, and the former was directed to give consideration to the application of electric welding instead of mechanical patching, which was then being used on the three ships in that port.

The following list gives the names, original and rechristened, of all the vessels that were in our ports and in Cuban waters at the date of the declaration of war:

HISTORY OF ENGINEERING DURING THE WORLD WAR. 81

United States name	German name	Taken over and repaired at—	Gross tonnage	Horse-power
Actaeon	Adamstrum	New York	5,000	2,000
Adelheid	Adelheid	Cuba	2,870	
Aeolus	Grosser Kurfurst	New York	14,102	8,400
Agamemnon	Kaiser Wilhelm II	do	19,361	45,000
America	Amerika	Boston	22,621	15,800
Amphion	Koln	do	7,109	3,540
Andalusia	Andalusia	Manila	5,471	2,980
Antigone	Neckar	Norfolk	9,835	5,860
Appelles	Elsass	Pago Pago, Samoa	6,591	3,900
Arcadia	Arcadia	Newport News	5,454	2,980
Armenia	Armenia	New York	5,156	2,980
Artemis	Bohemia	do	8,414	7,340
Artigas	Wiegand	Cebu	4,990	
Ascutney	Pisa	New York	4,967	4,858
Astoria	Frieda Leonhardt	Jacksonville	2,789	2,492
Bath	Andromeda	New Orleans	2,554	2,337
Bavaria	Bavaria	Cuba	3,805	2,500
Beaufort	Rudolf Blumberg	Pensacola	1,769	1,364
Black Hawk	Rheatia	Philadelphia	6,599	3,195
Bridgeport	Breslau	New Orleans	7,521	4,479
Calabria	Calabria	St. Thomas, Virgin Islands	3,004	2,736
Camden	Kiel	Charleston	4,491	4,967
Casco	Elmshorn	Manila	1,591	2,800
Chattahoochee	Sachsen	do	8,232	1,000
Constantia	Constantia	New Orleans	3,026	2,727
Corsa	Loonginoon	Honolulu	1,971	1,770
Cormorant[1]	Cormorant	Guam	(¹)	(¹)
Covington	Cincinnati	Boston	16,339	10,900
De Kalb	Prinz Eitel Friedrich	Philadelphia	7,889	7,000
Farn Geraux	Farn Geraux	San Juan	4,393	3,216
General Ernst	Sachsenwald	Colon	3,559	2,130
General Goethals	Gruenwald	do	4,707	3,612
General Hodges	Savoia	do	6,214	3,260
General Gorgas	Prinz Sigsmund	do	4,689	2,900
George Washington	George Washington	New York	25,570	21,000
Gulfport	Locksun	Pearl Harbor	1,657	1,220
Hercules	Bulgaria	Norfolk	11,110	5,500
Hermes	Hermes	Honolulu	118	(²)
Houston	Liebenfels	Charleston	4,525	3,402
Huron	Friedrich der Grosse	New York	10,771	6,800
Iosco	Johanne	Manila	1,731	1,144
Iroquois	Wittekind	Boston	5,640	4,641
Isonomia	Nassovia	New York	3,662	2,174
Itasca	Netos	Honolulu	1,730	2,730
Kittery	Praesident	Philadelphia	1,819	1,800
Leviathan	Vaterland	New York	54,282	90,000
Long Beach	Hohenfelde	Savannah	2,974	1,750
Madawaska	Koenig Wilhelm II	New York	9,110	7,400
Mercury	Barbarossa	do	10,984	7,200
Minnow	Neptune	Oakland, Calif	197	(²)
Moccasin	Prinz Joachim	New York	4,760	3,450
Montpelier	Bochum	Manila	6,161	3,052
Monongahela	Dalbek	Portland	2,723	(²)
Montauk	Matador	New York	1,168	(²)
Monticello	O. J. D. Ahlers	Hilo	7,490	2,052
Moshulu	Kurt	Portland, Oreg	3,109	(²)
Mount Vernon	Kronprinzessin Cecilie	Boston	19,503	45,000
Muscoota	Ottawa	San Francisco	2,659	(³)
Nansemond	Pennsylvania	New York	13,333	6,276
Neuse	Magdeburg	do	4,496	3,130
Newport News	Odenwald	San Juan	3,537	2,730
Nipsic	Borneo	Zamboanga	2,168	1,170
Oconee	Mais	New York	2,535	1,626
Olivant	Olivant	Cuba	1,014	1,660
Orion	Prinz Oskar	Philadelphia	6,026	3,630
Osage	Serapis	San Francisco	1,756	2,590
Ostego	Prinz Eitel Friedrich	New York	1,650	2,580
Owasco	Allemania	do	1,630	3,100
Pawnee	Harburg	do	4,172	3,150
Pensacola	Nicaria	Charleston	3,974	2,100
Pequot	Ockenfels	Boston	5,621	4,600
Pocahontas	Prinzess Irene	New York	10,893	9,000
Powhatan	Hamburg	do	10,893	9,000
Princess Matoika	Princess Alice	Cebu	10,984	9,000
President Lincoln	President Lincoln	New York	18,168	8,500
President Grant	President Grant	do	18,072	8,500
Quantico	Freemoon	Manila	1,625	1,500
Quincy	Voggesen	Pensacola	3,716	1,835
Quinnebaug	Fongtong	Manila	1,641	938
Rajah	Rajah	do	2,028	1,085
Rappahannock	Pommern	Hem'l M	5,573	3,885

[1] Blown up by own crew   Sunk by ...
[2] Gasoline   [3] ...

United States name	German name	Taken over and repaired at—	Gross tonnage	Horse-power
Raritan	Carl Diederichsen	Manila	1,243	135
Sachem	Coblenz	do	3,130	2,000
Samoa	Staatssekretar Solf	Samoa	304	125
Savannah	Saxonia	Winslow, Wash	4,124	2,500
Seneca	Tubingen	Manila	5,586	3,330
Schurz (gunboat)	Geier	Honolulu	1,630	
Susquehanna	Rhein	Norfolk	10,058	9,520
Suwanee	Mark	Manila	6,579	3,850
Tacony	Staat Kraetke	Honolulu	2,009	2,660
Tonawanda	Indra	New York	1,746	(²)
Ticonderoga	Camilla Rickmers	Manila	5,130	2,800
Tippecanoe	Holsatia	Honolulu	5,644	2,800
Tioga	Clara Jobson	Manila	1,735	1,260
Tunica	Sambia	do	1,765	2,520
Von Steuben	Kronprinz Wilhelm	Philadelphia	14,908	31,500
Wachusett	Suevia	Manila	3,780	1,900
Wacouta	Prinz Waldemar	Honolulu	3,227	2,200
Wamsutta	Dorvel	Zamboanga	1,508	1,225
Wasgenwold	Wasgenwold	St Thomas, Virgin Islands	4,708	3,612
Watoga	Goveneur Jaeschke	Honolulu	1,738	1,440
Wyandotte	Willehad	New Orleans	1,761	1,610
Yazoo	Marudu	Zamboanga	1,514	1,225
Yadkin	Clara Mennig	Manila	1,685	910
Yucca	Portonia	New York	2,778	1,260
Yuma	Tam Tau	Cebu	1,635	920

² Sailing ship

In addition to the German merchant vessels and gunboat given in the list above, the following Austrian merchant steamers were later seized similarly and refitted for United States service:

United States name	Austrian name	Taken over at—	Gross tonnage	Horse-power
Anna	Anna	New Orleans	1,575	1,400
Dora	Dora	New York	7,037	2,590
Erny	Erny	Boston	6,513	2,590
Ida	Ida		4,730	1,787
Martha Washington	Martha Washington	New York	8,312	6,940
Borneo	Borneo	Tampa	3,621	1,900
Nyanza	Esslinger	Manila	4,902	2,850
Teresa	Teresa	New Orleans	3,789	2,100

Tonnage of vessels seized.—The tonnage of the German merchant ships taken over is 592,195 gross tons, and that of the eight Austrian ships is 40,461, making a total of 632,656 gross tons of shipping placed under the United States flag from these two sources.

Ports where vessels were seized.—These vessels were taken over in various American ports throughout the world, such as Boston; New York; Philadelphia; Baltimore; Norfolk, Charleston, Savannah; Pensacola, Jacksonville; New Orleans; St Thomas, Virgin Islands; San Juan, P. R ; Colon, San Francisco and Oakland, Calif ; Portland and Clifton, Oreg ; Winslow, Wash.; Honolulu, Pearl Harbor, and Hilo, Hawaii; Pago Pago, Samoa, and Manila, Cebu, and Zamboanga, P. I In addition, ships seized in Cuban ports were delivered to our Government The wide distribution of these seizures is noted to show the extent to which German sea-borne commerce with our ports had grown.

Vandalism prearranged and simultaneous on all ships.—The machinery of practically all of these vessels was damaged by their crews for the very evident purpose of placing them out of service during a period of at least a year or 18 months. From the general nature of the vandalism thus perpetrated—the same parts being broken or otherwise damaged on practically all of the ships, no matter in what ports they were—it is clear that the order for this destructive work must have been given by high authority and sent out broadcast and simultaneously to all German vessels interned in United States ports. And yet a close analysis indicates that the instructions to vessels in Atlantic ports may have differed from those in Pacific ports. In the case of the former the vandalism was confined almost entirely to injury to the cylinders and valve chests, to destruction of throttle valves and engine valves, the breaking of circulating pump casings, and in general to injury to iron castings, and only in rare cases to injury to boilers, none of those in the large ships being damaged at all. In the Pacific, however, it was unusual to find boilers that had not been dry fired, and in such cases the extent of injury to the engines was far less in extent than was the case with vessels in Atlantic ports.

The extent to which the attempted wrecking of the machinery of these ships was carried may be indicated by a few examples, as follows:

America (ex-Amerika).—Both high-pressure cylinders broken, one low-pressure cylinder head broken, two low-pressure piston rods bent, other minor damages.

Astoria (ex-Frieda Leonhardt).—High-pressure piston rod and throttle missing. All receiver flanges, low-pressure cylinder head, high-pressure steam nozzle, high-pressure receiver pipe, low-pressure receiver pipe, exhaust trunk and steam gauges broken. Hole cut in shell, both boilers. Hole cut in outboard furnace, both boilers. Both boilers dry-fired, back end of tubes and stay-bolt nuts badly burned; seams, rivets, and tube leaking. Stop-valve bonnets missing. Water column destroyed.

Bath (ex-Andromeda).—Intermediate-pressure and low-pressure cylinder liners broken; high-pressure piston, valve, rings, follower, etc., missing; low-pressure piston valve, rings, and packing missing; low-pressure valve stem missing.

Camden (ex-Kiel).—Throttle missing, low-pressure cylinder, first intermediate-pressure valve, second intermediate-pressure valve, and low-pressure valve broken. All steam pipes cut at the flanges. All boilers fittings smashed. All valve stems of double bottom manifolds bent. Engine telegraphs damaged.

George W. ... High-pressure cylinder, ... nozzle,

low-pressure valve chest of both engines broken, also both circulating pump casings

Madawaska (ex-Koenig Wilhelm II).—On both engines, main-engine stop valves broken; high-pressure, first intermediate-pressure, second intermediate-pressure cylinders broken, valve chest broken.

Mercury (ex-Barbarossa)—Following parts broken on both engines High-pressure cylinder heads and flanges; first intermediate-pressure cylinder head and flanges, first intermediate-pressure cylinder, second intermediate-pressure steam nozzle, low-pressure cylinder, circulating pump casings

Quincy (ex-Vogensen).—Boiler stays and stay bolts sawed through; connecting rods sawed half through; piston rods sawed half through. Other cases of vandalism, but of minor character.

Damage of much moment to the great *Vaterland*, now the *Leviathan*, apparently proved to be beyond the capacity of her engineer force Her machinery was, however, in bad order, owing to poor design, incompetent operation, and her long stay and lack of overhaul in port.

That the engineers of these German ships believed the damage they inflicted to be irreparable is shown by the frequent note "Cannot be repaired" in the following literal translation of a memorandum found by our officers on the *Hamburg*, now the *Powhatan*, summarizing the damages to the machinery of that vessel

S S HAMBURG,
New York, January 31, 1917

1 Starboard and port h p cylinder with valve chest, upper exhaust outlet flange broken off (Can not be repaired)

2 Starboard and port 1st m. p cylinder with valve chest, upper exhaust outlet flange broken off. (Can not be repaired)

3 Starboard and part 2d m p valve chest, steam inlet flange broken off (Can not be repaired)

4 Valve chest cover damaged; balance cylinder broken (Can not be repaired)

5 Four (4) relief valves from second m p destroyed

6 Starboard 2d m p piston guide rod damaged (Can not be repaired)

7 Port 2d m p stuffing box gland of piston rod guide destroyed.

8 Starboard and port low-pressure valve chests, steam inlet flanges broken off (Can not be repaired)

9 Valve chest cover damaged Balance cylinder broken. (Can not be repaired)

10 Two (2) relief valves destroyed

11 Port low-pressure stuffing box gland of the piston rod guide destroyed

12 Port and starboard main engine stop valve, with bypass valves, and reversing engine valves destroyed.

13 Low-pressure relief valves and two guides of valve stem destroyed

14 Port and starboard exhaust nozzles (outlets) from high pressure to first m p, three (3) flanges broken off, two (2) relief valves destroyed

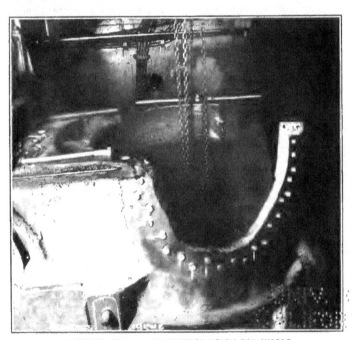

PRINCESS IRENE, H. P. CYLINDER READY FOR INSERT.

PRINCESS IRENE, H. P. CYLINDER; INSERT IN PLACE READY FOR WELDING.

PRINCESS IRENE, H. P. CYLINDER WELDED.

PRINCESS IRENE. BROKEN I. P. VALVE CHEST.

PRINCESS IRENE. I. P. VALVE CHEST READY TO WELD.

PRINCESS IRENE. I. P. VALVE CHEST WELDED.

15 First m p starboard, exhaust pipe exhaust line to 2d m p flange broken off (Can not be repaired)

16 Guide of the valve stem, relief valve on cylinder destroyed

17 First m p port, exhaust pipe of exhaust line to 2d m p. flange broken off (Can not be repaired)

18 Exhaust line to 2d m p damaged, guide on valve stem and relief valve destroyed

19 Starboard and port low-pressure exhaust pipe damaged (Can not be repaired)

The seeming complacency with which the Germans regarded the effectiveness of their work is also indicated in an entry made four weeks later in the log of the *Prinz Eitel Friedrich* (*De Kalb*), which was interned at the Philadelphia Navy Yard. It follows:

After the work done to-day, the condition of the cylinders of both engines is such that there is no possibility whatever of starting them

And yet the damage on the *Prinz Eitel* was far less in extent and much more easily corrected than that on any other of the large ships.

The illustrations indicate clearly the typical character of the damage and the general method of repair by electric welding. This method consisted in general of welding to each surface of cast iron a layer of steel, thoroughly calked down to insure that a good union has been made, and then welding these layers of steel to a cast-steel filling piece fashioned to fill as nearly as possible the intervening space. It will be noted that the iron casting is studded and the welding metal carried over beyond the studs. While it is stated that this is done merely as a precaution and to insure that the strength of the weld be not less than that of the part to be welded, the presence of the studs does no harm, and, whether necessary or not they, at least, have not militated against the integrity of any weld that was made

Importance of rapid repairs —The Navy Department speedily recognized that the large passenger ships thus taken over must be our chief reliance in transporting our troops to France, and that their quick repair was a matter of the greatest national importance. In fact, as the following table shows, 20 of these vessels—transferred to and repaired by the Navy—were capable of transporting an aggregate of about 70,000 troops in one trip:

	Troops
Leviathan (ex-Vaterland)	10 000
George Washington (ex-George Washington)	6 000
America (ex-Amerika)	4,100
Agamemnon (ex-Kaiser Wilhelm II)	3 500
Mt Vernon (ex-Kronprinzessin Cecilie)	3,600
President Lincoln (ex-President Lincoln)	4,000
President Grant (ex-President Grant)	4,900
Covington (ex-Cincinnati)	3,800
Aeolus (ex-Grosser Kurfurst)	2,800
Mercury (ex Barbarossa)	.)
Pocahontas (ex Prinzess Irene)	...
Princess Matoika (ex Prinzess Alice)	700

	Troops
Huron (ex-Friedrich der Grosse)	2,600
Powhatan (ex-Hamburg)	2,300
Susquehanna (ex-Rhein)	2,300
Antigone (ex-Neckar)	2,300
De Kalb (ex-Prinz Eitel Friedrich)	1,600
Von Steuben (ex-Kronprinz Wilhelm)	1,300
Madawaska (ex-Koenig Wilhelm II)	2,800
Martha Washington (ex-Martha Washington, Austrian)	2,700
Total	69,900

Ships repaired by the Navy.—In addition to the 20 transports noted above, the following ex-German vessels were transferred to the Navy for repairs and conversion into Navy auxiliaries:

Present name	Former name	Where repaired and fitted out	Duty
Astoria	Frieda Leonhardt	Charleston	Navy auxiliary
Bath	Andromeda	New Orleans	Do
Beaufort	Rudolf Blumberg	..do..	Do
Bridgeport	Breslau	New Orleans and Boston	Repair ship
Camden	Kiel	Charleston and Philadelphia	Do
Gulfport	Locksun	Pearl Harbor	Navy auxiliary
Hermes	Hermes	..do..	Do
Houston	Liebenfels	Charleston	Do
Kittery	Praesident	Philadelphia	Do
Long Beach	Hohenfelde	Charleston	Do
Newport News	Odenwald	Philadelphia	Do
Pensacola	Nicaria	Charleston	Do
Quincy	Vogensen	Pensacola and New Orleans	Do
Samoa	Staatssekretar Solf	Samoa	Do
Savannah	Saxonia	Puget Sound	Repair ship
Schurz	Geier	Pearl Harbor	Gunboat

Also the Navy repaired and fitted out for the United States Shipping Board Emergency Fleet Corporation the following ex-German ships:

Present name	Former name	Where repaired and fitted out
Adelheid	Adelheid	New Orleans (received from Cuba)
Appeles	Elsass	Mare Island
Bavaria	Bavaria	New Orleans (received from Cuba)
Chattahoochee	Sachsen	Olongapo and Puget Sound
Constantia	Constantia	New Orleans (received from Cuba)
Itasca	Setos	Mare Island
Nyanza	Easlinger	Cavite
Olivant	Olivant	New Orleans (received from Cuba)
Philippines	Bulgaria	Norfolk
Quantico	Lyeemoon	Olongapo
Rajah	Rajah	Mare Island
Rappahannock	Pommern	Do
Raritan	Carl Diederichsen	Olongapo
Suwanee	Mark	Do
Tacony	Staatssekretar Kraetke	Pearl Harbor and Mare Island
Teresa (Austrian)	Teresa	New Orleans and Norfolk
Ticonderoga	Camilla Rickmers	Olongapo
Tippecanoe	Holsatia	Mare Island
Tunica	Cambria	Olongapo, Cavite, and Mare Island
Wacouta	Prinz Waldemar	Puget Sound

In considering the repair and refit of these ex-German ships, it should be borne in mind that the engines had not only been damaged, but that normally they should have been in poor condition, since the ships had been laid up in various American ports for three years, with very inadequate upkeep during that period. Hence deterioration as well as damage had to be corrected, and as no drawings of plans of any kind were available, the actual time taken in getting the ships ready for service was consumed less in repairing vandalism than in general overhaul and in conversion to the special service they were to perform

One condition which next to welding, contributed most to the rapidity with which the work was done was that the Navy Department, upon the recommendation of this Bureau to the Chief of Naval Operations, put the ships in commission as soon as they were taken over. In this way not only did the crews become familiar with the ships, but they also assisted materially in the detection of vandalism and in the rapid preparation of the ships for service

Upon completion of this work of repair and overhaul every important piece of machinery, boilers, and other equipment was submitted to the original design tests under the supervision of the ship's officers. Then the customary dock trials were held, and finally, before the ships were pronounced ready to engage in the responsible work of transporting troops, they were taken to sea and subjected to a continuous full-power test of 48 hours' duration. The purpose of this was to test the effectiveness of the unusual repairs that had been undertaken to determine whether any important operating feature had been overlooked, and finally to familiarize the crew with the handling of the ship and the operation of the machinery. So well had the work been done and so satisfactorily had the engines operated that upon completion of the sea trial the transports usually proceeded to the point of embarkation of troops to begin a service which was epoch making in our national history.

The military value of this work in the transport of troops is particularly interesting. The last of these ships was in service for nearly a year before hostilities ceased, and this represents approximately the time saved by the use of welding methods They alone transported nearly 600 000 troops to France, the *Leviathan* heading the list with upward of 94 000 But for them the Allies would have been seriously embarrassed

The total number of troops transported by each ship is given below

Ships	Total trips	Total troops	Ships	Total trips	Total troops
Aeolus	8	24,340	Mercury	7	18,292
Agamemnon	10	45,392	Mount Vernon	9	33,628
America	9	39,678	Princess Matoika	6	21,329
Antigone	8	16,476	Powhatan	7	11,547
Covington[1]	5	21,755	Pocahontas	9	22,579
De Kalb	11	9,779	President Grant	8	39,422
George Washington	9	46,446	President Lincoln[1]	4½	23,149
Huron	8	20,771	Susquehanna	8	18,394
Leviathan	10	94,109	Von Steuben	9	15,929
Madawaska	9	18,931			
Martha Washington	8	21,902	Total		537,537

[1] Torpedoed on

The throwing into France of 500,000 United States troops a year ahead of the time estimated by the Germans for their arrival had unquestionably a most important effect on the shortening of the war. It was these ships which enabled this huge force to reach France early and be trained at the front, so that they might be ready to do their share in turning the tide of war.

The financial aspect of the matter is minor. It has been estimated, however, that if used wholly as freight carriers, these ex-German ships would have effected an economy of more than $20,000,000.

The *Rhein*, the *Neckar*, the *Bulgaria* (renamed the *Susquehanna*), the *Antigone*, and the *Hercules* were repaired at the Norfolk Navy Yard. The damage to their engines was similar to that of the other ships, but in this case repair was made for the greater part by oxy-acetylene welding, only a few welds having been made by the electric method. In the case of oxy-acetylene welding it was, of course, necessary to remove the cylinders from the ship in order to heat them to the temperature necessary to secure a good weld, and while the use of this process added greatly to the expense and the time necessary for making repairs, the welds that were so made have proved equally as reliable as those done by the electric arc.

In what has preceded, the reference is chiefly to the reciprocating engined ships, which comprehends all except the *Leviathan* (ex-*Vaterland*), the most powerfully engined merchant ship afloat. She was the only turbine vessel of the German fleet that fell into our hands, and her prospective value as a troop transport transcended that of any other of this big fleet, not only on account of her speed but because of her passenger capacity. Her boilers were uninjured, and while damage was in evidence in her turbines, it was not clear that this was the result of vandalism; it was of such a character as might have been charged to an accident of operation. Several rows of blading had to be renewed, and some rows were cut out altogether. Cracks were also found in the casing of one of the backing turbines, and these were welded.

There were many minor evidences of vandalism, all of which were disclosed by the thorough examination that was made of every portion of this superb ship, and it is greatly to the credit of those concerned in the work on her, as well as on all the others, that not a single case of vandalism was undiscovered.

Secretary Daniels in commenting on this work in his annual report for 1918, says:

This decision (to use welding), so far-reaching in its application and so fraught with danger to the professional reputation of the officers concerned, was made in the face of opposition by engine builders and by marine insurance companies, but with such confidence in the ultimate result as left no room for doubt of its success.

S. S. NECKAR, 2D I. P. CYLINDER; CAST IRON PATCH READY FOR WELDING.

S. S. NECKAR, I. P. CYLINDER WELDED.

S. S. SANTOS, SECOND I. P. CYLINDER.

S. S. SANTOS.

S. S. SANTOS

S. S. SANTOS.

S. S. SANTOS:—SECOND I. P. VALVE CHEST AFTER WELDING AT NAVY YARD, PHILADELPHIA, PA.

S. S. SANTOS, I. P. VALVE CHEST READY FOR WELDING.

The electric welding was done by the Wilson Welder & Metals Co., New York City, and the oxy-acetylene welding by the Davis-Bournonville Co., Jersey City, N. J.

In addition to this work on German vessels that were interned in our ports, work of a similar character was done at the Philadelphia Navy Yard on the cylinders of the *Santos* (ex-*Santos*) which had been interned in Brazilian waters. She had been leased to the French Government, but the engine cylinders had been so badly wrecked that it was considered to be impossible to repair them in Rio, and the several parts were, therefore, shipped to Philadelphia where the work of repair was undertaken and completed in time for installation after the vessel reached that port in tow.

Another vessel, the *Itu* (ex-*Cap Roca*) which had been similarly transferred to the French, had extensive boiler work, the result of vandalism, undertaken at New York under the direction of the industrial manager of the navy yard.

RADIO TELEGRAPHY.

INTRODUCTORY

During the war, the functions of the Radio Division covered the maintenance of the transoceanic high-power radio systems, of the radio navigational stations, and of the coastal ship and shore radio stations. It included also the design, installation, and upkeep of all radio apparatus on naval vessels, on those of the Shipping Board, and, in fact, on all vessels and aircraft operated by the Government, except those owned by the Army. To these duties—almost world-wide in their scope—were added continuous and urgent research and development in all lines relating to radio apparatus.

RADIO DEVELOPMENTS DURING THE WAR

The principal developments in radio apparatus by the Navy during the war were

1. An increase in the efficiency of the transoceanic radio service, together with such a growth in the number of stations that radio must now be considered as a competitor of the ocean cables

2. The development of the radio compass to aid in navigation, and also its installation for practical operation

3. The development of radio equipment for aircraft from ranges of 100 miles to a range of 500 miles

4. The concentration, with resultant conservation, of the radio personnel and radio facilities for all departments of the Government—except the Army, whose service was distinct—by placing all radio design and maintenance under the Navy. This system permitted an immense amount of work to be carried on effectively in connection with the design, purchase, installation, and upkeep of radio equipment for practically all Government and merchant vessels operating from ports in this country.

5. The taking over and maintenance for traffic use of all privately owned radio stations.

6. The establishment of repair facilities abroad at the various naval bases for installing and maintaining radio equipment at naval bases

7. The installation of radio telephone equipment on all naval vessels and aircraft

As a basis for carrying on the work noted above, the Bureau adopted the policy of using the available facilities and engineering personnel of existing firms, even though these facilities were at times inadequate. It was decided that such a system would be more advantageous than starting an entirely new company on the large scale necessary to meet the urgent requirements of war. This policy proved to be a sound one. There is no known case in which any vessel was delayed through failure to provide promptly a radio installation.

It is a pleasure to make acknowledgment of the hearty and thorough cooperation of the radio engineers in civil life and the various radio manufacturing companies, who gave their whole time to Government requirements during the war, and who carried out willingly every request and suggestion made by the Bureau.

HIGH-POWER RADIO TRANSMISSION

In order fully to appreciate the recent developments in the art of high-power transmission it is desirable to review briefly its progress prior to the commencement of the war.

Historically, the first long-distance transmission by radio was effected in 1901 by Marconi between Newfoundland and Ireland; in 1908 he established a commercial radio service between Nova Scotia and Ireland. In 1911, the Federal Telegraph Co. started experiments, and in 1912 established a circuit between San Francisco and Honolulu, which was immediately opened to commercial service. At about this time the Navy Department had completed the installation of a large equipment at Arlington, Va., which communicated across the Atlantic and a German company established a station at Sayville, Long Island, which communicated with Germany. In 1914 the American and English Marconi companies established stations in Hawaii, California, New Jersey, and Massachusetts, and also in England and Norway, and a German company opened a station at Tuckerton, N. J., for communication with Germany.

Until the beginning of the European war most of the high-power radio equipments in existence—other than those of the United States Navy—were of the "spark" or damped-wave type, the only exceptions to this being the installations of the Federal Telegraph Co. and of the foreign-owned company at Tuckerton, which were arc and alternator systems, respectively, or of the undamped-wave variety.

Prior to this period the advantages of the undamped equipment over the damped became very apparent, and the Navy, acting through the Bureau of Steam Engineering, adopted the arc system, the first station erected being at Arlington, Va., and followed by others at Darien, Canal Zone; San Diego, Cal.; Pearl Harbor,

Hawaii, and Cavite, P. I. These new naval radio stations were by far the largest ever erected and have been in successful operation since their completion. A large number of medium-powered stations were also built.

Conditions when the United States entered the War.—At the time of the entry of the United States into the world war the following large radio stations were in use:

U. S. Navy, for trans-Pacific work:
    Cavite, P. I.
    Pearl Harbor, Hawaii
    San Diego, Calif.
U. S. Navy, for trans-Atlantic work:
    Arlington, Va.
U. S. Navy, for other work:
    Darien, Canal Zone
Private companies in United States:
    Federal Telegraph Co., for trans-Pacific work—
        Lents, Oreg.
        South San Francisco, Calif.
        Heeia Point, Hawaii
    Marconi Co., for trans-Pacific work—
        Bolinas, Calif.
        Kahuku, Hawaii.
    Marconi Co. for trans-Atlantic work—
        New Brunswick, N. J.
    German-owned station for trans-Atlantic work—
        Sayville, Long Island
    Foreign-owned, other than German—
        Tuckerton, N. J.

Upon the declaration of war, the Navy Department seized all of the above privately owned properties.

The stations in Europe capable of trans-Atlantic communication were English, Carnarvon, Wales; Norwegian, Stavanger; German, Nauen; Eilvese.

DEVELOPMENT DURING THE PERIOD OF THE WAR

Communications in the Atlantic.—In August, 1917, owing to the necessity for increased trans-Atlantic communication, a joint conference was arranged by the Bureau between representatives of the Navy Department, the War Department, and of members of the French Communication Service then in the United States. This conference was called at New London, since that was the point where experiments were being conducted by the Navy Department in connection with antistatic devices for receiving purposes.

During the conference, a plan was submitted by the Bureau which was subsequently adopted, concerning necessary developments for trans-Atlantic communications. The elements of the plan were as follows:

RADIO STATION, DARIEN, CANAL ZONE.

ANNAPOLIS STATION.

FOUNDATIONS AND ERECTING TOWER, LAFAYETTE STATION.

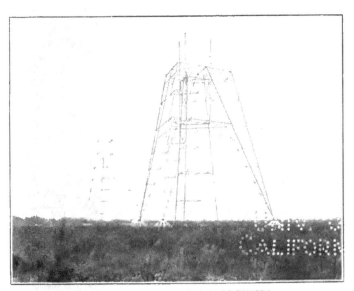

LAFAYETTE STATION, ERECTION OF TOWERS.

LEAD-IN INSULATORS, NEW BRUNSWICK STATION.

ARC MACHINE AT ANNAPOLIS.

1. The establishment of three receiving stations along the Atlantic coast of the United States connected with Washington by leased wires

2. The enlargement of, and duplication of, equipment in existing high-power stations

3. The erection of an additional station in the United States so that a final plan of five transmitting stations might be fulfilled.

4. The provision of sleet-melting equipment for the various transmitting station antenna systems, in order to assure freedom from ice during the winter season.

5. The recommendations to the French representatives, for development in the allied countries, of the multiple sending and receiving station plan agreed upon for the United States

6. The further recommendation that a superhigh-power station be erected abroad as an additional channel for trans-Atlantic communication

The adoption of this plan led to the erection of the Annapolis station in the United States and the Lafayette station in France, as mentioned subsequently.

In order to increase the reliability of trans-Atlantic radio communication, the Bureau let contracts for the erection of a large station at Annapolis, Md., to be a duplicate of the Pearl Harbor station, with a power of 350 kilowatts. This installation was later increased to a size of about 500 kilowatts. The plant was to be equipped with four 600-foot towers. The Annapolis station was completed in September, 1918, and has been in continuous use since that time.

The construction of the Lafayette (Bordeaux) station was an imperative war measure, since enemy operations might cause failure of the trans-Atlantic cables. The tower foundations and buildings were to be furnished by the French Government. The project was started, and a working detachment of nearly 600 officers and enlisted men was sent to France. On the day of the armistice, practically all material had been delivered, and the towers and buildings were well under way. This plant, as finished, contains two 1,000-kilowatt arc transmitters and has an antenna system 1,320 by 5,280 feet supported by eight 820-foot self-supporting steel towers. The station has been completed by the Navy Department under contract with the Republic of France. It was tested in September, 1920.

In 1918, when it became evident that overseas communications might be interrupted by the attack of enemy submarines on the cable systems, steps were taken to erect on the Atlantic coast of the United States a station which would have sufficient power to insure communications with Europe at all times. The site selected was at Monroe, N. C. and on November 11, 1918, the project had been developed to the point where all essential design work was complete, and contracts were ready to be awarded for the entire plant. The station was to have been equipped with four 500-kilowatt radio transmitters and four antenna systems, supported on a total of 20 600-foot self-supporting steel towers, each antenna being 5,000 feet long. This plant would have been from two to four times more powerful than any existing radio station. The project was, however, abandoned after the signing of the armistice.

The German-owned station at Sayville, Long Island, was turned over to the Navy Department by the Alien Property Custodian, and equipped with a 200-kilowatt arc transmitter and other improvements, which were ready for use in July, 1918. The foreign-owned station at Tuckerton, N J, was supplied with a 100-kilowatt arc transmitter, and an additional boiler and generator, which equipment was required in order to insure reliable communication from that station.

The Bureau also had under construction at Cayey, P R, a 200-kilowatt station.

The Marconi station at New Brunswick, N J, was being provided with a new type of equipment when taken over by the Navy. A temporary installation was made in 1917, which rendered valuable service for trans-Atlantic work in the winter of 1917-18. In September, 1918, a permanent transmitter was installed and put in operation, which has been in almost continual use ever since. This is the best station operated by the Navy Department during the war.

During the year 1917, some communications with European stations were carried on by the Sayville and Tuckerton stations. Other communications were carried on at various times with the experimental equipment at New Brunswick. The severe winter of 1917-18 wrecked the antennas at nearly all of these stations, and up to July, 1918, the Tuckerton station constituted the main reliance. The French Government meanwhile established a new station at Nantes, France.

In July, 1918, the control of the American stations was moved from Belmar, N. J., to Washington, D C, where it was centralized. At the date of the armistice, trans-Atlantic communications had become very well organized, and continuous transmission was carried on from Sayville, New Brunswick, Tuckerton, and Annapolis, in the United States, and in Europe from Carnarvon, England; Nantes and Lyon, France; Rome, Italy; and Nauen, Germany. The Nauen station was operated, of course, by the enemy, and all of its communications were intercepted in the United States.

Trans-Pacific communications.—The need for additional radio communication facilities in the Pacific was felt because of military

WHEATSTONE AUTOMATIC TRANSMITTER, BELMAR, N. J.

STANDARD NAVY RECEIVER, AUDION AND AMPLIFIER, RADIO STATION, BELMAR, N. J.

operations in Eastern Siberia, and consequently, at the request of the commander of the Asiatic Fleet, a former Russian station on Russian Island, Vladivostok, was occupied, and the *Saturn* detailed to transport the equipment and installation crew from San Francisco, Calif. The equipment was temporarily removed from the Heeia Point station, Hawaii, which station the Navy Department had meanwhile acquired from the Federal Telegraph Co. by purchase. The Vladivostok station when put in operation was of material assistance to our troops in Siberia.

A new equipment was installed in the Heeia Point station, Hawaii, and that plant is again in operation. Subsequent to the date of the armistice, commercial radio service was opened between the trans-Pacific stations, and this service still continues.

Summary of chief results.—The period of the war has seen a rapid development toward higher powers in radio stations for long-distance communication. This higher power is required for reliability in communication, particularly when heavy "atmospherics" exist. From a military viewpoint, this requirement is absolute. Prior to February, 1917, 350 kilowatts in power was considered the upper limit. The Annapolis station of 500 kilowatts, however, represented a material increase. The Lafayette station has a further rise to 1,000 kilowatts, and the proposed Monroe station was designed for a total power of 2,000 kilowatts. The Navy is thus emerging from the war with a 1,000 kilowatt station to its credit, whereas, but for the war, 350 kilowatts would probably have been the upper limit.

The war period has also seen the complete abandonment of "spark" transmitters for long-distance communication. The development of "arc" transmitters has been rapid. The Federal Telegraph Co., of San Francisco, Calif., has been the only organization which has furnished equipment of this type. During the war, the General Electric Co. developed the most efficient type of high-power transmitter thus far produced, namely, the Alexanderson alternator with which the New Brunswick station is equipped.

Personnel.—Lieut. Commander George C. Sweet, U. S. Navy (retired), whose experience in high-power radio work had been extensive, was placed in direct charge of the radio work on the Annapolis and Lafayette stations, and in July, 1918, was ordered to France as commander of the radio detachment for the construction of the latter. It is due in no small measure to his efforts that work was well advanced when the armistice was signed. He was assisted by Lieut. A. M. Stevens, U. S. Naval Reserve Force. Upon Lieut. Commander Sweet's return to the United States, the work was placed under the direction of Capt. A. St.C. Smith, U. S. Navy.

The design and erection of the towers of these stations was under the direction of the Bureau of Yards and Docks.

Contractors.—The Bureau was given hearty support and assistance by the Federal Telegraph Co. and the General Electric Co. The former designed and installed the radio equipment at Sayville, Tuckerton, and Annapolis, and also designed the equipment for the Lafayette station The latter, with the equipment of the New Brunswick station, made available to the Navy Department its best station during the war Mr. Alexanderson, of the General Electric Co, also gave some assistance in the design of the proposed Monroe station

THE RADIO COMPASS

In the early part of 1916 the desirability of having a means for ascertaining the location of radio transmitting stations became apparent to all persons having to do with the radio system of communication. Apparatus for this purpose had already been developed to some extent abroad, the system employed being known as the Bellini-Tosi system of radio direction finding Its early operation was complicated and subject to many inaccuracies, which made it unsuitable for naval vessels

With a view of improving apparatus for this purpose, Dr F A. Kolster, of the Bureau of Standards, made a study of the problem and discovered that a coil of wire wound on a rectangular frame mounted in such a way that it could be rotated was adapted for ascertaining the direction of radio waves His experiments proved that a coil placed in a plane at right angles to incoming radio waves is unaffected and current is not induced in the coil Turning this coil through an arc of 90 degrees results in a maximum flow of current in its winding He applied this principle to an instrument which was called the Kolstermeter. Its operation was simple, inasmuch as the only adjustment necessary was the regulation of the receiver to the proper tune for the incoming wave and then to rotate the coil and notice on the dial attached to the shaft the number of degrees displacement of the coil from a true north and south line The coil system was adopted by the Navy, on account of its simplicity of operation and accuracy within prescribed limits, after exhaustive tests and comparisons had been made with it and the Bellini-Tosi apparatus then manufactured

The Bureau secured the exclusive rights to the patents from Dr. Kolster for a period of two years in order to keep it confidential, and the Philadelphia Navy Yard was authorized, about the middle of 1916, to proceed with the manufacture of 30 Kolstermeters of the coil type. The principle and details of the apparatus were kept closely guarded. As one of the precautions, the name was changed from Kolstermeter, by which it had become known, to that of "radio compass" Experiments were begun at the same time at the Pensacola

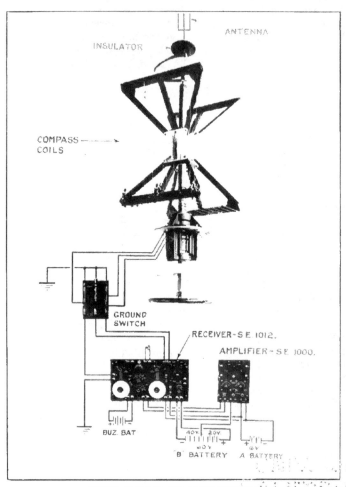

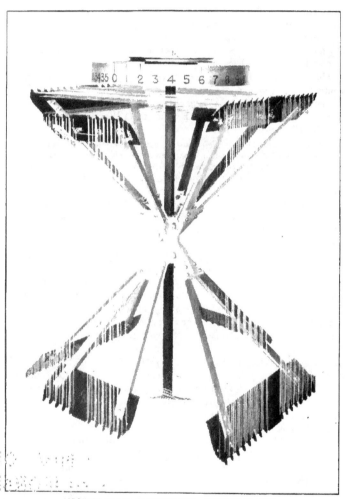

AIRCRAFT RADIO COMPASS COIL, REVOLVING TYPE.

and Philadelphia Navy Yards with a view to developing this compass for use in connection with the navigation of aircraft.

Such success was obtained with the experimental apparatus first installed at the Philadelphia radio station that in November, 1916, the Director of Naval Communications requested that the apparatus remain as a permanent installation in order to locate unneutral radio stations. As other sets were completed they were installed on vessels of the Atlantic Fleet.

The value of the radio compass in locating enemy craft and making contact with convoys during thick weather was demonstrated on numerous occasions. As an example of the assistance given in such cases the following quotation, "Extract from War Diary, 11 November, 1918," may be cited:

> The commanding officer *Benham* has reported concerning an instance of the successful use of the radio compass on that vessel when *Benham* gave a bearing from convoy to *Parker*, which had been unable to regain a lost contact. *Parker* set her course by the bearing given and rejoined the convoy without difficulty.

The apparatus placed upon the first vessels was of a more or less unwieldy type, but further experiments and development resulted in the design of a more compact coil, suitable for installation on destroyers and smaller vessels.

The early installation of the radio compass apparatus brought out the fact that incoming radio waves received from a distant ship or shore station are distorted by surrounding metallic objects or wires and that it was necessary to calibrate the compass for these errors. This work was assigned to the navy yard at Boston, and was done principally at Newport, in order that the ships might be calibrated when they went to that place to receive a supply of torpedoes.

This work was considered of such importance that an officer, Ensign Bowden Washington, U. S. Naval Reserve Force, was detailed to the Boston Navy Yard to supervise radio compass calibration and installation, with orders to travel to any yard or station on the Atlantic coast. The work grew so rapidly that other officers of the reserve had to be detailed to assist.

For vessels in foreign waters complete installations were shipped to Queenstown, Ireland, where they were installed under the supervision of Lieut. A. Forbes, U. S. Naval Reserve Force.

In June, 1918, sites were selected for radio compass shore stations and preparations were made for their equipment, but the necessity for concentrating the available employees on ship installation work prevented any of these stations from being finished before the signing of the armistice, though the most important ones—for Boston, New York, Delaware Bay, Chesapeake Bay, and Charleston—to which troopships returned, were completed shortly thereafter, the ones for New York in time to furnish bearings to our battleships on their return December 26, 1918. The sites for these stations were so selected that three stations would cooperate to furnish cross bearings.

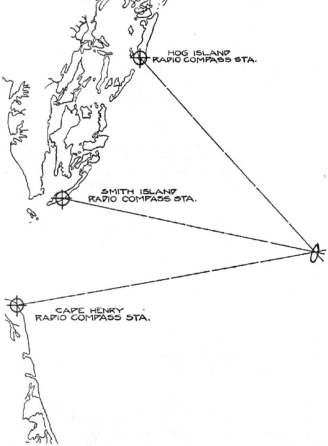

Data of much practical value have been obtained by the establishment of these stations and there is no doubt that they are destined to become a most important aid to navigation.

THE RADIOTELEPHONE.

Prewar work.—Prior to the war, the radiotelephone activities of the Navy Department had included the long-distance experiments carried out at Arlington in conjunction with the Western Electric

Co In these experiments, telephone conversations were held with Darien, Canal Zone, 2,100 miles away, and with Mare Island on the Pacific coast a distance of 2,500 miles. Speech was also transmitted to Paris, 3,600 miles distant, and to Honolulu, 6,000 miles

Tests had also been made between Arlington station and the *New Hampshire*. In these experiments, conversations were conducted by remote control between the Navy Department, Washington, and the battleship while she was 50 miles off Cape Henry. Similar conversation also took place between this ship and the Great Lakes naval station In this case, the communication was carried from Washington to the Great Lakes station over the long-distance telephone lines.

The possibilities of the radiotelephone for naval uses had been realized by the Bureau and arrangements had been made with the Western Electric Co for that organization to develop an equipment suitable for standard installations on battleships The first two of these sets were placed on the *Arkansas* and *Florida* in February, 1916, and a satisfactory two-way conversation was held over a distance of 30 miles. Other sets, designed by the Western Electric Co, were installed on the *Pennsylvania*, *Wyoming*, and *Seattle*. These latter sets were capable of multiplex operation, so that nine conversations could be carried on and three wave lengths utilized

War activities.—The first radiotelephone equipment constructed for war purposes was built by the Western Electric Co, in March, 1917. It comprised 15 experimental sets for possible use on submarine chasers. These sets were of the continuous-wave, vacuum-tube type, and were intended primarily for telegraphic communication, but were equipped also with telephone and modulating attachments

These sets were soon replaced by a highly improved type which consisted essentially of a complete telephone transmitter and receiver, arranged to operate on wave lengths from 200 to 600 meters, with a normal operating distance between vessels of 10 nautical miles It was provided with an extension designed originally for the pilot house of submarine chasers The installation is shown in figure 1. During the war, approximately 1,000 of these sets were placed on submarine chasers, destroyers, and battleships, and were of inestimable value in the antisubmarine campaign

One of the most important developments in radiotelephony during the war was the installation of a 200-kilowatt high-frequency alternator of the Alexanderson type at the former Marconi station, New Brunswick, N. J., and the adaptation of apparatus to this equipment to permit its use as a long-distance telephone transmitter This alternator is shown in figure 2 It is of historic interest that this transmitter was used to direct the first message to Germany after our entry into the war.

For operation with the New Brunswick station, the *George Washington* was equipped with a radiotelephone transmitter of the vacuum-tube type, whose controls are illustrated in figure 3. In the extreme lower section of the panel shown, there are located the smaller vacuum tubes for amplifying the feeble electrical currents from the microphone transmitter, together with auxiliary apparatus. The power is obtained from the ship's direct-current mains. The high voltage for the plate circuits of the vacuum tubes and the low voltage for the filaments are supplied from motor generator sets. The receiving apparatus is shown in figure 4; it is operated from a separate antenna. "Two-way," or duplex, operation with this system has been entirely satisfactory. The entire transmitting and receiving equipment was developed and manufactured by the General Electric Co., working in cooperation with Lieut (j g) W. Lemmon, United States Naval Force, of the Bureau of Steam Engineering.

Numerous telephone tests were made between the *George Washington* and the station at New Brunswick throughout a period of three months. To supervise these tests, Lieut Lemmon was assigned to the ship as representative of the Bureau, and Messrs J H Payne and H. H. Beverage as technical representatives of the General Electric Co.

Telephone conversation from New Brunswick was heard by the *George Washington* while lying in the harbor of Brest, a distance of 3,200 miles, and conversation was carried on both ways while the ship was still 1,300 miles at sea. The New Brunswick station transmits on 13,600 meters and the *George Washington* on 1,800 meters.

This radiotelephone system also enabled the President and various officials traveling on the *George Washington*, to keep in touch with our shores. To effect this, New Brunswick's radiotelephone was connected up to land wires, so that direct conversation with Washington and other points could be had at sea.

In one case, Secretary Daniels spoke from the Navy Department to President Wilson while the ship was 400 miles from our coast. Figure 5 gives a photographic representation of the variation of modulation and antenna currents in this conversation. Secretary Baker, also, returning on the *George Washington*, called up Acting Secretary Roosevelt while the ship was 200 miles at sea, and arranged some plans for his return to Washington.

It should be noted that, in addition to the radiotelephone developments which have been described, there have been carried on also, during the war, all of the applications of this telephone to aircraft. These applications will be considered in another section.

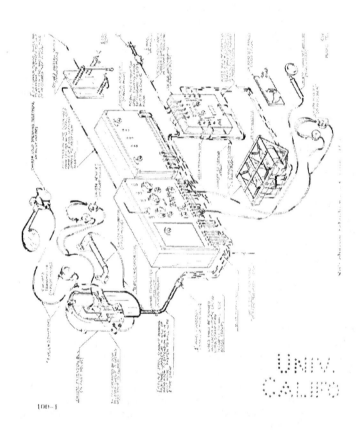

MAGNETIC AMPLIFIER.

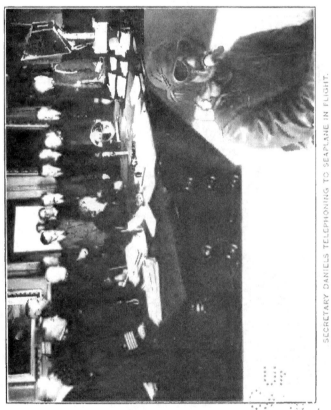

SECRETARY DANIELS TELEPHONING TO SEAPLANE IN FLIGHT.

FIGURE 1.

FIG. 2.—ALEXANDERSON ALTERNATOR, NEW BRUNSWICK, N. J.

FIG. 3.—TELEPHONE TRANSMITTER CONTROLS, U. S. S. GEORGE WASHINGTON.

FIG. 4. TELEPHONE RECEIVING EQUIPMENT, U. S. S. GEORGE WASHINGTON.

FIG. 5.

UNDERGROUND AND UNDERWATER RADIO

Development.—On May 31, 1917 a conference was held at Hyattsville, Md., between Mr. J. H. Rogers, inventor of the underground radio system, and Commander S. C. Hooper, U. S. Navy, Lieut. Commander A. Hoyt Taylor, U. S. Naval Reserve Force, and Expert Radio Aid G. H. Clark, as representatives of the Bureau of Steam Engineering. During this conference, the merits of the system were presented, and, as a result, it was decided that the Navy would investigate underground radio thoroughly to determine its availability for naval use.

For this investigation, the Bureau authorized Lieut. Commander Taylor to establish a laboratory at Great Lakes, Ill. This laboratory was organized on August 1, 1917, with the following personnel: Lieut. Commander Taylor, director; Radio Gunner (later ensign) A. Crossley, U. S. Naval Reserve Force, officer in charge; Chief Electrician R. G. Matthews, U. S. Naval Reserve Force, electrician; and a detail of five enlisted men.

Experiments at Great Lakes.—The laboratory was not completed until October, 1917. Since early results were necessary, experiments were begun immediately at the main radio station, Great Lakes. Combinations of insulated wire and bare antenna wire were tested, and the results proved that the underground system had fair possibilities. Signals were received from long-wave arc stations with readable intensity, while very poor signals came from spark stations. It was possible to copy arc stations through local electrical storms, and to copy as many as six stations while using the same set of underground wires. The use of a series condenser in the primary circuit gave better results and sharper tuning.

Experiments were next conducted on the shore of Lake Michigan to determine the feasibility of receiving signals on underground and underwater wires. Poor results were obtained with bare wires laid in sand, while better ones were had with wires a part of whose length was insulated. It was found that rubber-covered wires acted better than weatherproof wires, and that when wires were submerged in the lake the signal strength was increased tenfold.

It was discovered that underground wires had an "optimum" or most favorable length for each of the different wave lengths. For example, two No. 12 waterproof wires, 300 and 600 feet long respectively, were buried 1 foot below the surface in wet sand; the 600-foot wire gave the best results on long wave signals; the 300-foot wire on short wave. Again, it was noted that a 150-foot length of No. 12 waterproof wire had a signal strength three times that of a 300-foot length when receiving signals from 600-meter stations.

During experiments conducted between the University of Wisconsin and Great Lakes—in which the university transmitted on two wave lengths, 425 and 1,150 meters—it was found that the best wire length per wave length, using No. 12 rubber-covered wire, was equal to one-eighth of the transmitted wave length. It was also found that the best length of wire per wave length was the same, whether the wires were buried in wet sand or immersed in water.

These experiments also showed that underground wires had directive qualities; that is, wires pointing toward transmitting stations gave the best results, while wires laid at an angle of 90° to those stations worked poorly. In extended experiments later it was found in all cases that wires laid in the same plane and extending toward transmitting stations gave maximum signal strength.

Again, a small rectangle, 18 by 24 inches, wound with 15 turns of No. 18 wire placed in series with the ground wires proved that it was possible to balance out to a great extent signals received from the main radio station when copying distant stations. Better balance was obtained when receiving instruments were placed in a screened receiving room.

On November 15, 1917, the first transmitting experiments were conducted through a half-mile distance on underground wires. The optimum wire length per wave length was found to be equal to the wave length, showing that the wires were not aperiodic. They had also extremely high capacity and very small inductance. When a ¼-kilowatt vacuum-tube transmitting set was used with the underground system it was possible to transmit through a distance of 30 miles from Great Lakes to Chicago. In comparative tests the same current was radiated into a 30-foot overhead antenna, with the result that the signal strength received at Chicago from the underground wires was twice that from the overhead antenna. A comparison was also made between the 11-foot rectangular antenna, wound with 18 turns of No. 13 copper wire, and the 2,300-foot underground wire on signals received from European stations. The results were that the underground system gave fifteen times the signal strength of the rectangle and also collected one-half the strays gathered in by the rectangle. Directive experiments with transmitting apparatus on underground wires showed that these wires have the same directive qualities for transmission as for reception.

A number of other primary experiments were conducted at Great Lakes by Lieut. Commander Taylor and later by Radio Gunner Crossley after the detachment of Lieut. Commander Taylor on October 20, 1917. On February 27, 1918, Gunner Crossley was ordered to Hampton Roads, Va., to install the underground system at the distant control station there.

Experiments at New Orleans.—Experiments were conducted during April, 1917, at New Orleans, La., by Mr H H. Lyons assistant to J H Rogers, originator of the underground system Mr Lyons, working under the direction of Lieut E H Loftin, U S Navy, made a series of experiments covering a period of three months, during which time promising results were obtained on short and long wave reception. As a consequence, recommendations were made and carried out to establish a distant control station at New Orleans This installation was the first of its kind in the world

Experiments at Piney Point, Va.—Dr. L W Austin and Gunner J. Allen, of the United States Naval Radio Laboratory, conducted a series of experiments with the underground system at Piney Point. Va., in which various lengths of wire were submerged in Chesapeake Bay, and the results compared with those from the small antenna used at that place. The underground wires were found to be slightly superior

Experiments at Belmar, N. J.—With regard to the experiments conducted at the Belmar trans-Atlantic receiving station, Lieut Commander A. H Taylor found that, by the use of the underground system, fair results were obtained in copying European stations up to the latter part of the spring of 1918, when, owing to heavy summer strays, he was compelled to resort to the use of balance circuits.

Experiments at the Rogers laboratory.—Ensign Crossley conducted a series of experiments at the laboratory of Mr J. H Rogers to determine whether there was a definite wire length for signals from long-wave stations. Tests showed that there is a sharply defined wire length for the reception of such signals Other experiments were made to ascertain the effect of an iron protection over wires It was found that the use of 20-foot iron pipe sections, insulated from each other by rubber hose through which magneto cable was run, gave practically the same results as Packard ignition cable buried in the earth, and that the use of continuous iron pipe covering over the wire reduced the signal strength to about one one-hundredth of that received on the other two wires.

General results from underground system.—In addition to the results noted, it should be stated that underground wires used at the main station, Great Lakes, to aid in the transcontinental traffic, gave satisfactory communication at all times between this station and those on the east and west coasts Long-distance experiments also produced excellent results in receiving signals from the Atlantic and Gulf coastal stations and from ships where a regenerative receiver and one-stage De Forest amplifier were used.

Underwater radio development.—From June 1, 1918, to September 20, 1918, Messrs. Willoughby and Lowell, of the Bureau of Standards, conducted a series of experiments on submarines at New London. They found that by the use of an insulated loop on submarines it was possible to transmit 9 miles when submerged, and also to receive signals from high-power European radio stations when the periscopes were submerged to a distance of 21 feet from the surface. It was also found that, when using the insulated loop on board submarines, a transmitting radius on the surface was much greater than that of the average submarine antenna, owing to the fact that the antenna was subject to frequent grounding of insulators from spray.

TRANSOCEANIC RADIO RECEIVING SYSTEMS.

Tuckerton.—The first work on transoceanic receiving done by the Navy after our entrance into the war was carried out at Sayville, Long Island, and at Tuckerton, N. J., both of which stations had been in the hands of the Navy for some time prior to April 6, 1917. In fact, both stations had carried on a good deal of traffic with Germany previous to the severance of diplomatic relations with that country. There was nothing unusual about the system at Tuckerton, except that receiving was accomplished, during part of the time at least, by the use of a 4-mile-long, single wire, which was part of an old telephone line. This antenna was almost aperiodic and probably had some directive properties, rendering it slightly superior to an ordinary antenna. The main antenna at Tuckerton was not used directly for receiving, but sometimes during reception. Improvement in signals was obtained by tuning this antenna to earth, so that it reradiated upon the receiving antenna, thereby increasing the strength of the signals.

The Zenneck receiving system.—At Sayville full advantage was taken of a special receiving system devised by Prof. Zenneck. This system utilized the Sayville counterpoise for receiving, with the latter split into halves for this purpose. The northeast section of the counterpoise was connected to one primary binding post and the southwest section to the other post; no ground connection was used. The secondary system was connected to a 2-stage radio-frequency amplifier thence to a detector, and thence to a 2-stage audio-frequency amplifier. The circuits were very complicated, very difficult to adjust, and adapted to operation on a fixed wave. Change of wave length was a difficult and laborious process. The system gave, however, fairly good signals, which we now know were due largely to the directive properties of the counterpoise system used as an antenna. This station was the best one we had during the winter of 1917–18; it had the best output rate.

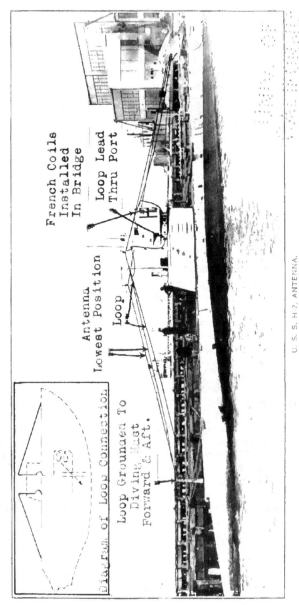

U. S. S. H2, ANTENNA.

Belmar.—The experience of the summer of 1917 was sufficient to demonstrate that communication with European stations during the summer period was extremely precarious and inefficient, owing to the summer phenomena of weak signals accompanied by heavy strays (static). The successful development at Great Lakes of the reception of radio signals on the Rogers submarine and subterranean antenna system induced the Bureau to install this system at Belmar, N. J., the radio station at this place having been taken over in April from the Marconi company, but not operated. By the end of October, 1917, Belmar was receiving on submerged wires laid on the inlet and on a 2,000-foot long land wire buried 2 feet deep. Belmar then became the control center for trans-Atlantic work.

The Weagant system.—Chief Engineer Roy Weagant of the Marconi company had been engaged in development work on trans-Atlantic receiving systems, whose principal purpose was the elimination of strays, and he was given every possible encouragement to continue this work at Belmar at the same time that Lieut. Commander Taylor was assigned to duty there (Oct 17, 1917), with instructions to install the underground system. The Marconi experiments at Belmar were continued until the latter part of November, 1917, without being brought to a satisfactory conclusion, when the Weagant work was moved to Miami, Fla., and finally completed in the summer of 1918 at Lakewood, N. J. The Weagant system was never used on actual traffic by the Navy Department in trans-Atlantic work. The completion of the system at Lakewood was mainly the work of the Marconi company.

The Chatham station.—Early in November, Lieut. Commander Sweet, U. S. Navy (retired), accompanied by Lieut Commander Taylor and Lieut J C Cooper, jr., U. S Naval Reserve Force, visited the Marconi receiving station at Chatham, Mass. It was decided to take it over for receiving purposes, the general idea at the time being that by having several receiving centers along the coast with wire connections to Belmar and Washington, it might be possible to get around local storms and strays, as receiving conditions would probably not be bad at all of these stations at the same time. The Chatham station also offered unusual opportunity—on account of the proximity of a salt-water bay and a fresh-water lake—to test the relative readaptability of signals on ground wires and wires immersed in salt water and in fresh water. A few weeks later the station was opened up and much data collected which showed that the salt-water wires gave the weakest, but at the same time the most readable, signals. Nevertheless, it was found almost invariably that Chatham could not make copy when Belmar could not make it, and therefore, in October, 1918, Chatham ceased to be used for trans-Atlantic reception.

The Otter Cliffs circuits —In the meantime the remarkable receiving conditions at Otter Cliffs radio station (Bar Harbor, Me), had been called to the attention of the Bureau, and early in 1918 the orders of Ensign A Fabbri, later lieutenant, U. S. Naval Reserve Force, the officer in charge, were altered in such a way as to take him out of the district organization so far as trans-Atlantic work was concerned and to place him under the orders of the trans-Atlantic communication officer Thus Bar Harbor was added to the chain of trans-Atlantic receiving centers, a step which was subsequently justified by that station proving to be the most ideally situated of all stations for the reception of trans-Atlantic signals The remarkable absence of strays at Bar Harbor and the ingenious system of loop antennas and counterpoises used by Lieut Fabbri gave early evidence that this station had great natural advantages. Figure 5 shows one of these circuits upon which much trans-Atlantic copy was made, the development of which is largely due to Chief Electrician W E. Woods. It will be noted that the secondary circuit is coupled both to the loop and to another inductance which leads through a high resistance to ground from one leg of the loop. Recent investigations show that this is probably not the best possible arrangement. as the phases of the two currents collected in the receiver are not quite right with respect to each other. Great credit is due Lieut Fabbri for the way in which this station was handled. In this he was ably seconded by Chief Electrician (radio) W E. Woods, U. S. Naval Reserve Force, and Gunner R Cole, U S. Navy

Belmar versus Otter Cliffs —So far as the relative advantages of the Belmar and the Otter Cliffs circuits are concerned, it may be stated that. for trans-Atlantic work, the use of ground wires and submarine wires was found insufficient to cope with summer static until the system of balancing out the static by combining a submarine wire with a rectangle was devised

Very satisfactory circuits were also devised whereby a submarine wire was balanced against one laid on the surface of the ground in lead-covered cable, or buried in dry earth The only reason Belmar was able to compete at all with Bar Harbor, and finally to excel Sayville, was because of the introduction of these special receiving systems Tuckerton was kept so busy transmitting that it had little opportunity for receiving Sufficient comparisons were made, however, to show that Tuckerton's receiving conditions, in spite of good personnel, were by no means equal to those at Belmar, even before the advent of the balanced circuits there. The best Bar Harbor circuits partially owe their success to the fact that they are partly or wholly blind in the southwest direction, from which come the worst of the strays on long waves.

The Alexanderson barrage receiver.—Not the least interesting of the circuits experimented with by the Navy Department for transoceanic reception was the Alexanderson barrage receiver. Mr. E. F. W. Alexanderson, of the General Electric Co., was given all information concerning the various antistatic systems in the hope that he might be able to utilize it in the development of his barrage receiver, the circuits of which are shown in figure 4. As a result of this conference, which was held at Belmar, Mr. Alexanderson was able to substitute with satisfactory results wires laid on the ground for antenna on poles, greatly simplifying the installation. Part of the success of the system is undoubtedly due to the fact that it also possesses barrage properties, as has been strikingly demonstrated by recent experiments at New Orleans. The Alexanderson system, however, not only possesses barrage properties but has a pronounced focusing property, which is of very great value in eliminating interferences coming from the same direction as that from which the signal arrives.

The Austin circuits.—During the summer of 1918, Dr. L. W. Austin, of the Naval Radio Laboratory, developed a number of interesting circuits, which may be called balanced circuits. None of these was, however, used on actual trans-Atlantic traffic, but they have been utilized in transcontinental work. Some of them are shown in figures 1, 2, 3, 6, and 7.

Summary.—During the Navy's connection with trans-Atlantic radio a large number of receiving circuits were devised and tried out, partly by officers and civilians connected with the Navy and partly by representatives of the Marconi company and the General Electric Co. Of these it may be said that the Rogers underground, the Weagant circuit, the Belmar circuit, the Alexanderson barrage system, the Otter Cliffs (Bar Harbor) circuits, and some of the Austin circuits gave very decided improvements. One of the Austin circuits has the advantage of permitting multiple reception on the same loop and ground wires. (See fig. 3.) Of all these circuits, those of Otter Cliffs and Belmar are the simplest in operation and were the ones which were actually used in making official trans-Atlantic copy. After Otter Cliffs had been properly equipped and new circuits installed the copy made at that station was so certain that the Belmar station was, in February, 1919, closed and returned to the Marconi company. Combined with the advantages due to the geographical location of Bar Harbor, the station there was amply able to care for trans-Atlantic copy.

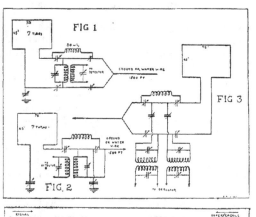
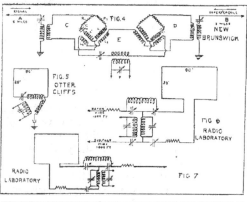
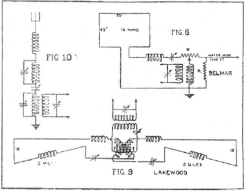

SHIPBOARD RADIO EQUIPMENT

Before the war, only a small number for each type of vessel was contracted for each year, and, hence, some latitude was permissible in the design of installation details, radio-room arrangement and antenna. With the advent of war and the consequent purchase of large quantities of standardized apparatus, uniformity of design in these respects became absolutely essential.

To effect this standardization, steps were taken immediately to secure and train the necessary personnel. This was, in itself, a considerable undertaking, since the number of employees familiar with the highly specialized needs of the Navy in these respects was very limited. There were, in fact, practically none who were not already employed in the various navy yards, where the pressure of work was such that they could not be spared for work in the Bureau.

This same shortage of trained radio engineering personnel was felt by the Emergency Fleet Corporation, and the Bureau therefore tendered its services to that organization. Plans were prepared for radio installation on the various standardized types of Emergency Fleet vessels, and the radio personnel at our navy yards was increased to provide for adequate technical assistance to the ship contractors who were charged with the installation of radio apparatus on the vessels they built.

In addition to the large number of merchant vessels thus cared for, plans were prepared for the new naval vessels provided for in the 1916 building program and in the various emergency acts. In each case this involved a thorough study of the duties and structural details of each class of vessel, and of the requirements of the types of radio apparatus assigned to that class. The performance of this work on many different types of vessels by the same men made possible a certain fixed similarity in arrangement and in the treatment of the various technical difficulties which were met.

In brief, then, the radio arrangements were standardized to the greatest possible extent. The value of such standardization is evident when it is considered that, with the rapid growth of the operating personnel, nearly three-fourths of it was entirely new to the service and could not be quickly brought to a high degree of efficiency if every ship to which a man were transferred differed from the one which he had just left. As a result of this policy of standardization, there were practically only two types of main radio rooms on destroyers built or contracted for during the war. The necessity for more than one arrangement was due to the fact that there was a change in the size of the radio room on later destroyers.

The following is an example of the many problems met in radio arrangements:

It was found that when a ship was torpedoed or struck a mine the shock of the explosion usually made the masts whip apart to such an extent that the halyards of the radio antenna would break under the strain; the antenna would drop, and the radio set would become useless at just the time when it was most urgently needed to send out an S O S call.

To meet this condition, a safety link was devised for location in the halyards at the ends of the antenna. The arrangement was such that the antenna was supported normally at each end by a wire which had approximately one-fourth of the tensile strength of the antenna proper. When the tops of the masts separated suddenly the safety link broke, and the antenna dropped a long distance until brought up by the halyards. In this way the antenna was lengthened about 5 feet at each end, and sufficient slack was provided to allow for the displacement of the mastheads. This safety link was fitted on all of our naval vessels which were on duty in European waters infested by submarines and mines, and also on ships of the Emergency Fleet Corporation.

The operation of vessels of our Navy with the fleets of the Allies made necessary many changes in the type and arrangement of the radio apparatus of our vessels.

COASTAL RADIO STATIONS, STATIONS FOR SHIPPING BOARD VESSELS, AND FOR PRIVATELY OWNED COMMERCIAL SHIPS.

The maintenance of the coastal radio stations, of radio stations for the vessels of the Shipping Board, and for privately owned commercial ships formed a very important part of the duties of the Bureau throughout the war.

When the United States entered the war the Bureau was, as noted previously, responsible for the maintenance in efficient condition of the 49 coastal radio stations of the Naval Communication Service, which were located along our Atlantic and Pacific coasts, in our outlying possessions, and at other strategic points, including one on the Great Lakes. These stations had been established, primarily, to provide communication facilities between the Navy Department and the Atlantic, Pacific, and Asiatic Fleets; and, secondarily, to safeguard life and property at sea.

Sixty-seven coastal radio stations had also been established at various points on the Atlantic and Pacific coasts, on the Great Lakes, and within the Hawaiian Islands, by commercial radio companies to supply facilities for communication between merchant ships and the coasts. These stations were maintained and operated by their owners. There were approximately 600 merchant vessels under American registry equipped with radio, which was maintained by either the commercial radio organizations or the owners of the vessels.

War measures: commercal stations taken over; shipping board stations provided —Upon the declaration of a state of war all shore radio stations within the jurisdiction of the United States, including the 67 coastal stations just noted, were taken over for operation or closed by the Navy in accordance with Executive order No 2885, dated April 6, 1917. This order was based on the "act to regulate radio communication," approved August 13, 1912.

This sweeping extension of the Bureau's duties as to shore stations was followed by directions that it maintain for efficient operation the radio installations on all privately owned vessels operating under the United States flag, on which armed guards had been or were to be placed

The Shipping Board had also commandeered about 450 vessels then building in American shipyards, and as it had neither the organization nor the technical personnel to install radio apparatus on these vessels, the Bureau offered to arrange for the purchase, installation, and subsequent maintenance and repair of this equipment for the account of the Shipping Board. The board accepted this offer and requested that the Bureau also arrange for similar service on the additional vessels for which contracts had been or would be let This was agreed to, and arrangements were made at once to design and provide standard radio installations for Shipping Board vessels Meanwhile all existing radio sets in the United States and Canada were purchased by the Navy for emergency installations on the vessels commandeered by the Shipping Board, since a number of these vessels were nearly or wholly completed, and except for a few, no provision for radio equipment had been made by their former owners.

Upon the subsequent requisitioning by the Shipping Board of virtually the whole American merchant marine, the Bureau was also charged with the maintenance of the radio installations on these vessels Arrangements were made, therefore, to relieve the various commercial radio organizations of this work, and to assign it to the radio material organizations at navy yards.

As a result of the several war measures noted, and of the subsequent chartering by the Shipping Board of a large part of the merchant marine of neutral countries, the Bureau, when the armistice was signed, was responsible for 229 coastal radio stations and approximately 3,775 ship radio stations. The aggregate of these, when compared with the 49 coastal stations under the Bureau's care when hostilities began, shows the wide extension of naval responsibility for the maintenance of radio communication which the war brought.

Contracts had also been let for radio apparatus sufficient to equip approximately 3,000 vessels for the Shipping Board. Some of these contracts were canceled, however, after the armistice was signed.

Major projects for shore radio stations during the war.—In addition to the great increase in the activities of the Bureau with regard to coastal and ship stations as outlined previously, various major projects were undertaken, during the war, as follows:

(*a*) The establishment of a number of new coastal stations to meet war emergencies, including 25 low-power stations in the vicinity of the several patrol headquarters, and also radio stations at the newly established naval air stations.

(*b*) The establishment of a radio station at Otter Cliffs, Me., and its development into a trans-Atlantic receiving station. Also the subsequent establishment of a transmitting station at Sea Wall, Me., to be distant controlled from Otter Cliffs, in order to give improved and increased facilities for communication between vessels—mainly transports—at sea and with the mainland.

(*c*) The removal of the Newport transmitting station to Melville, R. I., and the establishment of a distant coastal and receiving station at Coasters Harbor Island. This change was made owing to the possibility that explosions which had occurred in the magazines at the torpedo station, Newport, might have been caused by sparks from the discharge of inductively charged conductors within the magazine, which conductors might have been charged by the functioning of the near-by transmitting station.

(*d*) The enlargement and relocation of the Norfolk radio station and its distant control from the Naval Operating Base, Hampton Roads.

(*e*) The establishment of distant control and the underground receiving system at the New Orleans radio station.

(*f*) The establishment of distant control and the underground receiving system at Great Lakes, Ill.

(*g*) The establishment of three radio stations in the Republic of Panama for operation by the United States Naval Communication Service.

(*h*) The establishment of a radio station at Port-au-Prince, Haiti.

Compensation for shore stations.—The taking over by the Navy, in conformity with the provisions of an act of Congress, of the commercial shore and ship radio stations involved the question of compensation to the owners for the shore radio stations and of special arrangements with regard to the cost of maintenance of the leased installations in ship stations.

Compensation for stations that had been in operation a sufficient length of time to enable their earnings to be determined was fixed on the basis of these earnings and the value of the property. For low-power stations, a fixed rental was agreed upon for those that were kept in operation and a much lower rate for those that were closed.

The Government assumed all expense incidental to the maintenance of the stations which it operated, excepting the payment of taxes, rentals, and insurance, while for closed stations the owner assumed all expense without exception.

In general, the basis of compensation for shore radio stations was adopted after negotiations with the Marconi company in regard to their stations, and a like system adopted in settlement with other commercial radio organizations.

Compensation for ship radio stations.—The taking over of the ship radio stations of the American merchant marine involved the question of payment by the owners of expenditures incurred for repair to these small installations. This was arranged on the basis of a small payment monthly to cover the average actual cost on all ships.

A large number of these ship stations comprised installations leased from commercial radio companies, for which a rental was paid by the steamship owners. A few of the stations were, however, the property of the owners of the vessels.

When it is considered that on very short notice the operation and maintenance organizations of the commercial radio companies were disrupted and their activities assumed by the Navy—involving an immensely increased volume of work and many complex financial adjustments, which were largely repeated when these ship and shore stations were returned to their owners—it will be apparent that very cordial cooperation existed between the commercial companies and the Navy Department in the successful accomplishment of this difficult undertaking.

Purchase of the Federal and Marconi stations.—About 10 months after our entry into the war negotiations were begun by the Navy Department with the Federal Telegraph Co. for the purchase of its patents and shore radio stations. These negotiations were concluded satisfactorily, and on May 15, 1918, the Government acquired the patents of this company and its shore stations—three high-power and five coastal—for the sum of $1,600,000.

Shortly after the purchase of the Federal patents the Bureau received a resolution passed by the Shipping Board authorizing the purchase of all leased radio stations on vessels owned or controlled by the board. In accordance with this resolution negotiations were entered into with the Marconi company with a view to the purchase for the account of the Shipping Board. These negotiations were not completed until about November 1, 1918; and, meanwhile, the Railroad Administration requested that the leased ship installations on its vessels be purchased also

The Marconi company would consent to sell their ship installations only on the condition that the Government buy also their coastal radio stations. This was agreed to, and the purchase of 330 ship installations and 45 coastal stations was effected, as of November 30, 1918, for the sum of $1,450,000. As this purchase had been for a lump sum, it was necessary to have a basis of value for the ship stations—to be paid for by the Shipping Board and the Railroad Administration—separately from the value of the coastal radio stations which were acquired for the account of the Navy. This was accomplished by appraising the ship installations at a figure representing 20 per cent less than the price paid by the Navy for similar radio sets bought in quantity when new. It was believed that this arrangement provided a generous allowance for the depreciation of the equipment, and, further, the average price represented about one year and nine months' rental on the equipment as charged previously by the Marconi company. On this basis of settlement the lump sum of $1,450,000 was divided as follows:

Shipping Board For the radio installations of 267 vessels_____ $519,200
Railroad Administration For the radio installations on 63 vessels____ 141,200
Navy. For 45 shore radio stations, including the Ketchikan, Juneau-Astoria Alaskan circuit, the South Wellfleet (obsolete) high-power station and the leased shore radio stations_____ 789,500

Summary—Notwithstanding the greatly increased activities of the Bureau with regard to coastal and merchant ship stations including those for the Shipping Board, all demands made with respect to these stations were satisfied promptly. The construction of additional coastal radio stations and the improvement of other similar stations to meet war emergencies were accomplished without delay, as was also the taking over and operation of the commercial shore and ship stations.

The equipment on short notice of all Shipping Board vessels, particularly the 450 commandeered ships, was accomplished successfully through the foresight and effective action taken to secure the prompt delivery of equipment and material, and the expansion of the naval radio matériel organizations at navy yards to meet all probable demands.

The expansion of radio matériel activities during the period of the war, with regard to coastal and ship radio stations and other matters, was such that district radio matériel officers were detailed to practically all navy yards and naval stations for supervising these activities under the direction of the Bureau.

MARCONI STATION, ASTORIA, OREG.

NAVAL RADIO RESEARCH LABORATORY.

The following improvements in radio apparatus and radio measurements were planned, in general, by Dr. L. W. Austin, head of the advance research laboratory, and were carried out experimentally under his direction.

1. A tuned telephone and a tuned audio frequency amplifier for receiving circuits, which give a considerable improvement in the reading of signals through static and interference

2 A study of underground and underwater antennas

3 Circuits for receiving from a number of stations on the same antenna or loop With this arrangement, the European stations at Lyons, Carnarvon, Nauen, and Rome are received at the same time at the trans-Atlantic office at the Navy Department

4. A visual method for the reduction of static disturbances in receiving. This method takes advantage of the difference in signal static ratio of surface wires water wires, and loops Chief Electrician L M Clausing also developed independently a variation in this circuit which gives similar results

5 A circuit for undamped reception with the audion in which plate circuit tuning is employed as well as the usual grid circuit tuning. This keeps out much interference which otherwise would make reception on certain wave lengths difficult or impossible.

There were also completed the following investigations, all by Chief Electrician W. F Grimes, which are not only of purely scientific interest but of practical value·

Experimental verification of the theory of loop antennas, including a formula and table for the calculation of the antenna height corresponding to any loop

A new and exceedingly simple formula for the predetermination of antenna capacity, and also for the calculation of "edge effect" of plate condensers

A new method of using contact detectors in the measurement of small radio frequency currents

RADIO TEST SHOP.

Under the direction of the Bureau the radio test shop at the Washington Navy Yard took a very active part in war work Its function is threefold, in that (1) it originates schemes for radio communication, especially in reference to methods and apparatus to be used in radio reception, and develops means and apparatus to put those schemes into ship and shore service; (2) it passes on ideas and apparatus along these lines developed outside its own organization, and (3) it receives, inspects and tests all the arc type of transmitters, and all the small transmitters which the Navy uses, and distributes these apparatus to the service

While this last class of work is the least interesting of the shop's activities, the greater part of its force is occupied in doing it From April 6, 1917, to November 11, 1918 the laboratory force tested 3,636 receivers, 1,100 amplifiers, 2,835 auxiliary apparatus, 789 small transmitters, and 26 arc transmitters

Receivers.—The biggest and most important problem that the shop was confronted with was that of standardizing the receiving equipment of the Navy. This standardization was made more difficult by the fact that, in the first year of the war, the range of wave lengths that was used was greatly increased, and apparatus had to be designed for operation over the entire range Furthermore, the era of the crystal detector was still with us and that of the vacuum tube was just beginning, so that all receiving apparatus had to be a compromise between the ideal designs for either of these types of detectors

However, a standard receiver layout was formulated, and on the basis of this arrangement a series of receivers was designed. The details of the standard panel are shown in figure 1 This was the first one built in the SE 143 receivers that were purchased in such large quantities, and it was later used in the design of three other receivers. The details of the SE 143 receiver are shown in figure 2 It was designed to cover the range from 300 to 7,000 meters, and was of great value for its general utility, since it covered the range of wave lengths most used Three other receivers were designed to meet the need for reception on extremely short wave lengths, and one of them modified, by the addition of a simple switch, for radio compass operation

Control boxes; amplifiers —With this development of receiving equipment came that of standard designs of auxiliary apparatus, as typified by the SE 1071 audion control box and SE 1000 amplifier. Control boxes that had been previously purchased were unsatisfactory in structural detail and were expensive As is usual, it was difficult to get the manufacturer to supply just what was required by the service, and when an acceptable approximation was finally received the price was found to be excessive However, when the Navy design was put into production it was found that the cost of control boxes was greatly reduced, and, as in the case of the receivers, a higher quality of product and one of greater uniformity was secured, while the rate of delivery was increased tenfold

The design of the SE 1000 was made to meet the needs of the service for an amplifier of moderate power Before its appearance in the service the only amplifier in use had proved so unsatisfactory that the various commercial companies capable of such design work

FIG. 1.

FIG. 2.

FIG. 4.

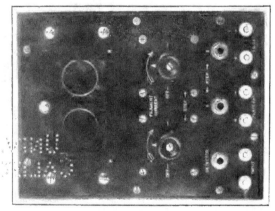

FIG. 3.—TWO STAGE AMPLIFIER.

FIG. 5.—PANEL, RECEIVER, TYPE S. E. 1012.

FIG. 6.—RECEIVER, TYPE S. E. 1012.

FIG. 7.—BACK OF BACK PANEL, RECEIVER TYPE S. E. 950

FIG. 8.

FIG. 9.

were requested to submit samples. These samples were so unsatisfactory that a Navy design was essential, and thus the SE 1000 audio frequency amplifier came into being.

The details of this amplifier are shown in figures 3 and 4. Modifications were made from time to time to improve the operation and to cheapen production, but at no time was the standard arrangement departed from, so that now all of the audio frequency amplifiers are electrically and mechanically interchangeable, and, in external appearance, are identical.

Radio compass receivers.—Besides these standard designs special designs were put into production to meet certain needs. Among these are the SE 1012 radio compass receiver and the SE 950 airplane radio compass receiver.

Figures 5 and 6 show the details of the SE 1012. It was designed to meet the need for a compact compass receiver for use on destroyer installations. There is incorporated in it all the tube equipment, so that it requires only the connection of battery and phones for operation. It was at the time of its design, and is still, unique in that it is the only receiver of commercial or Navy design capable of undamped reception below 100 meters.

The details of the airplane radio compass receiver are shown in figure 7. It was designed for radio compass work on planes and has all of the tubes and tube apparatus for the operation of the receiver and the 2-step amplifier, which is integral with the receiver, and also the switching and balancing apparatus for use in radio compass work. It is of interest to note that this receiver was designed in a shorter time than any single device that this laboratory ever turned out. In less than two weeks from the time of the order by the Bureau for an airplane compass receiver the complete apparatus was designed, the model built, minor changes made, and the device tried out. It is still the best receiver for aircraft radio reception in the service.

Improved receivers.—About a year and a half after the SE 143 type of receiver had been standardized this laboratory had gathered enough data to build an improved receiver which differed from the SE 143 type in greater sensibility, selectivity, and lesser bulk and cost. The first of this type to be built was the SE 1420, shown in figures 8 and 9. The chief characteristic of this apparatus is that the receiver is thoroughly shielded both against external interference and undesirable interactions in the receiver. It occupies about one-half of the volume of the SE 143 receiver, has all the tube apparatus integral with it, is designed for damped and undamped operation between 235 and 7,000 meters, and has features which make it the best receiver for general radio service, and probably the world, has ever seen This was the first of a new series of receivers for the service, the others of this series being SE 1412, SE 1530

Coincident with the second series of receivers came the development of high-power amplifiers. The need for these was especially urgent in aircraft, and the demand was met in the SE 1605 and the SE 1405 amplifiers. The report of the aircraft radio laboratory shows these amplifiers to be of higher power than any in general use in the military service here or abroad.

Personnel.—The development of the receiving apparatus was under the direction of Lieut W. A. Eaton, U. S Navy, with Gunner T McL. Davis, U. S Navy, as his assistant. Working under him were Expert Radio Aids Horle, Israel, and Priess, and Radio Electricians Shapiro, Carpenter, and Worrall, with Prof. L A. Hazeltine as consulting engineer.

Summary —Briefly, the work of the radio test shop during the war has been the design of radio equipment of the highest quality compatible with the space, cost, production, and personnel limitations The shop has succeeded in making the standard of receiving equipment of the Navy equal to, or superior to, that of any other nation, and vastly in advance of any equipment in commercial use. It has made possible also the procurement of this apparatus in large quantities at a high production rate and at very low cost.

RADIO FOR AIRCRAFT.

The great importance of radio for military aircraft is too evident to require comment. One of the most important functions of military airplanes and dirigibles is that of observing, and the primary importance of such observation lies in the ability to transmit results instantly to a distant point. To this very great advantage, radio adds that of being able to control the movement of aircraft from the ground or from other aircraft, and that of transmission of distress signals from disabled craft.

The naval aircraft radio problem is of a different character in many ways from that of the land military forces in that it introduces the use of this communication, in connection with antisubmarine and other coastal patrol duties where larger craft are used, and where larger and longer range radio sets are required This patrol duty involves the reporting of position as the aircraft covers its patrol territory, and the reporting of enemy craft or mines sighted, or of vessels in distress In connection with these duties, there is involved that of convoy, in which radio enables the aircraft to communicate directly with the vessels under escort.

The other and very important phase of the naval aircraft problem in which radio enters is that of fire control for battleships In this case the craft used are smaller, the radio is usually operated by the pilot, and the transmitting distance required is relatively short Thus, from a radio viewpoint, naval aircraft radio is divided into two distinctly separate phases, each calling for apparatus and equipment of a widely varying character

Development; installation; operation —At the beginning of the war there was no field of radio work newer than that of its application to aircraft. As with a number of other novel technical questions introduced by the war, that of aircraft radio was attended by many difficulties In solving the problem presented there arose the development difficulties of providing new methods of investigation as applied to aircraft, and of training personnel to conduct these investigations from a basic knowledge which was extremely meager It was necessary to have a large number of aircraft of the various standardized types for radio testing purposes, and this was difficult, owing to the general lack of such craft at the beginning of the war. It was also found that in this development work, it was necessary to employ pilots who were sympathetic with the radio investigations, in order to obtain the most satisfactory results in the shortest possible time.

After the preliminary investigations had been conducted it was required that the apparatus pass rapidly from the development to the standardization stage In standardization it was necessary to combine compactness, light weight, and simplicity of manufacture with ease of control, watertightness, and the highest degree of solidity to withstand shocks of a widely varying nature Standardization was also attended by the difficulty of its simultaneous application to the radio equipment and that of the aircraft itself.

Installation difficulties were largely solved by the careful choice of complete equipments, including all detailed fittings and material necessary for a standard installation The installation work required however, the special training of personnel who would be familiar with aircraft so that the general utility would not be impaired The initial installations were made in a standard manner by equipping each plane before it was shipped from the factory

The matter of operation also involved the special training of personnel Operating radio apparatus on aircraft is of a very special and unusual nature The operator must usually work in a space which is more or less restricted and with a large number of conditions such as motor noise and rough flying, which seriously distract his attention from his radio duties The use of more recent forms of apparatus, such as vacuum-tube transmitt— — — — receivers, and the radio compass, has still further necessitated special training.

Prewar transmitters and receivers.—At the beginning of the war the radio equipment for aircraft which had been developed consisted of a few types of spark transmitters and one-tube transmitters, all of which had proved rather unreliable, heavy, and bulky. The only equipment which appeared at all promising was the spark transmitter and receiver designed and manufactured by E. J Simon, New York, N. Y., and illustrated in figure 1

A reel was supplied with this set which was made entirely of insulated material so that tuning of the antenna circuit could be accomplished by the variation of the length of trailing antenna while the transmitter was operated Power was supplied from a propeller-driven generator mounted on the wing of the airplane, a brake being provided to prevent the propeller from revolving when the radio set was not in use This set, completely installed, weighed approximately 100 pounds. During the summer of 1917 signals were transmitted a distance of 150 nautical miles with this transmitter The receiver employs a single vacuum tube with a regenerative circuit.

Work of aircraft radio laboratory —Both of these apparatus were tested out in their development at the aircraft radio laboratory, naval air station. Pensacola, Fla., where, from the beginning of the war until January 1, 1918, all development work of this nature was conducted under the direction of Expert Radio Aid B. F. Meissner. During this period, measurements were made of antenna constants on seaplanes, and the directive effect of trailing wire antennas was investigated A very satisfactory intercommunicating system of the voice-tube type was developed, together with suitable helmets for the pilot and radio operator. The radio compass as applied to aircraft and the use of high-tension ignition magneto as a radio transmitter were also investigated Development of installation fittings, such as antenna reels and antenna weights, was also undertaken.

In May, 1917, the experimental laboratory was moved from the station at Pensacola to that at Hampton Roads, Va., and development work was undertaken on a far more extensive scale with a view to accomplishing standardization of equipment and quantity production as soon as possible Great stress was laid also upon the development of vacuum-tube transmitters for telephone use and the radio direction finder And, further, there became available flying boats of the latest standardized type, thereby permitting the standardization of radio installations

The preliminary experimental work at Hampton Roads involved a large number of fundamental investigations in connection with

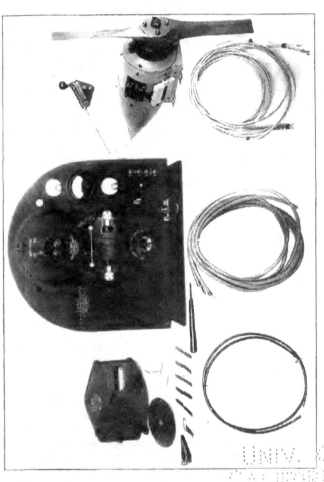

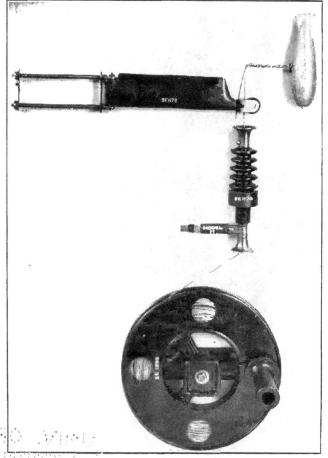

FIG. 2.—STANDARD AIRCRAFT TRAILING ANTENNA.

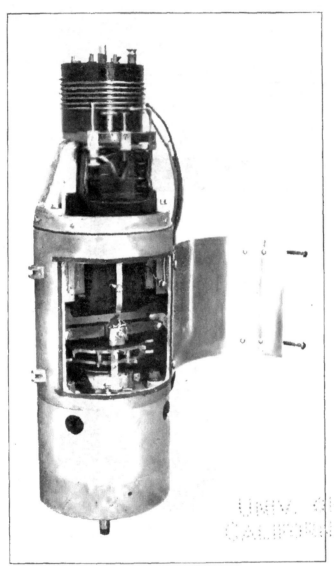

FIG. 3.

FIG. 4.

FIG. 3.

FIG. 6.

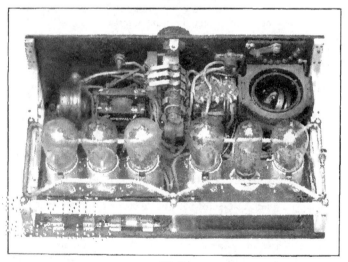

FIG. 7.

various details, such as all forms of power generating apparatus, including propellers, storage batteries, generators, and dynamotors, all forms of antenna and ground systems, electrical communicating systems, helmets, microphones, and the many other units forming a part of complete equipments.

Transmitters.—The principal sets tested at Hampton Roads consisted of two vacuum-tube transmitters developed by the Western Electric Co., a vacuum-tube transmitter made by the DeForest Radio Telegraph & Telephone Co., and spark transmitters submitted by E. J. Simon, New York (designed by L. Israel), and by the National Electrical Supply Co. In addition to the above experimental sets, there were tested at Hampton Roads all of the present standardized aircraft radio equipments for aircraft. A sample of such standard equipment is the trailing wire, reel, insulators, and weight, illustrated in figure 2.

The standard spark transmitting equipments consist of three types. The 200-watt type and the 500-watt type are manufactured by the International Radio Telegraph Co., and were designed by Mr. F. H. Kroger, formerly chief engineer of that company. These transmitters represent the most satisfactory spark transmitter of the propeller-driven form ever developed for aircraft use. The equipment in each case consists of a radio assembly embodying the main elements of a rotary gap transmitter, mounted within a streamline case, as illustrated in figure 3, and a tuning variometer illustrated in figure 4. The 200-watt set weighs 65 pounds complete and has a transmitting range of 100 nautical miles. The 500-watt set weighs 85 pounds complete, and on the trans-Atlantic flight was used for communicating 1,450 miles to land and 500 miles to destroyers.

Another 500-watt spark transmitter is that manufactured by Cutting & Washington (Inc.) This set is of the impact excitation type and consists essentially of a panel, illustrated in figure 5, and a propeller-driven generator.

Of the vacuum-tube transmitters developed for naval aircraft, the most satisfactory have been supplied by the General Electric Co. In the development of these sets there were utilized three types of tubes—a 5-watt output tube using a plate voltage of 350, a 50-watt output tube using a plate voltage of 500 and 1,000, and a 250-watt output tube using a plate voltage of 1,500 and 2,000.

The smallest tube transmitter developed by the General Electric Co. is illustrated in figures 6 and 7, and consists of a combined telephone transmitter and receiver for use by spotting airplanes for directing the fire of battleships within an operating radius of 30 miles. The set is very small, and completely installed weighs only 50 pounds. Power is supplied from a propeller-driven generator. Another similar equipment embodying that matter only shown in figures 8 and 9, is operated on a storage battery and has a telegraph range of 100 miles in addition to its telephone features

The highest power set developed for aircraft is the one illustrated in figure 10, which is operated on a combination of a storage battery and a propeller-driven generator; it has a telephone range of 200 miles and a telegraph range of 400 miles

Another type of medium-power tube transmitter developed during the war is that shown in figures 11 and 12 and designed by the Marconi Wireless Telegraph Co This transmitter has a telegraph range of 150 miles and telephone range of 60 miles.

A low-power vacuum-tube transmitter of 5-watt antenna input was designed by the General Radio Co., and was utilized in service to a limited extent. Another low-power vacuum-tube transmitter and receiver, illustrated in figure 13, was also used. It was manufactured by the Western Electric Co

A very important advance in connection with telephone transmitters was that of a suitable microphone transmitter The best one developed, and that which was adopted as standard, is shown in figure 14 This transmitter is manufactured by the Magnavox Co, of San Francisco

Receivers—The reception of radio signals on aircraft is an entirely different problem from that of any other form of radio reception The difficulties encountered may be classified as acoustic disturbances, consisting of wind rush, engine noise, and vibrational noises, and electrical disturbances resulting from vibration of vacuum tubes and other apparatus, and from induction from engine ignition systems

The electrical disturbances are provided against by the proper design of receiving apparatus, suitable flexible mountings, the shielding of ignition systems, and so on. The problem of acoustic disturbances has its solution in the design of a suitable helmet holding the radio telephone receivers. Although several helmets had been designed for this purpose, none was found satisfactory, and it was necessary to design one which would be suitable for the needs of the naval service This helmet is illustrated in figure 15 It is made of soft leather with a flannel lining, the central rear seam being left open in manufacture to allow for fitting to the head The main feature is the deep soft rubber ear cup which incloses the radio telephone receiver and fits closely to the head, excluding external noises. The helmet is fitted tightly to the head by a strap running around the forehead and the back of the neck instead of by a chin strap. The design of this helmet was perfected by Lieut Commander A H. Taylor, U S Naval Reserve Force; Lieut (j g.) W R Davis, U. S. Naval Reserve Force; and Ensign C D. Palmer, U. S. Naval Reserve Force.

FIG. 8.

FIG. 9.

FIG. 10.

FIG. 11.

FIG. 12

FIG. 13.

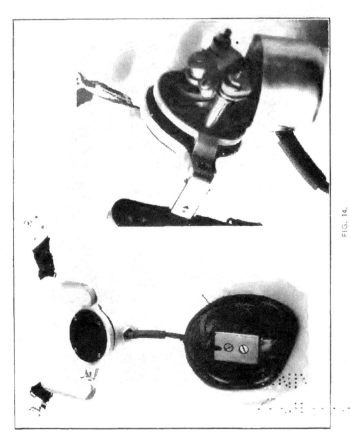

FIG. 14.

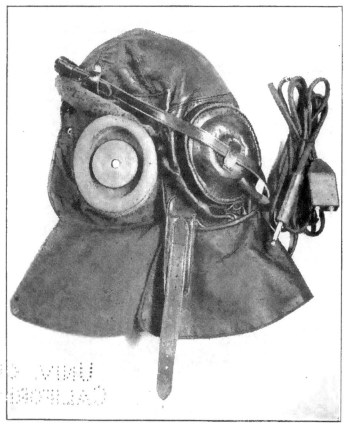

FIG. 15.

FIG. 16.

FIG. 16.—AIRCRAFT RADIO RECEIVER, TYPE 950.

FIG. 18.

FIG. 19.—RADIO COMPASS COILS IN WINGS OF AIRPLANE.

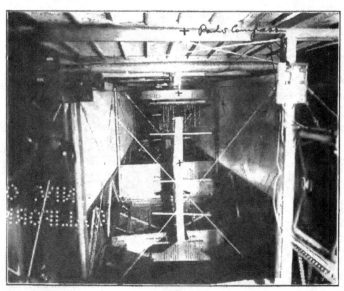

FIG. 21.—SEAPLANE, SHOWING SKID FIN ANTENNA.

FIG. 22.

The first standard naval aircraft receiver was developed during the early part of the war, and is shown in figure 16. It consists of an inductively coupled vacuum-tube receiver of a wave length range from 300 to 2,500 meters, provided with static tube coupling for attaining regeneration and oscillation, with two stages of audio-frequency amplification. The receiver is also provided with proper switching and a compensating inductance to adapt it for radio compass use. This receiver was designated at the radio test shop and manufactured by the National Electrical Supply Co.

Another aircraft radio receiver of simpler construction is illustrated in figure 17. It consists of a conductively coupled receiver of wave length range of 200 to 3,000 meters with inductive tube coupling for regeneration and oscillation, and it is provided with two stages of audio-frequency amplification. In this receiver the tubes are not provided with any individual flexible mounting, but the entire receiver is mounted in a rubber suspension. This receiver was also designed at the radio test shop, and is manufactured by the Westinghouse Electric & Manufacturing Co.

Another very interesting piece of apparatus used for radio reception on naval aircraft is the audio-radio frequency amplifier illustrated in figure 18. This amplifier is designed primarily for use in connection with radio compass apparatus, but may be used successfully for any radio reception within the wave length specified. It is very small, weighs but 10 pounds, and consists of three stages of radio-frequency amplification. The amplification is made in two ranges of wave length, 600 to 1,800, and 1,800 to 5,400 meters.

Radio compass or direction finder.—One of the most interesting features of naval radio for aircraft development during the war was the radio compass or direction finder. The standard equipment designed consists essentially of a coil system fixed in the wings of the planes as illustrated in figure 19, or of an independently revolving type as shown in figure 20, a control panel involving a reversing switch and tubing condensers, and the amplifier just described. The form of coil fixed in the wings of the planes has not been widely used in the naval air service itself, but has been employed in the development of radio-compass equipment for airplane use by the Post Office Department. In this case, satisfactory radio direction finding has been accomplished, utilizing the signals of a 5-kilowatt spark station at a distance of 50 miles. Bearings within 1° have been taken at a distance of 300 miles on Arlington 100-kilowatt spark signals on 2,500 meters. This is the maximum distance attempted with these signals during the war, the results obtained indicate that accurate results could be had at a much greater distance

The aircraft radio compass development work was conducted under the direction of Lieut Commander A H Taylor. The final design of the independently revolving coils is the work of Mr F. H. Kroger, of the International Radio Telegraph Co.

Radio apparatus in the trans-Atlantic flight—A complete aircraft radio installation of particular interest is the special one adopted for the type NC flying boats used on the trans-Atlantic flight, and which was a development of war experience The radio equipment consisted essentially of a 500-watt propeller-driven spark transmitter supplied by the International Radio Telegraph Co., a low-power battery-driven General Electric Co telephone transmitter, a standard aircraft receiver, and a large independently revolving set of radio compass coils, together with compass control panel and amplifier. Arrangement was made for transmission or reception either on a skid fin antenna, illustrated in figure 21, or on a single wire trailing antenna

The intercommunication telephone systems on the boats were arranged so that the radio telephone could be used by either the commanding officer, located forward in the craft, or the radio operator, thereby permitting radio conversation directly between the commanding officers of the various boats. Arrangements were also made for the navigator to receive the radio signals, which allowed the checking of chronometers by radio from signals sent by Arlington The complete radio equipment weighed 200 pounds. The interior installation is illustrated in figure 22

During the trans-Atlantic flight, record-breaking communication results were obtained The planes were heard on shore when 1,450 miles distant, and communication was conducted between the planes and shore for 700 miles and between planes and destroyers for 500 miles Signals were received on board the planes from stations 1,600 miles distant.

The radio preparations for the trans-Atlantic flight were conducted by Lieut Commander R. A Lavender, U. S. Navy, Lieuts (j. g) H Sadenwater, U. S. Naval Reserve Force, and C. B Mirick, U S Naval Reserve Force, Ensigns C. D. Palmer, U S Naval Reserve Force, and H. C. Rodd, U. S. Naval Reserve Force, Chief Electricians R M Wise and F P. Jones, and Electricians W A. Parks and O C Dresser Radio operation was conducted on the trip by Lieut Sadenwater and Ensign Rodd

Similar radio apparatus was used on the dirigible *C-5* in its thousand-mile trip to St. Johns, Newfoundland, on which a T interval antenna was used. Excellent communication was established by the operator, Lieut (j g) M H. Esterly, U. S. Naval Reserve Force, who also supervised the installation.

Antennas.—During the latter part of the war a very complete and careful investigation of aircraft antennas was conducted by the General Electric Co. under the direction of the Navy Department. Extremely valuable results were obtained which were not available previously in any form. This investigation resulted in the adaptation of an interior T form of antenna for dirigibles. The development work on this form of antenna was conducted by Lieut (j g.) M. H. Esterly, U. S. Naval Reserve Force.

In addition to the work on power generating apparatus for radio for aircraft sets done by the General Electric Co during the war, considerable development work was undertaken by the Crocker-Wheeler Co.

RADIO WAR WORK AT OVERSEAS NAVAL BASES.

It was soon realized that the radio equipment of our naval forces overseas would have to be maintained by organizations to be established at each of the United States naval bases in Europe. In September, 1917, Lieut. P H. Bastedo, U. S Navy, who had recently been detached from the Bureau of Steam Engineering, was accordingly assigned by the force commander, Vice Admiral Sims, to duty as force radio matériel officer.

Later, when aviation, mining, and sub chaser forces were added to our vessels overseas, it became the duty of the radio officer of each force to study its communication requirements, to modify the existing, or obtain new, radio apparatus to meet these requirements, and to establish a maintenance and repair base.

When our battleships joined the Grand Fleet, the squadron had difficulty in operating efficiently as a unit of the fleet until radical changes were made in its radio equipment. These changes were effected with the assistance and cooperation of the British, and complete recommendations were submitted to the Navy Department covering the alterations necessary in our vessels for such service.

As soon as it was known that a United States naval aviation force was to be established in Europe, a study of British practice in this respect was made, and complete data covering the following points were forwarded to the Navy Department

(a) Apparatus used in all types of seaplanes
(b) Apparatus used at seaplane bases
(c) Description of organization, giving personnel engaged in radio material work. This description covered the organization at headquarters in London, and the personnel employed in experimental work, in production, installation, and maintenance, in operation of the planes, and at the bases

Full recor... ... ... al aviation requir... ... ...

On this subject, and also on British radio material practice, the British Admiralty furnished our officers all the information requested. For valuable assistance rendered as to naval aviation, especial acknowledgment is due the then Commander Warrington-Morris, R N, now colonel, R. A F. and deputy director of instruments, while with regard to British radio practice, a similar acknowledgment is due Commander Geoffrey Candy, R N.

The radio officer on the staff of the force commander acted as permanent liaison officer with the British until the headquarters of the United States naval aviation were removed from Paris to London After this, the liaison work was performed by the radio officer in the technical section of aviation under the force commander.

When headquarters were in Paris, the same liaison was effected with the French radio service under the direction of Gen Ferrié, through whose courtesy the radio officers detailed to the various air stations in Europe were given a short course of instruction and granted an opportunity to inspect the several shops engaged in manufacturing and testing French aviation radio material

Samples of all aviation radio apparatus developed by the French were purchased and shipped to the Bureau as aids in the design and manufacture of our own aviation radio apparatus Requisitions were also made from time to time on the French Government for radio supplies, and while it was at first difficult to secure a sufficient quantity, this condition soon improved and our needs were readily satisfied The assistance thus rendered by the French was very opportune, and made possible the prompt equipment of our air stations in France

In June, 1918, the radio section was removed to Pauillac, and in September to Brest, where it remained until hostilities ceased.

Destroyer base, Queenstown, Ireland —As an example of the character and magnitude of the radio work done at these overseas naval bases, that carried on at Queenstown may be cited This base was the first established in European waters, and had its beginning early in May, 1917, when several United States destroyers arrived. Each of these vessels carried an excess of radio spare parts and material, with which she was self-supporting

After the arrival of the *Melville* and *Dixie*, the *Melville* alone maintained the base from July to September, 1917, while during that period the *Dixie* furnished supplies to destroyers from a sub-base in Bantry Bay From September, 1917, until the cessation of hostilities, these two ships worked together at Queenstown

The work accomplished by them was very extensive. In many cases extensive alterations in our radio installations were required because of the necessity of adapting our vessels to the Admiralty system of communication.

Great Britain aided this base during the interim between its establishment and the regular receipt of stores from the United States, besides furnishing the special material required to make the alterations necessitated by the adoption of the British communication system. In all cases the work of repair, alteration, or installation was done by the radio personnel of the repair ship, aided when necessary by that of the vessel under repair.

United States naval base, Gibraltar.—The radio department of the United States naval base, Gibraltar, was established on January 18, 1918, and placed in charge of the squadron radio officer, Lieut. B. F. Jenkins, U. S. Navy, whose duties comprised the organization of radio work by ships, the control of the radio personnel, and the maintenance, repair, and installation of all radio equipment.

From February 10, 1918, onward, the radio outfits on all American vessels passing through the Mediterranean were maintained and repaired. Considerable work was also done at various times for the British, such as the installation of radio apparatus at the Summit and at Europa Point, and the tuning up of the Rock wireless tower and North Front wireless tower stations.

Naval radio repair bases in France.—Eight radio repair bases were established in France, as follows:

	Date of establishment		Date of establishment
Brest	December, 1917	La Pallice	May 15, 1918
Lorient	February, 1918	Gironde River	May 30, 1918
St Nazaire	December 1917.	Le Havre	June 1, 1918
Rochefort	February 1918	Marseille	June 15, 1918

Of these stations the two most important were Brest and St Nazaire—the former because of the large force of warships based there; the latter, owing to the great number of United States transports, chartered transports, and merchantmen which discharged in that port.

In general, the governing policy of these European repair bases in France and elsewhere was:

To inspect the radio installations of all American ships making the port a discharging point, to make repairs and replacements, when necessary, to bring all radio installations inspected to the highest efficiency possible to the base; and in order to conserve the ship space required for the transport of new apparatus from the United States, to issue new equipment only when repairs were wholly impracticable.

Submarine chaser bases.—Shortly after the first United States submarine chasers arrived in European waters Lieut. Commander E C Raquet, U. S. Navy, under the direction of Capt R H Leigh, U S Navy, was placed in charge of the maintenance of the radio apparatus on these vessels.

Standard radio repair bases were established at Plymouth, England; Queenstown, Ireland; and Corfu, Greece. The repair facilities of the destroyer force at Queenstown were available for the chaser force based at that port.

RADIO PATENTS.

For a number of years prior to the entrance of the United States into the war, the radio field had been a particularly active one in the matter of patent litigation and of other efforts to establish certain patents as being basic and controlling in the various types of apparatus commonly used in radio communication. Some of the suits are noted in the history of patent litigation from the number of famous physicists, technicians, and inventors arrayed against each other, and from the volume and high character of the testimony presented. It is apparent that such elaborate litigation was carried on only at great cost.

That such expensive litigation should have occurred in the radio field at that time can be accounted for only by the hope that radio had a wide field opening up in the displacement of the cables or the limitation of future cable laying over new communication routes.

The Government, more particularly through the Navy, has always been the largest purchaser of radio apparatus, and, since the consumer must eventually pay all costs of production, including patent litigation, it was manifestly the Government's duty—and this was done—to take as active interest as possible in such suits.

When the United States entered the war there were a number of suits pending in the Court of Claims, and many forming, some of them against the Government. It was early realized that to permit these suits to continue during the war would interfere materially with the increased production necessary for war purposes, since a suit always lessens the attention to normal affairs in any organization and requires the time and thought of its expert engineers. As expert radio engineers were none too numerous and many of them had entered the military services or were engaged in Government war work, the Navy Department demanded, in letters to the various litigants and in some cases to the courts, that all such litigations be suspended for the period of the war, which demand was acceded to in all cases.

Act of June 25, 1910.—The act of June 25, 1910, reads as follows:

That whenever any invention described in and covered by a patent of the United States shall hereafter be used by the United States without license of the owner thereof or lawful right to use the same, such owner may recover reasonable compensation for such use by suit in the Court of Claims.

This, it was interpreted by some to relieve the contractor from any liability for infringement in meeting Government orders, and hence an attempt was made to return this liability to the contractor by a clause in contracts to the effect that the contractor would hold the Government harmless from claims for patent infringement In a suit, Marconi v. Simon, for infringement in some radio transmitters furnished by Simon to the Navy Department, Simon defended under the act of June 25, 1910, maintaining that the Government, by right of eminent domain, could order radio apparatus from him which he was compelled to manufacture, but that the plaintiff only had a right of action against the Government under the act. Simon was upheld by the United States District Court in which the case was tried.

Supreme Court's reversal of decision by lower court.—With the decision of the district court in Marconi v. Simon to encourage contractors and with no interfering litigation, war production progressed rapidly until March, 1918, when the Supreme Court—to which tribunal the Marconi vs Simon case had been appealed—reversed the decision of the lower court, holding that a contractor for the Government was liable to the patent owner in so far as manufacturing and selling were concerned, and remanded the case to the lower court for the establishment of facts as to whether or not the apparatus manufactured and sold to the Government was infringing or constituted contributary infringement (The appeal to the Supreme Court was not objected to by the Navy Department, as it did not involve any new testimony, being simply a review by a higher court of the case as heard in the lower court)

The Supreme Court decision gave serious concern to the radio manufacturers, who were all working on large orders for the Government, and the Navy and War Departments soon found themselves confronted by their threat to cease production unless some way could be found to afford them protection

Therefore, to prevent delay, the Secretary of the Navy wrote letters to the various manufacturers directing them to continue production on their existing orders with all possible expedition, and so modified the terms of their contracts as to place all patent liability upon the Government.

Act of July 1, 1918—The act of July 1, 1918 reads as follows

Whenever an invention described in and covered by a patent of the United States shall hereafter be used or manufactured by or for the United States without license of the owners thereof or lawful right to use the same, such owners remedy shall be by suit against the United States in the Court of Claims for the recovery of his reasonable and entire compensation for such use and manufacture

This act cleared up the situation brought about by the reversal by the Supreme Court of the lower court's decision in the case of Marconi v. Simon and upheld the action of the Secretary of the Navy and the Secretary of War in directing that production continue on the Government's liability, since it so modified the act of June 25, 1910, as to place the liability for manufacture as well as use on the Government

Interdepartmental radio board.—The Munitions Patent Board had been formed early in the war to hear patent claims and make recommendations to the various departments concerning their settlement. but, on account of the number of these claims in the radio field, their value and duration, the complex state of the art, and other considerations, a special organization, the Interdepartmental Radio Board, composed of two members from the Navy Department, two from the War Department, and one from the Department of Justice, was formed in August, 1918, to judge radio claims Unfortunately, its personnel had to be selected from officers already occupied with war work, and the two original Navy members were detached from duty in the Department a short time after the board was formed, so that not much was accomplished in the early months of its existence.

The Bureau of Steam Engineering made an early effort to have Lient. Commander E. H. Loftin U S Navy, released from duty overseas in order that a specialized radio officer might be assigned to this board and be practically unhampered by other duties However, it was not until after the armistice was signed that this officer was released from foreign service and reported for duty in the Bureau on January 14, 1919.

The officers who served in the Radio Division during the war were:

In charge of division · Commander S C Hooper, U. S. Navy; Lieut. Commander H. P LeClair, U S Navy

High-power section Lieut Commander G. W Sweet, U. S. Navy (retired); Lieut. Commander R. G Coman, U. S. Navy, Lieut. (j g) A H. Vanderhoof, U. S Navy (retired); Gunner D. Mc-Whorter, jr, U S Navy

Design section Lieut G H. Lewis, U. S Naval Reserve Force; Lieut. C. T. Anderson, U. S. Naval Reserve Force.

Ship section · Lieut Commander P H Bastedo, U. S. Navy; Lieut. Commander U W. Conway, U S Navy; Lieut (T) H J. Mineratti, U. S. Naval Reserve Force; Lieut Edw J. Neary, U. S. Naval Reserve Force

Compass section · Lieut Commander R A Lavender, U. S. Navy; Lieut W. Dann, U. S. Naval Reserve Force, Ensign G. A. Graham, U S Naval Reserve Force; Ensign H S Murdock, U. S Naval Reserve Force

Aircraft section. Lieut. Commander R A. Lavender, U. S Navy; Lieut. (j g) H. Sadenwater, U S Naval Reserve Force; Ensign H M Anthony, U S Naval Reserve Force; Ensign M A Bishop,

U. S. Naval Reserve Force, Ensign M. H. Esterly, U. S Naval Reserve Force, Ensign A. Peter, 3d, U S. Naval Reserve Force; Ensign J Shoolbred, U S. Naval Reserve Force; Ensign T J. Styles, U. S. Naval Reserve Force.

Supply section Lieut V. Grieff, U. S. Naval Reserve Force; Ensign G. M. Hannah, U. S. Naval Reserve Force; Ensign F L. Koplin, U S. Naval Reserve Force.

Patent section Ensign J B Brady, U S Naval Reserve Force Research section. Ensign A Crossley, U. S. Naval Reserve Force.

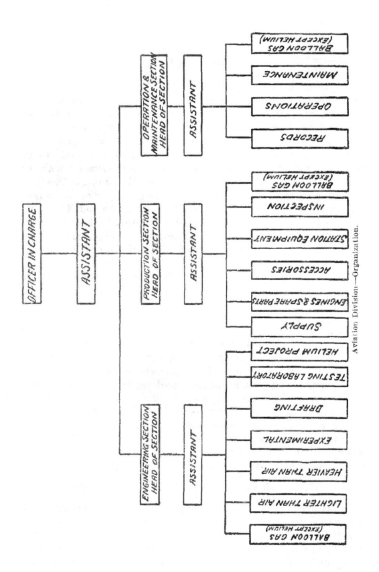

Aviation Division—Organization.

AVIATION.

The function of the Bureau during the war was to take the responsibility for the design and development of the power plants of all naval aircraft, to conduct the inspection, expedite the production, and supervise the operation and maintenance in service of all aviation material under the cognizance of the Bureau. The above duties also included the equipment for the manufacture and storage of balloon gas. In carrying on the work, close cooperation with the Army and other aviation activities was essential, and for this purpose the head of the Aviation Division was a member of the following agencies: (1) Aircraft Board; (2) Joint Army and Navy Airship Board; (3) Joint Army and Navy Aircraft Technical Board; (4) power plant committee of the National Advisory Committee for Aeronautics (5) aeronautical section of the Society of Automotive Engineers

Attendance upon the meetings of these boards and committees was a serious encroachment upon the duties of this officer, but no doubt this loss of time was compensated for by the close touch that was kept with all other activities that were pursuing the same line of endeavor. Frequent conferences between all offices of the Navy Department connected with aviation tended to closest cooperation

The principal difficulties encountered during the war were largely due to the fact that practically 90 per cent of the personnel connected with aviation were inexperienced reserves unfamiliar with naval customs and procedure, but this condition rapidly improved from month to month Transportation and shipping conditions were a source of great trouble during the summer of 1918, particularly in connection with the foreign stations. A special board was sent from the Navy Department to study conditions abroad and to make recommendations for such relief as was necessary.

PERSONNEL AND ORGANIZATION

At the beginning of the war, the personnel of the Aviation Division was composed of one officer and one stenographer, occupying one-half of one room in the State, War, and Navy Building There were three officers in the field on inspection duty As the aviation policy of the Department began to shape itself and and facilities for the production of aircraft became a necessity, it was apparent that an organization must be formed that could handle the design, the production and inspection, and the operation and maintenance of all aircraft material for which the Bureau was responsible.

From a force of one officer and one stenographer, occupying half a room, the Aviation Division expanded in a few months to a force of approximately 40 officers and 60 clerks and stenographers, requiring approximately 7,500 square feet of floor space. Office space at no time was adequate and could not be obtained until the New Navy Building was completed. The personnel worked under the most unfavorable conditions, all the officers being obliged to keep unusually long office hours, and most of them continuously working at night in order to keep up with their work.

The inspection force in the field expanded from 3 to approximately 150 officers in addition to the necessary enlisted force, civilian inspectors, clerks, and stenographers.

The Department had established 20 air stations abroad, in addition to 10 in the United States, all of which required a volume of detailed attention in connection with their operation and maintenance. The establishment of these bases, and their equipment with the necessary tools and material, was a major undertaking, requiring the sole attention of several officers. The proper equipment of the various schools that were established by the Bureau of Navigation required the attention of one complete section of the office.

The work was divided into three divisions, i. e., (a) engineering, which was responsible for the design or approval of the design of the power plant installations and power plant accessories on all naval aircraft; for balloon gas equipment; and for experimental and development work; (b) production, which was responsible for the production, inspection, and shipment of material; (c) operation and maintenance, which was responsible for all that pertained to the proper care, operation, and maintenance of all aviation material. A chart of the organization of the Aviation Division is shown on page 132.

LIBERTY ENGINES.

The Navy's program of service machines for the war was based upon the Liberty engine. Careful survey of the aviation engine field in the United States showed there was no engine in the country at the beginning of the war that was then developed or in process of development which had the qualifications for use by either the Army or the Navy that could cause it to be considered as an engine fitted for war service. There was no engine of sufficient power and proven reliability that would withstand transplanting to the United States from abroad and be manufactured in sufficient quantities to

INSPECTION OF VALVES FOR LIBERTY ENGINES, PACKARD COMPANY.

WELDING WATER JACKETS OF LIBERTY ENGINES, PACKARD COMPANY.

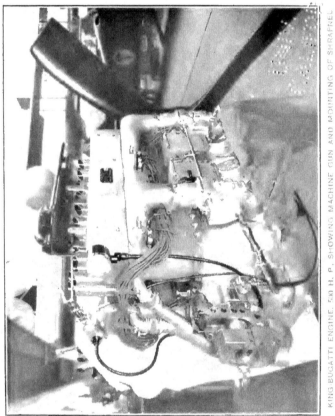

KING BUGATTI ENGINE, 500 H. P., SHOWING MACHINE GUN AND MOUNTING OF SHRAPNEL

enable the country's air service to be a factor in the struggle. The General Vehicle Co was building the 110-horsepower Gnome, which was not in especially good favor and was of little value to the Navy, and the Wright-Martin Co was not yet in successful production of the 150-horsepower Hispano-Suiza. The various commissions that went abroad reported that the trend of air planes for Army use was toward a two-seated fighter, and the more powerful the engine the better. The development thus indicated was a 400-horsepower engine, which was decided upon. The Liberty engine was laid out and designed to embody all the best features of all the known engines, to be particularly applicable to American manufacturing methods, making for large quantity production, and to be known as the United States standard engine

This engine was intended to eliminate the difficulties of having a large number of different types in the field, thus simplifying the question of spare parts and interchangeability It was originally planned to build the engine with 12 cylinders, 400 horsepower (maximum) · 8 cylinders, 275 horsepower (maximum); 6 cylinders, 165 horsepower (maximum), and 4 cylinders, 135 horsepower (maximum), thus using it for all purposes in both the Army and the Navy.

The engine drawing as originally designed was exhibited at a joint meeting of the Aircraft Board and the Joint Army and Navy Technical Board on June 4, 1917, and an opinion as to its merits was requested from the Navy members present. The consensus of opinion was that, as far as could be told from the drawing, it would be satisfactory except for the piston there shown; a flat-top piston was recommended to reduce the compression in order to satisfy the requirements of the Navy's lower altitude work, to reduce sparkplug difficulties, and simplify the question of cooling With the single exception of the piston, it was expected that the Army and Navy engines would be identical Later the Army had to offset their propeller hub 3 inches owing to the radiator shutters on the De Haviland. This offset hub gave the Navy considerable trouble later from the fact that the offset-hub engine would not fit into the HS flying boat, as it became necessary at one time to accept Army engines to keep production going.

The Navy had on order during the war approximately 4,370 Liberty engines, and practically all of these were delivered. The Aircraft Board recommended that all aircraft production for the Navy to be used for antiaircraft warfare should have priority in delivery. This recommendation was approved by the Secretary of War, and the Navy thus obtained the first production of Liberty engines, which began from the Packard company in January 1918 approximately two months behind the estimated time. Practically all of the Navy's Liberty engines came from the Packard company.

Considerable trouble was experienced with the first few engines owing to crank-shaft failures, but this soon disappeared by the use of a heavier design. Because of the great pressure brought upon the Packard company, the first run of engines also showed the lack of careful inspection and workmanship, and many arrived at the naval air stations in Europe that were in bad condition and short of essential equipment but these troubles were soon corrected.

The real outstanding difficulty was the shortage of spare parts, which were so essential while the personnel were getting acquainted with the engines. It became necessary to authorize the air stations to tear down unused engines for spare parts, and it was not until shortly before the armistice that the situation was relieved. The Liberty engine gave the Navy generally excellent service, and good results were obtained by all stations. The Army endeavored to cooperate with us in its improvement, and to this end detailed an officer for duty in the Aviation Division to note the troubles that we might have with the engine.

The Liberty engine being direct drive, was not entirely satisfactory in the large twin boats, owing to its high propeller speed. This pointed to the advisability of securing a geared engine. As production of this engine was under the direction of the Army, the Bureau, in June, 1918, took steps to work with the Army in the development of a geared type. The Army was, however, loath to take it up because of the limited production facilities in the country, the slower production of geared engines than of the straight drive, and the pressure of foreign Governments for more of the latter engines than could be produced. Experimental work was carried on at a slow rate at McCook Field on the geared engine, but the Navy was not able to get hold of the work and bring it to a definite conclusion, and at the time of the signing of the armistice the geared engine was still undeveloped. This instance illustrates a serious objection to a common aviation agency for both services. The geared engine was almost a vital need for the Navy, but the Army could not understand this need and would neither permit the Navy to go ahead and develop the geared engine nor do it itself.

As in other fields, inventors were much in evidence in that of aviation, and especially was this true with respect to aviation motors. Most of these inventors, carried away by enthusiasm but with little else to commend their activity were eager to supply the department in an incredibly short time with engines which in their opinion would excel anything that had either been built or projected. All the designs submitted were given the closest investigation, which was a line of action that was consistently followed only to find that the inventor, as a rule, knew little of the art and still less of the exacting conditions that had to be fulfilled. He was, however, always alive to the financial consideration involved in the use of his invention, which was generally in inverse proportion to its merit

TRAINING SEAPLANES.

The Navy's preliminary training program was based mainly upon the use of the Curtiss 100-horsepower engine. A few seaplanes with the Hall-Scott 100-horsepower engine and with the Curtiss 200-horsepower engine were purchased. The two latter types were found unsuitable for training, and preliminary training work was, therefore, all done with the Curtiss 100-horsepower engine. Approximately 1,000 of these engines were purchased in lots of 500 down to 50. The price of the early engines was $3,400, but this was reduced to $1,725 by the Navy order later placed with the Curtiss Co.

Extreme difficulty was encountered in getting a sufficient supply of spare parts, and the training stations were very much handicapped during the early part of the war. The Curtiss Co. could not make deliveries on spare material, and after several conferences on the subject the company finally agreed to permit the use of their plans, and thus allow the Navy to establish new sources of supply for this material independent of the Curtiss Co. This required an enormous amount of work on the part of the Aviation Division, but it was productive of excellent results, as all companies except one came through with their orders in good time. The prices that were paid were considerably lower than the amount previously paid contractors, and the character of the product was in most cases superior to that previously supplied.

The Wright-Martin Co. was able to satisfactorily produce the Hispano-Suiza 150-horsepower engine in quantity late in 1917, and this engine was adopted for use in the N-9 seaplane as a secondary training seaplane for use in gunnery practice. This engine gave excellent service when the personnel became accustomed to it. The usual difficulty was experienced in obtaining a supply of spare parts, which condition continued until practically the end of the war.

About one hundred 110-horsepower Gnome engines were contracted for by the Navy to be manufactured by the General Vehicle Co. They were delivered in the first year of the war, and a few put to service in speed scouts. The balance was turned over to the Army, as the engine found no real use in the Navy. A small number of 80-horsepower Le Rhone engines were obtained from the Army and used by the marines for training at the marine flying field at Miami, Fla. The marines were also given a small number of high-compression Liberty engines for use in Army airplanes in connection with the training for service with the Northern Bombing Group in Europe.

The early output of service seaplanes equipped with low-compression Liberty engines was used for training purposes in this country before any seaplanes were sent abroad. In this way a large number of men received service knowledge of the Liberty engine before going overseas and arrived abroad in time to assist in handling and installing the power plants of the first Navy seaplanes sent to European stations.

SERVICE SEAPLANES

The Navy program contemplated the use of a single-engined flying boat known as the HS type, and of a twin-engined flying boat, the H-16 type, for antisubmarine work overseas. Both of these seaplanes were to be equipped with Liberty engines. A total of 1,185 HS type was ordered, and a total of 864 of the H-16 type. This required an approximate total of 4,870 Liberty engines to be delivered to the Navy during the year 1918.

The HS seaplane was an untried product, but the H-16 type, equipped with Rolls-Royce engines, had been used by the British, though it was an American-designed machine. The adaptation of these seaplanes to the Liberty engine would have presented no unusual difficulties if time had permitted tests of the installation to be made before putting it into production. The production of boats, however, was faster than that of engines, and hence it was necessary to complete the final design of all power-plant installations and proceed on a productive basis, with the expectation of improving the equipment from information gained from the results of the first tests. This was a very unsatisfactory method of procedure, but in view of the pressing need of the boats, it was necessary. Great difficulty was experienced later in getting the required improvements into production and pressing the output of the parts of the seaplanes that had been manufactured on a limited scale pending their trial.

During the year 1917 the Curtiss Co. was working under contract, in cooperation with the Bureau of Construction and Repair and the Bureau of Steam Engineering, in preparing designs for a flying boat with three engines that might be delivered overseas under it own power. These plans were completed late in the year, and on December 21, 1917, the Bureaus prepared a joint requisition for four of the three-engined boats, which were known as the *NC-1*, *NC-2*, *NC-3*, and *NC-4*. The *NC-1* came through for her preliminary trials shortly before the close of the war and was found to be a very satisfactory machine.

PROPELLERS.

The question of the propeller design for the Liberty engine was one upon which there was not much data to be obtained until the propeller itself had been tried. The problem of designing a propeller to absorb 400 horsepower at 1,800 revolutions per minute was one that no other country had to face. There was at that time no equipment which could be located in this country that was capable of testing the strength of such propellers for service use. The first propellers designed for the H-16 were made in limited numbers only, and when tested allowed the engine to turn up too rapidly. Changes were made and further tests held. The modified propellers gave good results in the air, but were found to be weak at the root of the blade. After further modification a good design was secured for production for war purposes.

The propeller problem on the HS seaplanes was more difficult, but was solved more quickly. This seaplane required a pusher propeller, but on account of the limited distance between the boat hull and the crankshaft it was necessary to use the 4-bladed form. The small diameter to which it was limited, and the many interferences on the plane to a free flow of air to it, made the design of an efficient propeller difficult. Fortunately, the first design gave a very good performance and was at once put into production. A second question that had to be met was the difficulty of handling, transporting, and storing the 4-bladed propeller. It was imperative that this propeller should be made in two parts, if only to meet the demands of limited transportation space for overseas shipment. After a certain amount of investigation, a 4-bladed propeller was devised by taking two 2-bladers and making a mortised joint at the hub by cutting partly through the first lamination on each blade. This propeller gave good service, but a tendency was found to split at the joint, and the design was abandoned in favor of two blades without the mortise, but with a slightly thinner hub so that they would fit the engine hub.

It is pertinent here to make acknowledgment of the very valuable assistance rendered by Mr. Watt, the chief of the British Admiralty airplane propeller section, in connection with the design and construction of propellers. An officer from the propeller section of the Aviation Division was detailed with Mr. Watt during his stay in the United States, to gain from him all possible information about the British methods and practices in connection with airplane propellers. The result was a great advance in our work from this knowledge of British experience. It became possible for the Aviation Division to take the lead in propeller work instead of depending upon the few propeller manufacturers in this country.

An allotment was made to the forest products laboratory of the Department of Agriculture, at Madison, Wis., for the purpose of investigating propeller materials, methods of manufacture, making of propeller glues, methods of storing and transporting propellers, etc. The work of this laboratory was of great assistance, especially in drawing up propeller specifications for the guidance and development of new sources of supply. In addition to walnut, oak, and Honduras mahogany, it was found that certain grades of Philippine mahogany were suitable for the Navy propellers.

At the beginning of the war, there were only about four companies who were prepared to manufacture propellers for the Navy, and all of these had a very limited production. It was necessary to encourage them to enlarge their facilities and also to establish new sources of supply. Several high-grade furniture makers and one or two piano manufacturers willingly took up the manufacture, and after careful instruction were able to turn out excellent propellers, and in larger quantities than the more experienced makers. This was due to their superior knowledge of the methods of quantity production.

The Westinghouse company at Pittsburgh, Pa., developed equipment by which it was possible to give propellers a whirling test to any overload desired. These tests were restricted to Saturday nights and Sundays, as there was no work in the shops at that time and the moving of a propeller on a whirling test at the loads desired for 10 or 12 hours continuously made so much noise that no other activity could be carried on. All new designs of Navy propellers and sample propellers from a new manufacturer were always given a whirling test at Pittsburgh before being used in service.

A great deal of trouble was experienced with metal tipping, and a special study had to be made of this, both as to the method of securing the tipping and the character of the metal itself. A solution was reached and each company carefully instructed in the details of the work.

In order to save shipping space for overseas, it was necessary to pack the propellers in the boxes containing the seaplane parts. This resulted in a large number of propellers arriving overseas in a condition unsafe for use, due to the treatment received in shipment and the long period of time the cases were exposed to the weather.

Continual experiments were carried forward, looking to the development of steel or other material for propeller construction, but no material was found that had even the approximate value of wood.

With the development of the *F–5* type of seaplane, which was an enlarged *H–16*, the question of getting these boats off the water with the direct drive Liberty engine became acute, and a compromise on propeller design between one that would pull the boat out of the water and another which would satisfactorily fly the plane in the air was necessary. A study was made looking to an adjustable pitch propeller, and was well under way at the signing of the armistice. The apparatus had had preliminary tests but needed improvement in its mechanical details before it could actually be used in flight. This method of obtaining the best propeller efficiency for both conditions would not be as satisfactory for Navy use as the geared engine.

RADIATORS

The use of the Liberty engine and the necessity of cutting down the power plant weights in naval aircraft to the last pound brought out many questions for the Bureau to consider in connection with the cooling system on all naval seaplanes. Heretofore the question of radiator design had been left entirely in the hands of the plane manufacturers, and it was found that there was no radiator manufacturer in the United States who had any actual information relative to aviation radiator design. A section for the study of radiator design was established by the Bureau, and a great amount of data collected from foreign sources. All radiator manufacturers were asked to submit samples of their radiators. Upon receipt of the samples they were tested in the wind tunnel and were given comparative ratings based upon an empirical formula that took into consideration the weight of the radiator, its head resistance, and its cooling qualities. On the results of these tests, basing the warmest temperatures to be encountered in European service as 90° F., all radiators for service machines were designed.

So far as cooling was concerned, the results were excellent, giving a good range of operating temperatures with the lightest weight and smallest frontal area of any airplanes of corresponding performance then in service, American or foreign. Constructional weaknesses developed in service at first that were troublesome, due to the time required to get the improved radiators in use. It was also found that radiators that had long periods of idleness between the time of manufacture and actual service nearly always developed leaks. Upon investigation this was found to be due to the acid used in manufacture which was allowed to remain undetected in the radiators. This acid attacked the radiator metal, and inside of a period of 10 days had spent itself in eating holes through the radiator core. A process of washing all radiators carefully in a neutralizing bath was put into use at the radiator plants that eliminated this trouble. Continuous studies were made of the metals, solders, fluxes and methods used in manufacture of radiators. At the end of the war the quality had improved considerably, and excellent performances were obtained from all of our radiators. The Navy adhered to the use of the ribbon-type radiators, as opposed to the heavier tubular type later adopted by the Army.

At the end of the war all seaplanes were being sent out with radiator shutters fitted for use in controlling the temperature of the cooling water during cold or cool weather.

Considerable difficulty was experienced in getting sufficient production in the early part of the program, due to the shortage of brass and the large demands upon the manufacturers by both the Army and the Navy All manufacturers were inclined to take on more work than they could turn out, and an arbitrary rearrangement of production schedules was worked out jointly by the Army and Navy until quantity production was reached.

INSTRUMENTS AND ACCESSORIES.

At the beginning of the war there was only one company that was producing a satisfactory type of tachometer and one company that manufactured oil and water thermometers. In view of the enormous number of these instruments needed, other companies began experiments at once. and very satisfactory types of both instruments were rapidly brought forward. The supply at first was not up to the production of boats, and many short shipments were made, but the shortages were made up, and there was soon an abundance of all these instruments

It had been planned to use air starters on Liberty-engined flying boats, but restrictions on weight caused their elimination at the last minute. It therefore became necessary to develop a hand starter in a very short space of time. This was done, but the results were not entirely satisfactory in service, owing to improper heat treatment of some of the parts The starter was modified, but the company producing it had labor trouble and fell down badly on production. This caused a serious shortage of these appliances, especially overseas. Every effort was made to get production, and a second company was put on the work, but the deficiency was keenly felt before the effects of renewed production reached the stations.

The need for an electric starter became evident, and the Bijur Co., in cooperation with the Bureau, developed an excellent starter of fairly reasonable weight This device was rapidly going into service on the multiengined boats at the signing of the armistice, and it is believed to be the first practical general application of an electric starter to airplane engines

A highly satisfactory leak-proof gasoline tank was developed with the assistance of Lieut. Imber, of the Royal Air Force, who was sent to the United States for the purpose. This tank had been thoroughly tested by rifle and machine gun fire and had just been put into production when the armistice was signed

Oil and water heaters for use in cold weather had been developed and were being sent to service by the end of October, 1918

Much difficulty was experienced with the wind-driven gasoline pumps supplied by the manufacturer for the original boats, and it was necessary to redesign them throughout. A substantial improvement was accomplished, but efforts were continued to find a substitute for the wind-driven pump, although without results. A vacuum system, similar to that used on automobiles, was devised and tested in service. While it gave promising results, it still needed considerable development before it could be called satisfactory.

LIGHTER THAN AIR.

Lighter than air development was very slow during the war; the first dirigibles brought out were of 80,000 cubic feet capacity, mounting one 100-horsepower Curtiss engine. These craft were underpowered and had only real use in training pilots. Their speed was approximately 45 miles an hour, they carried a very small load, and were not safe to be flown in a very strong breeze on account of the lack of power, and because they were equipped with but one engine. These first dirigibles led the way to a large type equipped with two engines. Two Hispano-Suiza engines, one mounted on each side of the car, were used and the capacity of the bag increased to 180,000 cubic feet. This gave a very good dirigible for service use that compared favorably with any of its class in the world. Thirty of these were ordered, but only one or two were delivered before the armistice. The Hispano-Suiza, though giving good service in these dirigibles were scheduled for replacement by the Union 125-horsepower engine, which was essentially a dirigible type.

Research was carried on with the Liberty engine looking to its use in larger dirigibles than any heretofore constructed in the United States. A type of craft of 400,000 cubic feet capacity, equipped with Liberty engines, was projected at the signing of the armistice.

STEAM POWER PLANTS

Realizing the advantages that would accrue from the use of steam power plants in aircraft, and learning of the interest of certain private parties in their development, the Bureau, in February, 1918, took up with the Department the question of proceeding with the investigation of this subject to supplement the work that had been previously accomplished by its Aviation Division.

In March, 1918, the Department approved the steam power plant project and authorized the expenditure of $50,000 to carry it out.

A committee of civilian experts was then appointed by the Bureau, which was authorized to proceed with the design of a 400-brake-horsepower steam turbine unit and reduction gear, applying two of these units to an H-16 type of flying boat, and further to design a boiler to supply the necessary steam for the two turbines. The fundamental idea of the committee was that it should coordinate all the talent in the country on the job of developing the proposed steam plant. It was realized that there were a great many men in the United States who had experience along the line of research contemplated, and it was desired to bring the sum total of their knowledge to bear on the work. The plant was to be designed to fit into an existing type of aircraft, so that a direct comparison could be obtained with the gasoline-engine drive, and the question of the availability of the steam drive definitely settled

The committee established itself in New York and proceeded with the work, and after many difficulties in connection with labor and material the boiler of the plant and its accessories were practically ready for its preliminary test at the signing of the armistice

EXPERIMENTAL ENGINES

In addition to the work on the geared Liberty engine. the Bureau was interested in the experimental development of three engines, namely, (1) the Kessler supercompression 125, 200, and 400 horsepower engine; (2) the Lawrence 60-horsepower air-cooled engine for small shipboard planes, (3) the Dusenberg 850-horsepower engine.

The Kessler engine gave promise, but mechanical troubles were recurrent, and the engine was still in an undeveloped state at the time of the signing of the armistice The Lawrence engine came through very well and was in use in two small planes, but did not render any war service. The Dusenberg engine made very good progress up to a certain period, when cylinder head. jacket, and ignition troubles began to develop. There were also difficulties in testing an engine of this power, as there was no existing dynamometer that could absorb the power.

ENGINE TESTING LABORATORY.

The aeronautical engine testing laboratory at the navy yard, Washington, D. C., rendered valuable assistance both to the Army and the Navy during the war. The laboratory was located in very restricted quarters, but was unable to make use of its dynamometer on account of the fire risk involved in the dynamometer's location. All apparatus submitted for aviation power-plant use was tested at the laboratory, and it was a big factor in the development work during the war.

A lubrication-oil investigation in cooperation with the War Department was carried on for three months by the laboratory to obtain data for specifications for oil for all aviation engines This investigation showed that castor oil was not an essential for the lubrication of any but rotary engines and that the threatened shortage of this oil was not vital. Extensive tests were carried out on the Liberty engine and on all engines for the Navy to determine their operating characteristics, the most favorable carburetor adjustments, and similar data relative to the operation and maintenance of the engines upon which to base instructions for the guidance of the personnel in the field.

HELIUM

While the United States remained neutral nothing was done with our deposits of natural gas containing helium. But as soon as we declared war the British Government referred to our military and naval authorities various research problems whose solution would aid in ending the war. Among those problems was that of securing an adequate supply of helium for use in observation and dirigible balloons.

Its recognized military value may be appreciated from the remark attributed to a British officer, that "if the Germans had had helium for their Zeppelins they would have knocked England out in six weeks." This statement, while sweeping, indicates the view held by experts in our Army and Navy that helium as a substitute for hydrogen would make the dirigible balloon a war weapon of the most deadly power.

In order to detract attention from the real work in hand, the name "argon" was adopted as the designation of this gas and of all activities connected with its production.

The hydrogen employed for floating observation and dirigible balloons has one vital defect—its inflammability. When struck by an incendiary bullet the balloon instantly bursts into volcanic flame and falls in smoking fragments to the earth. Helium, on the contrary, is an inert gas like nitrogen. It will neither burn nor aid in the combustion of other materials. Its use in balloons means therefore, that the fire risk is eliminated and that a helium filled airship could be brought down or seriously injured only by driving an airplane into it.

The fire-damping qualities of this gas were strikingly shown in an experiment conducted by order of this Bureau. Two exactly similar model balloons were made; one was filled with hydrogen, the other with helium. Then, into both, explosive bullets were fired. The hydrogen-filled balloon vanished in an instant in a flash of flame and smoke; but the other balloon remained virtually intact, since when the ring of covering around the bullet hole took fire, the helium poured out like a stream of water and quenched the flame.

The use of helium entails comparatively little reduction in the airship's cargo capacity, for helium has 92 per cent of the lifting power of hydrogen, and, next to that gas is the lightest one known

Acting upon the representations of the British Government, the Director of the Bureau of Mines addressed a letter to the Chief Signal Officer of the War Department on July 19, 1917, stating that the question of the production of helium has been carefully gone into by that Bureau, and that a plant for the production of 27,000 cubic feet of helium per day, at a cost of from $2.10 to $3.80 per thousand cubic feet, could be built in a few month's time for $28,000. This letter was presented to the Joint Army and Navy Airship Board at a special meeting a few days later, and it was the opinion of the representative of the Aviation Division of this Bureau present at the meeting that $100,000 should be allotted for this purpose. The Board, accordingly, made a recommendation to the Aircraft Production Board on July 26, 1917, that $100,000 be allotted, in equal shares by the Army and Navy, the undertaking of the production of helium to be carried out by the Bureau of Mines. The attention of that Bureau had been drawn to a proposed new process for air separation that was dependent on some novel and striking features, invented by Mr Fred E Norton, of Worcester Mass. This process had not yet been through a successful practical demonstration, but the Bureau of Mines was convinced that the Norton process was the most hopeful method to be used for obtaining helium. Mr. Norton was, accordingly, employed by that Bureau to design the separation plant, and a field survey was made to determine the best location for it.

About this time information was conveyed to the British Admiralty that the United States Government had taken steps looking toward the production of helium. The Admiralty sent a commission to this country to get first-hand information as to our action. Its members impressed upon everyone with whom they talked the importance of proceeding with the utmost vigor toward the production of helium; and from the data that was furnished it, the commission seemed to have the opinion that the Norton process was the method to use, as the results claimed were far superior to those that had been obtained in 1916, by the Canadian experiments on a gas very lean in helium, using the Claude system. The Canadian experiments were not successful, and indicated a very high cost of production.

Acting upon the impression obtained from the British Commission the Bureau was of the opinion that further funds should be allotted for general helium development, particularly in connection with the employment of the only two companies in the United States who had extensive experience in the daily operation of liquefaction problems that were akin to the processes with natural gas to obtain helium. These companies were the Linde Air Products Co and the Air Reduction Co.

Accordingly, a conference was held in the office of the Director of the Bureau of Mines, attended by a representative of the Aviation

Division of the Bureau, at which it was decided to recommend that $500,000 in addition to the amount already allotted to the Bureau of Mines and used by it for the Norton process be allotted in equal shares by the Army and the Navy for further vigorous prosecution of helium development. The Aircraft Production Board passed a resolution on October 17, 1917, recommending the above allotment for further helium work, with the proviso that none of it was to be used for the Norton process. This resolution was acted upon favorably by the War and Navy Departments, but, upon objection by the Director of the Bureau of Mines, the Aircraft Board at a special meeting again considered the matter and decided that if further funds were required for the Norton process by the Bureau of Mines, consideration would be given to a request from that Bureau for additional funds when needed.

The Aircraft Board adhered unanimously to its decision to restrict the use of the $500,000 to other than the Norton process, and the Director of the Bureau of Mines formally requested that $100,000 in addition to the first $100,000 be allotted for that process. The Aircraft Board recommended to the War and Navy Departments the allocation of the funds requested by the Bureau of Mines, but as the war-time production of helium by this process seemed a very remote possibility, the technical advisers of the Bureau were of opinion that success by the Norton process could be hoped for only after a long series of experiments and changes, and that by that time the war would probably be ended. As, however, the experts of the Bureau of Mines were unshaken in their faith in the early production of helium by the Norton process, the Navy Department, upon the recommendation of the Bureau of Steam Engineering, requested the National Research Council to give an opinion on the merits of that process. This opinion was favorable, and the second allotment of $100,000 was promptly made.

In connection with the $500,000 for helium work other than the Norton process the Linde Air Products Co and the Air Reduction Co were found to be the only agencies that were qualified to undertake the work of experimenting in helium production. The Linde air plant was known as plant No. 1, and was set up at Fort Worth, Tex., at a cost of approximately $245,000. Its estimated capacity was 5,000 cubic feet per day. The air reduction plant was known as plant No. 2, and was established adjacent to the Linde plant at Fort Worth, at a cost of approximately $135,000, with an estimated capacity of 3,000 cubic feet per day. The Bureau of Mines (Norton) plant was known as plant No. 3, and was built at Petrolia, Tex., at an approximate cost of $150,000, with an estimated capacity of 300,000 cubic feet per day.

Plant No. 1 began operations on March 6, 1918, and in a few weeks was obtaining helium 70 per cent pure under continuous operating conditions. By reprocessing the 70 per cent gas a purity of 92½ per cent was obtained. These results indicated that helium could be produced.

Plant No. 2 began operations on May 1, 1918, and under steady conditions produced a limited quantity of gas of approximately 66 per cent purity, which was processed by plant No. 1 to 92½ per cent purity.

As plant No. 3 was not ready for operation upon the completion of the above runs and could not be ready for several months, it was decided that a committee composed of three members, one from the Navy Department, one from the War Department, and one from the Interior Department, visit the plants and make a study of the experimental results obtained, and make recommendation to the Aircraft Board as to what should be done in connection with helium production. The member of this committee for the War Department had also been a member of the committee of the National Research Council which had made a favorable report on the Norton process, so the committee was well constituted to cover all phases of the helium problem.

This committee recommended that a large production plant with a capacity of 30,000 cubic feet per day, based on the Linde process, be built at Fort Worth; that a larger experimental unit of the Air Reduction Co. type be constructed at Fort Worth; and that the experimental work with plant No. 3 be carried to a definite conclusion. The committee also recommended the construction of a pipe line from the Petrolia gas pool to the helium plants at Fort Worth, and the consummation of a lease of 10 years for the Petrolia pool, in order to conserve the gas. The committee stated that in its opinion the cost of the helium would not exceed $80 per thousand cubic feet, based upon a production of 30,000 cubic feet per day. The recommendations of the committee were approved by the Aircraft Board, and were being carried into effect when the armistice was signed. The task of carrying out these recommendations and operating the plant was turned over to the Navy Department and placed by the Department in the hands of this Bureau.

Shortly after the signing of the armistice the Aircraft Board recommended that all experimental helium work, except three months' operation of plant No. 3, be stopped and that the construction of the production plant proceed. This plan was approved by the War and Navy Departments.

The net result in helium production at the signing of the armistice was 20 cubic feet of helium by plant No. 1 and plant No. 2 and none by plant No. 3.

HYDROGEN.

The Department had a few small single-engined dirigibles on order at the beginning of the war which were to be placed at the proposed air stations. Accordingly, steps were taken at once to develop and expand our hydrogen facilities and supply

In view of the danger surrounding the use and production of hydrogen, it was necessary that this work should be handled with the utmost care. It was assigned to Mr G O Carter, a graduate of the Naval Academy, who had become an authority on compressed gases in civilian life, and who had reported to the Navy Department the day after war was declared, asking for an assignment in that connection Steps were taken at once to rush to completion the iron-contact hydrogen plant then building at the air station at Pensacola, to acquire an adequate stock of hydrogen cylinders, and to make contracts with the proper companies for a supply of commercial hydrogen. The design of an experimental, portable hydrogen generator using the ferrosilicon process was also started, using as a basis a line drawing and some French photographs of such a generator then in use on the front The experimental plant came through in about three months' time and gave sufficient data to enable the manufacturer of 12 portable plants to be started shortly thereafter These plants, with one or two others shipped from France, took care of the hydrogen production at the air stations in the United States By careful attention to details, their designed production per pound of material was practically doubled. As these plants were the first of their kind to be seen in this country, their successful production was a very creditable piece of engineering

The question of hydrogen personnel was solved by the Bureau of Navigation in the establishment of a school at the naval air station, Rockaway Long Island, in the summer of 1917, and in sending there a number of men who had had experience in the generation and handling of hydrogen Upon completion of the course the graduates were graded and given a commission, or were made hydrogen petty officers, depending upon their qualifications.

Advantage was taken of the hydrogen manuals of the Allies, and the experience and recommendations of the French and English were carefully studied in putting in our hydrogen equipment at the air stations and in operating it In consequence, we profited by their experience and therefore our hydrogen work was eminently successful. Precise and minute instructions were issued by the Bureau, and tests to further our knowledge were repeatedly made; and so closely were these instructions followed that during the war we did not have a

In order possible, a

more about foreign methods. After careful investigation, he returned with the report that we were then ahead of European practice. Much of our success in this respect is due to the advice and assistance given by Commander P. L. Teed. R. N. V. R., who was detailed by the British Admiralty for the purpose and whose services the Bureau desires thus publicly to recognize.

THE TRANS-ATLANTIC FLIGHT

Although this remarkable performance was made some months after the cessation of hostilities, the flight from Trepassey, Newfoundland, to the Azores was the result of plans that were made during the war to deliver planes in Europe under their own power and thus to solve some of the most annoying difficulties of transportation that had to be faced. The incorporation in this narrative of the engineering features attendant upon the preparation for the flight would, therefore, seem to be particularly appropriate.

Three flying boats of the NC type participated in the flight. They had not been built for such a test, but were of an experimental character, designed to provide a craft of wide radius of action and good weight-carrying ability for patrol operation which naval experience had shown to be necessary.

The proposal to transfer them to the war zone under their own power presented many novel engineering problems, for it was realized that the success of such a flight was dependent upon a satisfactory power plant; and although the inadequacy of the one contemplated in the original design was recognized, the solution of the problem was undertaken with absolute confidence in ultimate success.

The undertaking was one whose success could not be based upon chance; it had to be predicated upon results obtained in actual practice, with a reasonable margin of reserve.

Before undertaking the feat it was necessary to know with certainty that these boats could attain a certain speed in still air upon a certain development of horsepower, a matter to be shown conclusively only upon their first trials; that the necessary horsepower to produce this speed could be developed upon a certain hourly fuel consumption; that the requisite engine power, not only to attain this speed in the air but to attain a sufficient speed upon the surface of the water to enable the boat to get into the air, could be provided within the necessary limit of weight; that sufficient fuel could be carried.

The boats had been designed for a 3-engine installation each operating a single propeller. It was apparent to this Bureau at the outset that an additional engine would be necessary; that is, that at least two engines must be installed in tandem, the forward one operating a tractor propeller and the rear one a pusher propeller. No such installations had ever been made in this country and there was almost

HISTORY OF ENGINEERING DURING THE WORLD WAR.   151

no data upon the efficiency of propellers so installed, which had to be of sturdy construction and show maximum efficiency at cruising speed, but which would exact sufficient thrust to lift the maximum load from the water. Special carbureter adjustment had to be made on the high compression Liberty engines in order to secure an economy of from 8 to 12 per cent which was so essential to success.

The first boat was delivered in November, 1918, and the last of the four contracted for in April, 1919. After delivery there were several accidents to the craft due to weather conditions, which interrupted the necessary preliminary work, but the modifications that had been determined upon, including the installation of a fourth engine with its auxiliaries and of a complete radio equipment, were completed in time to allow the boats to leave the United States for Newfoundland on May 8, 1919.

Completely manned and equipped, the weight of the boats as they left the water at Trepassey was 28,700 pounds each. The total fuel capacity was 1,800 gallons. The NC-4 had 1,610 gallons at starting and 270 remained upon arrival at the Azores.

The bureau's estimate of fuel consumption was 1.25 gallons per knot; the actual consumption was 1.12 gallons.

Schedule of times and distances.

	Start.		Arrival.		Departure.	
	Date.	Time.	Date.	Time.	Date.	Time.
Rockaway, Long Island:						
NC-1	May 8, 1919	10.00 a.m.				
NC-3	do	10.00 a.m.				
NC-4	do	10.00 a.m.				
End of first leg, Halifax (540 nautical miles):						
NC-1			May 8, 1919	6.00 p.m.	May 10, 1919	7.47 a.m.
NC-3			do	6.00 p.m.	do	8.08 a.m.
NC-4			May 14, 1919	1.10 p.m.	May 15, 1919	8.52 a.m.
End of second leg, Trepassey (440 nautical miles):						
NC-1			May 10, 1919	7.41 p.m.	May 16, 1919	6.09 p.m.
NC-2			do	6.31 p.m.	do	6.01 p.m.
NC-3			May 15, 1919	5.38 p.m.	do	6.07 p.m.
End of third leg, Horta, Fayal, Azores (1,196 nautical miles):						
NC-1			May 20, 1919	(¹)		
NC-3²						
NC-4			May 17, 1919	9.25 a.m.	May 20, 1919	8.10 a.m.
Ponta Delgada (150 nautical miles):						
NC-3			May 19, 1919	1.50 p.m.		
NC-4			May 20, 1919	10.24 a.m.	May 26, 1919	6.18 p.m.
End of fourth leg, Lisbon, Portugal (800 nautical miles):						
NC-4			May 27, 1919	4.02 p.m.	May 30, 1919	2.23 a.m.
End of fifth leg, Plymouth, England (775 nautical miles):						
NC-4			May 1, 1919			

¹ Sank at sea.
² The NC-3 arrived at Ponta Delgada but was unable to .... ed at sea.

The officers of the Bureau who took part in this memorable flight were: *NC-4*, Lieut J. L Breese. U. S. Naval Reserve Force, *NS-3*, Lieut. Commander R A. Lavender. U. S Navy, *NS-1*. Lieut (j. g) H. G. Sadenwater, U. S Naval Reserve Force

PERSONNEL

The following list gives the officers attached to the Aviation Division at various times during the war

Head of division, Commander A. K Atkins, U S Navy.

Executive assistant, Lieut (j g) L T Hemenway. U S Naval Reserve Force

ENGINEERING SECTION

Commander H T. Dyer U S Navy, head
Lieut Commander S. M. Kraus, U. S. Navy, heavier than air.
Lieut. J. L. Breese, U. S. Naval Reserve Force, heavier than air.
Ensign E. B Koger, U. S Naval Reserve Force, heavier than air.
Capt of Engineers T H Yeager, Coast Guard. lighter than air
Lieut (j. g) W. R Davis, U. S Naval Reserve Force, lighter than air.
Mr G. O. Carter, U. S. Naval Reserve Force, balloon gas.
Lieut R W. White. U. S Naval Reserve Force, balloon gas.
Lieut P. H Dole. U S Naval Reserve Force, balloon gas.
Lieut (j g) D. W Kent, U S Naval Reserve Force. balloon gas.
Lieut (j. g) C G. Pardee, U. S. Naval Reserve Force. balloon gas
Lieut. (j. g.) L. J. Platt, U. S. Naval Reserve Force, balloon gas
Ensign P. S Barnes. U S Naval Reserve Force, balloon gas.
Ensign E. R Burns, U S Naval Reserve Force. balloon gas
Ensign C I Stefanowich. U S. Naval Reserve Force, balloon gas.
Lieut (j g.) G S. Murray, U S Naval Reserve Force, propellers
Ensign A. J Mummert, U. S. Naval Reserve Force, plans
Ensign F. W. Morrow, U S Naval Reserve Force, experiments and tests.
Ensign C F Taylor, U S Naval Reserve Force, experiments and tests

PRODUCTION SECTION

Lieut. H. R. Naylor, U. S Naval Reserve Force. head
Lieut (j. g) F. P. Scully, U S. Naval Reserve Force, assistant
Lieut. (j. g) E. B. Hall, U. S Naval Reserve Force, engines and parts
Ensign E L Adams, U. S. Naval Reserve Force, engines and parts
Ensign E T. Condon. U. S. Naval Reserve Force. engines and parts.

Ensign A W Pope, U S. Naval Reserve Force, engines and parts
Ensign R. A Watkins, U. S Naval Reserve Force, engines and parts
Lieut. (j g.) J. W. McCausland, U. S Naval Reserve Force, propellers.
Lieut. (j. g.) D. W Monteith, U. S Naval Reserve Force, propellers
Ensign R. S. Wentworth, U S Naval Reserve Force. radiators.
Ensign L W Lee, U. S Naval Reserve Force field work
Lieut (j g) H F. Butler, U S. Naval Reserve Force, requisitions and shipments
Ensign E. J. B Gorman, U S. Naval Reserve Force, requisitions and shipments.
Lieut (j g.) A H Bunker, U. S. Naval Reserve Force, public bills
Ensign W. G Ebersole, U S. Naval Reserve Force, records.

OPERATION AND MAINTENANCE SECTION.

Lieut G M. Brush (U. S Naval Reserve Force), head.
Lieut. W A. Edmundson (U S. Naval Reserve Force), fuel and oil.
Lieut (j g.) N. F. Osburn (U. S. Naval Reserve Force), instruments and accessories
Ensign C. Brettell (U. S Naval Reserve Force), instruments and accessories.
Ensign C L Russell (U S Naval Reserve Force), instruments and accessories.
Ensign O W. Toll (U. S. Naval Reserve Force, instruments and accessories.
Ensign J R Johnson (U. S. Naval Reserve Force), gasoline tanks.
Ensign L. A. Bohacket (U. S Naval Reserve Force), training schools
Ensign H R. Green (U S Naval Reserve Force), information.
Ensign W. N Harris (U S Naval Reserve Force).

ANTIAIRCRAFT DEFENSE.

As in the case of all other types of offensive machines, the necessity for making provision for defense against aircraft became apparent and was intensified by the reports of destruction wrought by German aircraft within the allied lines This led, in the summer of 1916, to the development of means for the defense of our shore stations, the Department assigning to the Bureau of Steam Engineering the duty of providing searchlights and the entire fire-control system, including therein the communication and control systems and the salvo firing systems, as also airplane detectors.

The air station at Pensacola, Fla., was selected as the place for the conduct of the early experiments with searchlights, and the New York Navy Yard was assigned the problem of developing a detecting device along certain lines suggested by the Bureau. It was recognized that this was the problem that presented the greatest difficulty; and as development work is necessarily slow, it was not surprising that a successful device was not immediately produced. Good results were however, obtained and further progress was being made when a device designed by Prof G. W. Stewart, of the University of Iowa, was brought to the attention of the Bureau As this device appeared to possess superior qualities to the one under development at New York, further experiment with that detector was abandoned and effort concentrated on the device of Prof Stewart. As soon as it was perfected tests were made at Pensacola and at Langley Field which proved so successful that the fact was immediately communicated to the War Department and further progress of the detector carried out for that Department under the direction of the Chief of Engineers of the Army.

In the conduct of these tests the Bureau received the most active cooperation of the National Research Council through Dr. (later lieutenant colonel) R. A Millikan, chairman of the committee on physics, as also that of the Bureau of Standards, through Dr H. F. Stinson; of the Weather Bureau through Dr. W. P. Blair; and of the Western Electric Co through Dr. Jewett and Messrs Maxfield and Horton.

Tests of several other devices were also undertaken, but the results that were obtained were not such as to lead to the belief that any of them could be made to give results as satisfactory as those that were obtained with the Stewart detector.

SUPPLIES AND INSPECTION.

It may well be imagined that the addition of such a large number of vessels to the Navy added greatly to the work coming under that division of the Bureau, which not only had to prepare allowance lists of necessary engineering supplies but to see that those supplies were ready when required. It thus had to anticipate the needs of our immense fleet, which now had been augmented by the addition of the vessels of the Coast Guard, the Lighthouse Service, the Coast and Geodetic Survey, and the Fish Commission of the Government service, and by the ex-German ships, the ships of our own merchant marine, fishing boats, yachts, mine sweepers, and tugs, and by a host of small gasoline motor boats and yachts, all having machinery differing in characteristics from the usual type of naval machinery and requiring an immense amount of investigation to acquire the information necessary for providing for their machinery needs.

Prior to our declaration of war, schedules of the most important supplies had been prepared and much material placed under order. These orders included every kind of engineering material and equipment, mechanical and electrical; and while much of it was purchased under standard specifications, a considerable portion of it required the preparation of special specifications. All of it needed inspection, for which the Bureau's prewar inspection service was well prepared, though certain districts were more or less embarrassed by the resignation of trained assistant inspectors to accept commissions under the War Department at much higher rates of pay and to be employed on practically the same kind of work.

For those who are not familiar with the Navy's method of providing supplies, it should be here explained that while the purchase of all engineering material and supplies is made by the Bureau of Supplies and Accounts as the general purchasing agent of the Navy Department, determination as to the character of the material and of the quantity to be purchased, the preparation of the specifications which it must meet, and the inspection of the material is all under the Bureau of Steam Engineering.

Great difficulty had also been experienced in obtaining prompt delivery of engineering supplies, and the time of delivery on large orders, which in normal times could be secured in three to four months, was not infrequently quoted at nearly as many years. One quotation for boiler tubes did, in fact, name 1,095 days After the declaration of war, however, this condition changed. and while questions of priority were constantly arising they were settled satisfactorily and reasonable delivery obtained.

Toward the end of the war difficulty was encountered in obtaining supplies of tin, tungsten, and mica, which points to the necessity of maintaining a war supply of such metals

The requirements of the overseas bases and of the section patrol bases also contributed in no small measure to the work of providing supplies and machine-tool equipment. The latter duty, not only for these bases but for the navy yards and for the contractors building vessels for the Navy, made it necessary to keep in close touch with the War Industries Board in order that questions of priority, which were constantly arising, might be quickly disposed of and that the Bureau might be kept advised of the condition of the machine-tool market. So close was this liaison that there was scarcely a tool under construction whose ultimate destination the Bureau was not cognizant of.

During the progress of the war it became known to the Bureau that a Dutch steamer at New York was laden with machine tools and that a large number of tools were also sequestered in various storehouses in that city. These were at once commandeered and put to use in our navy yards and elsewhere in industrial work for the prosecution of the war. Another large shipment destined for Russia after the government of the Czar had collapsed was similarly commandeered.

A liaison was early established between the Bureau and the War Trade Board by which applications for export license for engineering material and equipment were referred to the Bureau for opinion as to the advisability of issuing the license. This liaison continued throughout the war and is believed to have been as helpful to the War Trade Board as it was of advantage to the Bureau.

In peace times it was the practice of the Bureau to maintain at west coast as well as at east coast navy yards a stock of important engineering material, such as boiler tubes, condenser tubes, shafting. and propellers, suited to the requirements of the vessels based on that coast As vessels were withdrawn from the Pacific this material was transferred to east coast yards and utilized as required.

One outstanding feature of the operation of the machinery of our naval vessels during the war was its freedom from breakdown, and this is attributed in no small measure to the strict specifications under which it is designed and the care that is bestowed upon its inspection The mass of our trouble was with the miscellaneous craft that were purchased and placed in service as patrol vessels either in home waters or abroad. These troubles were, almost without exception, attributable to material and were of such a nature that an officer familiar with them expressed the opinion that if one thing more than any other served to justify the practice of the Bureau in insisting on minute inspection of material and equipment it was the condition of the machinery of the yachts and other small craft purchased and assigned to patrol work at Brest as compared with that of strictly naval vessels employed on the same duty.

In an endeavor to expedite delivery, it was found necessary in some cases to waive certain requirements that had hitherto been strictly enforced, and in some cases to accept material which in normal times would not be considered, but in no case was inspection relaxed. In fact, the Bureau insisted that the special conditions necessitated even closer inspection, if possible, than had formerly been the practice.

The number of inspection districts that were in being at the outbreak of the war was insufficient to handle expeditiously the large volume of work, and especially was this the case in the Middle West, which had been administered from the Pittsburgh office. Other districts were, therefore, established at Buffalo, Cleveland, Chicago, Milwaukee, Cincinnati, Harrisburg, and Baltimore.

An idea of the volume of work handled by the inspectors may be gained from a consideration of the fact that 306 officers and civilians were engaged on the work, which required visits to more than 2,000 manufacturing establishments.

It early became apparent that, if Navy interests were to be properly protected, it would be necessary to have in the field of manufacture officers whose sole duty it was to expedite delivery of Navy material, and be independent of the regular inspection force. Accordingly, a number of officers were enrolled in the reserve for the special purpose of following up Navy orders for engineering material. They were in all cases engineers of experience, and by their knowledge and ability they contributed greatly to prompt delivery of material. A corresponding "follow up" section was established in the Bureau, and in this way it was possible to know the exact status of any important engineering work that was on order.

To meet more effectively the requirements of the Government, the Iron and Steel Institute, composed of the United States Steel Corporation and its subsidiaries and practically all the other steel companies in the United States, established in Washington, under the direction of Mr James B Bonner, an office for the express purpose of expediting work reconciling conflicting orders, and generally to coordinate the business of the Government with manufacturers of steel material by so placing orders that there would be the least possible interference with maximum production In everything that affected work for the Bureau of Steam Engineering, the services of Mr. Bonner were in the highest degree helpful, and contributed so much to orderly procedure in the production of material that it is a pleasure thus to give expression of the appreciation which is felt for the public service he performed.

The following-named officers served in the Supply Division of the Bureau.

Commander H. T. Winston, U. S Navy.[8]
Lieut. Commander C. K Mallory, U S Navy, retired [9]
Lieut Commander C. S. Gillette, U. S Navy.
Capt. of Engineers E. Reed-Hill, U. S. Coast Guard.
Lieut H. W. Ameli, U. S. Naval Reserve Force.
Lieut E. C. Bliss, U. S. Naval Reserve Force
Lieut W C. M Clark, U. S. Naval Reserve Force.
Lieut L. Lindenberg, U. S. Naval Reserve Force.
Lieut. F R. Shamel, U. S. Naval Reserve Force
Lieut. D. H Skeen, U. S. Naval Reserve Force
Lieut. J H. Steedman, U. S. Naval Reserve Force.
Lieut. S Turner, U. S. Naval Reserve Force.
Ensign (T) E R. Adams, U. S. Naval Reserve Force.
Ensign (T) I R Eustis, U. S. Naval Reserve Force
Ensign F J. Hearty, U S. Naval Reserve Force.
Ensign P C. Mayer, U. S Naval Reserve Force.
Ensign W M. Troy, U S. Naval Reserve Force
Ensign M. S Unger, U. S. Naval Reserve Force
Ensign E. C. Weller, U. S Naval Reserve Force.

The officers of the Inspection Division were.
Commander M A. Anderson, U. S. Navy, in charge
Lieut Commander C A Gardiner, U S. Navy, retired
Ensign J. K. Cooney, U. S. Naval Reserve Force
Ensign F. A Dixon, U S Naval Reserve Force.

The inspectors of engineering material were:
Boston district: Commodore B. T Walling, U. S Navy, retired
Hartford district Capt. R. B Higgins, U. S. Navy
Brooklyn district: Rear Admiral W. F. Worthington, U S Navy;
First Lieut N B Hall, U. S Coast Guard (Aeronautics).
Philadelphia district Capt F W Bartlett, U. S. Navy
Bethlehem district Capt C. M. Knepper, U. S. Navy, retired
Pittsburgh district Commodore R. G. Denig, U. S Navy, retired;
Lieut. L E. Isaacs, U. S. Naval Reserve Force, at Erie.
Cincinnati district: Commodore W C. Eaton, U S Navy, retired
Chicago district: Commander Howard Gage, U S. Navy, retired.

Detroit district Ensign W. W Walsh, U. S Navy, retired (Aeronautics).

Cleveland district. Commander Ward Winchell, U S Navy, retired

Buffalo district Commodore George R. Salisbury, U. S Navy, retired; Lieut. H. W Schofield U S Naval Reserve Force (Aeronautics).

Harrisburg district: Lieut. G W. Danforth, U S. Navy, retired.

Berkeley (Calif.) district. Commander George H Stafford U S Navy, retired (Aeronautics)

The inspectors of machinery at Schenectady, San Francisco, and Milwaukee were also the inspectors of engineering material for those districts.

FUEL.

With such a large increase in the fleet and in the number of vessels operated by the Navy, it was out of the question to supply Navy standard coal to all, and accordingly investigation was made of the product of mines that were not on the acceptable list in order to prepare another list of coal that would be suitable for use in auxiliary vessels of the Navy and in merchant steamers manned by the Navy. Such coal, while below the standard required for the best performance of naval vessels, was in every respect satisfactory for the merchant ships to which it was supplied, since it had a good thermal value As practically all of these vessels sailed in convoy and at reduced speed, no difficulty was to be expected from the use of a lower grade fuel This list proved quite satisfactory and was the means of insuring a supply of good coal to all vessels under the control of the Navy.

Modifications in the specifications for fuel oil were made to take care of merchant ships fitted with oil-burning equipment, and also in the specifications for gasoline in order to provide a high grade for aviation purposes, and, at the same time, by the use of a lower grade for other purposes, to permit of greater production and thus meet the ever-increasing demand The modifications in the fuel-oil specifications were such as allowed the use of a heavy oil in certain Navy transports and cargo carriers, by which means the supply of lighter oils was conserved Those in the gasoline specifications provided for three grades of aviation gasoline, denominated aviation domestic, aviation export, and aviation fighting The modifications in each case were made in conference with the Fuel Administration and with other agencies of the Government concerned in their use, as well as with the representatives of the Allies

The following-named officers served in the Fuel and Personnel Division.

Commander N. H Wright, U. S. Navy, in charge [10]
Commander H A Stuart. U. S. Navy in charge.[11]
Lieut. (T) C. E. Briggs, U. S. Navy.
Lieut L N Crichton, U. S. Naval Reserve Force
Lieut M Pendleton, U. S Naval Reserve Force

---

[10] Until Aug 12, 1918.   [11] After Aug 1, 1918

Lieut. O. F. Purcell, U. S. Naval Reserve Force.
Lieut. T. A. Nicholson, U. S. Naval Reserve Force
Ensign R. T. Denman, U. S. Naval Reserve Force.
Ensign G. L. Ellis, U. S. Naval Reserve Force.
Ensign N. W. Garrett, U. S. Naval Reserve Force
Ensign C. R. Hughes, U. S. Naval Reserve Force.
Ensign W. R. Irish, U. S. Naval Reserve Force
Ensign R. R. Reutlinger, U. S. Naval Reserve Force.
Ensign L. W. Sydnor, U. S. Naval Reserve Force

LOGS AND RECORDS.

This division is responsible for the supply of steam log books and blank forms to all vessels of the Navy and has to see that the proper forms are sent to each. With the large number of ships and the varied types of machinery this duty was one requiring much care and the exercise of foresight in looking out for the wants of all vessels. As all blank forms are printed at the Government Printing Office, and as the demands made on that office by all departments of the Government were extremely heavy, it was no easy matter to anticipate the wants of such a big fleet and to keep it supplied with the requisite engineering forms and instruction pamphlets.

Bureau pamphlets regarding the proper care and management of machinery installations on shipboard were revised from time to time and issued to the seagoing personnel of ships, to naval training schools, and to camps for the training of men for engineering duties afloat. This was supplemented by the "Confidential Bulletin of Engineering Information," which was published and circulated at intervals as material became available.

The examination and the custody of the logs was a work of great importance, as serious questions not infrequently hinge on an apparently insignificant remark in the steam log.

The work of this division increased in direct proportion with the increase in the number of ships.

The officers of this division were:

Commander W. W. White, U. S. Navy.
Lieut. Commander W. T. Conn, U. S. Navy, until June 4, 1917
Lieut. J. F. Robbins, U. S. Naval Reserve Force

INDUSTRIAL.

Industrial conditions were much disturbed during the early days of the war, and many contractors appealed to the Bureau to assist in securing some action that would prevent employees from being accepted by recruiting officers, or, if accepted, to return them to their former employment. At one time a scheme of industrial enrollment was prepared and some progress made with it, but this was soon abandoned Meanwhile the conditions were becoming more and more unsatisfactory, because patriotic young men were chafing under the epithet of "slackers" and enlisting in either the Army or Navy, which action frequently caused a suspension of work on Navy contracts. Upon proper representation to the War Department exemption was secured, but the time involved in the transaction was a serious matter and resulted in no little delay in the prosecution of some important contracts However, this difficulty was removed upon the passage of the selective-draft act, employees whose services were essential in the production of war material being granted exemption under the Emergency Fleet classification

The suspension of the 8-hour law enabled work to be prosecuted to the limit, though some delay resulted from strikes. The number was, however, comparatively few.

In June, 1918, a serious disturbance occurred at the works of the Macbeth-Evans Glass Co , at Charleroi, Pa. This firm was engaged almost exclusively on war work, much of their product being for the Bureau of Steam Engineering. This disturbance resulted from a misapprehension of the people as to the Government's attitude respecting exemption under the Emergency Fleet classification, and it was due in no small measure to the action of Commodore R. G Denig, U S. Navy, retired, the inspector of engineering material at Pittsburgh, that the situation was cleared up and normal conditions restored He called a conference of representative citizens, explained the working of the exemption clause, and made a clear statement of what was demanded of the people as loyal citizens The result was highly beneficial, and in a short time labor troubles ceased

Commodore Denig also rendered very effective service at Pittsburgh in improving street railway conditions, which at the time were seriously impeding the progress of work on Government contracts

Throughout the war the need was felt for some distinguishing badge which would indicate that a man was exempted from military service because of the fact that he was engaged on war work. One firm engaged upon Navy work supplied its employees with a handsome bronze badge inscribed "Navy War Workers' Badge," the wearing of which had an excellent influence.

The most serious handicap experienced was in the winter of 1917-18, when the intensely cold weather and its duration so seriously retarded all new undertakings and crippled transportation facilities to such a degree as to affect all industrial work because of lack of fuel.

The increase in the machine-tool equipment of our own shops and of those of Navy contractors, as well as the enormous demand on the part of the Army, created such pressure on manufacturers as to make it impossible for them to determine which orders should receive priority. This situation led to the creation under the Council of National Defense of a Priorities Committee, to which such matters were referred and with which committee the Bureau maintained the closest possible liaison.

Later on the creation of the War Industries Board, under the direction of Mr. S M. Vauclain, served to bring the contractors in closer touch with the conditions confronting us, and also to materially assist in expediting the completion of work This was especially true in the case of the new equipment—forging presses, boring and turning lathes—required for increasing the production of forgings.

One of the most gratifying events of the war was the promptness with which industrial firms generally tendered their services and that of their plants upon the first indication of trouble.

PLANT IMPROVEMENTS.

Soon after our entry into the war it became apparent that if our building program was to be extended it would be necessary to make large additions to existing manufacturing facilities or to create new ones, as all available industrial establishments were working to maximum capacity. The situation was brought prominently to the front when it was decided greatly to increase our destroyer force. In order to get a comprehensive estimate of the situation, the Secretary of the Navy called a conference, on August 20, 1917, of shipbuilders and others concerned in the production of important parts of destroyers, at which was discussed their ability to build 150 more destroyers, and the additional facilities that it would be necessary to provide in order to carry out the program which the department had in mind. This was followed by a second conference September 9, 1917, as a result of which additions to plant facilities, or the erection of entirely new ones, were undertaken in connection with the machinery for destroyers as enumerated in the following statement, mention of which has been made in the chapter on destroyers

TURBINE SHOP AT BUFFALO, N Y

This shop was built and fully equipped with machine and hand tools specially selected for use in the construction of the Fore River design of Curtis turbines for some of the destroyers building at the Fore River plant of the Bethlehem Shipbuilding Corporation. The entire cost of the building and its equipment was borne by the Government

GENERAL ELECTRIC CO, ERIE, PA

The General Electric Co had just completed the construction of a suitable building at Erie, Pa, and arrangements were made whereby this company would build the machinery for 40 destroyers for the Union Iron Works, San Francisco, Calif This contract provided that the tool equipment for this shop be furnished by the Government, the General Electric Co. having an option to purchase any or all the tools upon completion of the contract, and after appraisal.

DE LA VERGNE MACHINE CO., NEW YORK CITY

In order to assist the William Cramp & Sons Ship & Engine Building Co in the construction of turbines for the destroyers for which they had contracts, the Navy Department, acting through the Cramp company, purchased the stock of the De La Vergne Machine Co and thus acquired ownership of their plant, which was placed under the Cramp company for operation, and was utilized for the manufacture of other articles as well as turbines for the Navy

UNION IRON WORKS, SAN FRANCISCO, CALIF

The construction of 40 destroyers of the new program was assigned this branch of the Bethlehem Shipbuilding Corporation in addition to the 26 already under contract. To enable the work on both contracts to be prosecuted energetically it was necessary to build and equip at the Alameda plant of the company a machine shop which would be capable of building the turbines, and to lease and equip a portion of the Risdon Iron Works for use as a boiler shop. These were carried under the "special rentals" clause of the contract.

BOILER SHOP AT PROVIDENCE, R. I.

A shop for the sole purpose of building Yarrow boilers was constructed under the direction of the Bethlehem Shipbuilding Corporation, acting for the Navy Department, on land owned by the city of Providence. It was completely equipped with tools for the manufacture of Yarrow boilers, and supplemented the expanded facilities of the Fore River plant for the construction of boilers for the destroyers which were built by that yard. The cost of its construction and equipment was borne by the Government, and the building and tools were its property. The city of Providence has an option of purchasing the building after appraisal.

BATH IRON WORKS, BATH, ME

At the Bath Iron Works important extensions were made to shops concerned in the production of engines and boilers and to the office building. This was done under the "special rentals" clause of the contracts, the total cost to be adjusted by the Compensation Board upon completion of the latter

NEW YORK SHIPBUILDING CO, CAMDEN, N J.

Many extensions and improvements were made at this plant, all indirectly affecting work for the Bureau of Steam Engineering. They were made as "special rentals" to be adjusted by the Compensation Board

NEWPORT NEWS SHIPBUILDING & DRY DOCK CO, NEWPORT NEWS, VA.

Of the improvements made at this place to carry on the building program and especially to expedite destroyer building, the construction of a pattern shop building was the one that pertained especially to work for the Bureau of Steam Engineering. Its cost was covered by the "special rentals" clause of the contract.

BABCOCK & WILCOX CO., BAYONNE, N. J.

This firm built 260 boilers for 65 destroyers of the new program and 108 boilers for 54 mine sweepers, in addition to the boilers for some of the destroyers that were under construction at the time, October, 1917. To accomplish this and to fill their large contracts with the Emergency Fleet Corporation, a large addition was made to their plant facilities. This was financed by the Babcock & Wilcox Co.

THE FALK CO., MILWAUKEE, WIS.

The enlargement of the plant of this company and the cost of the additional tools necessary to produce the gears required for the 45 destroyers which were to be built at Fore River was borne by the Government. The contract provided for an appraisal of the improvements upon completion of the contract.

CONSOLIDATED SAFETY VALVE CO., BRIDGEPORT, CONN.

To this firm was assigned the manufacture of all the safety valves—1,200—for the 150 destroyers. It required only an addition to their tool equipment, which was paid for by the Government, the tools remaining as its property.

WORTHINGTON PUMP & MACHINERY CO., CAMBRIDGE, MASS.

The enlargement and remodeling of this plant at Cambridgeport, Mass., was financed by the Government. The terms of the contract provided for the taking over by the Worthington company of the Government's interest upon completion of the work and after appraisal.

WELLMAN-SEAVER MORGAN CO., AKRON, OHIO

To this firm was assigned as a part of their work the manufacture of condensers, and of boiler uptakes for some of the destroyers. The improvements necessary therefor were financed by the Government.

WILLIAM CRAMP & SONS SHIP & ENGINE BUILDING CO., PHILADELPHIA, PA.

The brass foundry at this place specializes in bronze screw propeller castings, and as it would be necessary for this foundry to produce about 400 propellers material additions had to be made to the foundry and its equipment in order to utilize to best advantage the experience of this firm. It was also necessary to construct a new office building. These were provided under "special rentals."

BORING PUMP CYLINDERS FOR DESTROYERS—WORTHINGTON'S

BORING PUMP CYLINDERS FOR DESTROYERS—WORTHINGTON S.

B F. STURTEVANT CO, HYDE PARK, MASS.

The forced-draft blowers for more than one-half of the destroyers were manufactured by this firm, and in order to insure their completion on time it was necessary to make provision for additional power and for minor additions to certain shops The cost was borne by the Government and the improvements taken over by the firm upon completion of the contract at their appraised value

GRISCOM-RUSSELL CO., MASSILLON, OHIO.

The distilling plants, comprising evaporators and distillers, and the feed water and oil heaters for about 150 destroyers were manufactured by this firm, who found it necessary to enlarge their plant in order to handle the work The cost was advanced by the Government and amortized as deliveries were made.

CHAPMAN VALVE CO, INDIAN ORCHARD, MASS.

This firm was given an order for a large number of gate valves, and in order to complete them in time it was necessary for the Government to make some additions to their tool equipment The tools remained the property of the Government

EDWARD VALVE CO, CHICAGO, ILL

To this company was assigned the manufacture of nearly all of the flanged steam and water valves for the destroyers to be built at Fore River, and to insure their production in time it was necessary to make a large addition to their tool equipment, the cost of which was borne by the Government, which retained possession of them upon completion of the contract.

ERIE FORGE & STEEL CO, ERIE, PA

There was built on ground belonging to the Erie Forge Co. a complete forging plant, with furnaces, forging presses, and machine-tool equipment for the manufacture of destroyer forgings for the Bureau of Steam Engineering and gun forgings for the Bureau of Ordnance.

Ground was broken for the erection of the plant November 9, 1917, and while the difficulties attending the construction of the buildings, as a consequence of the severe winter weather, operated to delay completion of the entire plant, manufacturing actually began May 17, 1918, thus making 189 days, or approximately six months, from the breaking of ground until the first heat of steel was tapped from the furnaces

The operation of the plant was under the direction of the Erie Forge & Steel Co, and a clause in the contract provided for the transfer of the Government's interest in the plant to that company upon the conclusion of peace at a price to be determined by appraisal

POLLAK STEEL CO, CINCINNATI, OHIO.

The forging facilities of this company were augmented by the construction of a building and the addition of suitable furnaces, a forging press, and the tools necessary for machining destroyer forgings Production was not as early as had been contemplated, nor as satisfactory as was desired; but conditions were very much improved, largely through the active cooperation and assistance of Mr. S M Vauclain, of the War Industries Board The agreement with this firm provided for the purchase of the machine-tool equipment upon completion of the contract

ALLIS-CHALMERS CO., MILWAUKEE, WIS

At the forge plant of this company it was necessary to make some additions, chiefly in the nature of heat-treating furnaces, to place them in position to make the forgings desired This was financed by the Navy Department

CAMDEN FORGE CO, CAMDEN, N. J.

The facilities of this firm were enlarged by the erection of an extension to their machine shop and the addition of necessary machine tools, the cost of which was amortized.

COLUMBIA STEEL CO, PITTSBURG, CALIF.

The steel-casting facilities of the Pacific coast were not sufficient for the production of all such material required by the Navy and the Shipping Board, and in order to meet this condition it was necessary to make extensive additions to the plant of the Columbia Steel Co, which supplied the castings for the destroyers building at the Union Iron Works and at the Mare Island Navy Yard

LANG PROPELLER CO, WHITESTONE, L I

The great demand for increased production of propellers for airplanes made necessary the extension of the works of the Lang Propeller Co, which was one of the plants assigned for Navy work. The cost of the building and equipment was borne by the Navy Department, the contract providing for an appraisal of the plant after the war

FORD MOTOR CO

Extensive additions were made to the construction plant of this company at River Rouge, Mich, and to an assembly plant at Kearney, N. J., to provide for the construction of "Eagles." The money was advanced by the Government, but the contract provided that the equipment should be appraised and taken over by the Ford Motor Co. at the appraised value upon completion of the contract.

NAVY YARDS.

The demands on the shops of the machinery divisions of navy yards made necessary important extensions, and in some cases—notably Philadelphia—the erection of new shops, as well as a large increase in their equipment. Electric steel furnaces were provided for four yards.

INDEX.

	Page
Aeronautics, Division of, duties	4
Aircraft, application of detection devices	68
experimental engines	144
instruments and accessories	142
propellers	138
radiators	141
steam power plants	143
Allis-Chalmers Co., additions to forging plant	30, 168
subcontract for destroyer turbines	28
Antiaircraft defense	152
Argon (helium)	145
Aviation Division, organization	133
officers of	153
personnel, method of obtaining	7
Babcock & Wilcox Co., addition to plant	166
boilers for destroyers	28
boilers for mine sweepers	41
number of boilers built	166
Bath Iron Works, extension of shops	165
Bethlehem Co., boilers for Squantum destroyers	27
Union Iron Works destroyers	28
Boilers for destroyers	28
Boiler shop at Providence	165
British Mission on submarine detection	8, 49
Busch-Sulzer Co., submarine engines	43
Camden Forge Co., extension of forging plant	30, 168
Cargo vessels, precedence in building	24
Chapman Valve Co., tool equipment	167
Civilian personnel	9
Clerical Division, duties	4
Coal, variation from standard	160
Coast Guard officers, duty in Bureau	7
Columbia Steel Co., plant improvements	168
Consolidated Safety Valve Co., tool equipment	166
Cramp & Sons, enlargement of foundry	30
operation by of De La Vergne Machinery Co.	28
plant improvements	166
propellers for destroyers	30
turbines for destroyers	28
De La Vergne Machinery Co., purchase of	28
Design, Division of, duties	4
officers of	45
Destroyers, authority to build 150 additional	26
boilers for	28
boilers, construction of spare	75
distribution of to shipbuilders	26
evaporators and distillers	29
forced-draft blowers	29
forgings, order for	75

INDEX.

	Page
Destroyers, general condition of machinery	75
precedence of, in construction	24
production of	31
propellers for	30
pumps for	28
reduction gear	29
refrigerating apparatus	31
safety valves	30
speed of 150 additional	25
standardization of design	27
Detection, sound, for defense against aircraft	152
Detection, submarine (*see also* Submarine detection)	47
Distillers and evaporators for destroyers	29
Division of Aeronautics, duties	4
Design, duties	4
Fuel and Personnel, duties	5
Logs and Records, duties	5
Repairs, duties	4
Duties of Bureau	1
Eagles, characteristics	38
precedence in building	24
proposition of Ford Motor Co	38
speed of	40
turbines and reduction gear	39
Electrical Division activities	45
duties	4
officers of	46
Electrical engineers, selection of	7
Electric drive	18
for battle cruisers	19
Electric generators for destroyers	31
wire and cable, conference on	45
Elia-Sperry net, experiments	50
Engineering representatives of contractors	39
Engines aircraft, Gnome	137
Hispano-Suiza	137
Le Rhone	137
Liberty	133
Rolls-Royce	138
testing laboratory	144
Erie Forge & Steel Co, new forging plant	30, 167
Evaporators and distillers for destroyers	29
Expenditures, 1918	3
Experimental station, naval, establishment of	54
Experiment station, Annapolis	3
Falk Co, enlargement of works	29, 166
Fans, forced-draft, for destroyers	29
Fessenden, Prof R A, sound detection	53
Fire-control activities	45
Ford Motor Co, plant additions	168
Forgings for destroyers	25
construction of plant for manufacture	30
French Mission on submarine detection	8, 49

INDEX. 173

	Page
Fuel and Personnel Division, duties	5
officers of	160
Fuel, modification of requirements.	160
General Electric Co, conference on submarine detection	48
contract for destroyer turbines	27
reduction gear	29
German ships, condition of machinery	77, 87
names of	81
nature of damage to machinery	83
ports where seized	82
repair by electric welding	79
repair by oxy-acetylene welding	88
troop capacity	85
troops transported in	87
Vaterland, condition of	88
Goggle, development of standard.	53
Griscom-Russell Co, evaporators and distillers	29
Helium, production of	145
Horsepower of the fleet.	3
Hydrogen, development of plants for manufacture	149
Improvement of navy yards, allotment of funds	17
Industrial conditions	162
Inspection Division, duties	4
officers of	158
Inspectors of engineering material	158
machinery	32, 42, 43
Iron and Steel Institute, cooperation	157
Jewett, Dr. F B, Board on Antisubmarine Devices	49
Kolstermeter	96
Lafayette radio station	93, 95
Lang Propeller Co, extension of works	168
Liberty engines	134
advisability of geared drive.	136
Light, development of standard goggle	53
Logs and Records, Division of, duties	5
importance of	161
Lyons-Atlas Co connection with subchaser machinery	34
Magnetic detection, board to investigate	48
limited range	48
result of experiments.	53
Millikan, Dr R A, detection devices.	47
Board on Anti-Submarine Devices	49
Mine sweepers, builders of.	42
machinery	41
precedence in construction.	24
Navy yard improvement, allotment of funds	17
Navy yards, plant improvements.	169
New London Ship & Engine Co, submarine engines	43
Newport News Co, shop improvements	165
turbines for destroyers.	28
New York Shipbuilding Co	165
	28
Oil, fuel, modification	160

174　INDEX

	Page
Organization of Bureau	3
Personnel of Bureau	5
Personnel Division	5
Plant improvements	164
Pollak Steel Co, extension of forging plant	30, 168
Powell, J W, connection with destroyer program	32
Preliminary preparations for war	11
Preparedness, plan of	13
Propellers for destroyers	30
seaplanes	138
Radiators for aircraft	141
Radio Board, Interdepartmental	131
Radio aircraft	118
compass	123
receivers	122
transatlantic flight	124
transmitters	121
Radio, amplifiers	116
arc system, adoption of	91
at overseas bases	125
compass	96
compass receivers	117
compass sites for stations	97
control boxes	116
control of stations moved to Washington	94
decision in case of Marconi vs Simon	129
developments during war	90
Division, duties	4
officers of	131
equipment of Shipping Board vessels	111
high-power transmission	91
observer in Europe in 1914	12
patents	128
purchase of Marconi and Federal stations	113
receivers	116
receiving systems, transoceanic	103
Alexanderson barrage	108
Austin	108
Belmar	106
Chatham	106
Otter Cliffs	107
Weagant	106
Zenneck	103
research laboratory	115
shipboard equipment	109
stations, Annapolis	93, 95
coastal for commercial vessels	111
Lafayette	93, 95
Marconi and Federal, purchase of	113
Monroe, projected	93
shore, compensation for use of	113
Vladivostok	95
tele, submarine chasers	71, 98
long-distance transmission	99

INDEX. 175

	Page
Radio, test shop	115
underground experiments at—	
Belmar	102
Great Lakes	100
New Orleans	102
Piney Point	102
Rogers laboratory	102
under water, experiments	103
Reduction gear for destroyers	29
Refrigerating apparatus for destroyers	31
Repairs and conversions	74
Repair Division, duties	4
officers of	78
ships, commendation of Admiral Bayly, R. N	76
equipment of	2
precedence in construction	24
Melville and Dixie, work of	76
Retired officers	6
School, gas engine for sub-chaser operators	35
hydrophone—listening	54, 59
Scout cruisers, machinery for	24
Special board, members	58
scope of activities	60
Squantum, destroyers built at	27
Standard Motor Construction Co., contract with	34
Standardization of destroyers	27
Steam power plants for aircraft	143
Sturtevant Co., fans for destroyers	29
plant improvements	167
Submarine chasers, endurance	35
equipment, general	37
with detecting divers	36
installation of detecting devices	57
machinery for	33
precedence in building	24
production of engines	34
reliability of machinery	36
tactics	58, 71
tenders	35
visual indicator	71
wireless telephone for	37
detection, apparatus mounted in boat and outside	67
binaural effect	50
British and French Missions	8, 49
Broca receivers	66
conference on	48
cooperation in development	54
C-tube development	55
development at Nahant	61
New London	62
devices in British craft	56
directional and nondirectional instruments	63
early tests	47
experiments with Elia-Sperry net	50

	Page.
Submarine detection, farming out investigations	52
general discussion of apparatus	62
K-tube, development	55
magnetic detection	48
mechanical and electrical	65
MV apparatus	51
resonant and nonresonant instruments	64
shore-station apparatus	69
single and multi-unit receivers	67
special boards on	49
station at Nahant	48
New London	51
supersonic work	50
Walzer apparatus	51
Submarines, benefits from listening devices in	73
construction of	43
new engines for H and K classes	44
precedence in building	24
Submarine Signal Co, station at Nahant	48
devices designed by Prof Fessenden	53
Supplies, cooperation of Iron and Steel Institute	157
inspection	156
procurement of	155
Supply Division, duties	5
officers of	158
Supreme Court, reversal of decision in Marconi v Simon	129
Terry Steam Turbine Co., fans	29
Transatlantic flight, engine equipment	150
Troopships, precedence in conversion of	24
Tubes, boiler and condenser, difficulty in obtaining	30
Tugs, builders of	42
construction	41
precedence in construction	24
Turbines for destroyers	27, 28
Turbine shop at Buffalo	164
Erie	164
Union Works, turbines for destroyers	28
Valves manufactured by Edward Valve Co	31
safety, for destroyers	30
Vaterland, condition of machinery	88
Vauclain, S M, aid in production of forgings	31, 163
Vessels, number in service	74
Welding, electric, on German ships	79
oxy-acetylene, on German ships	88
Wireless (See Radio)	
Wellman-Seaver, Morgan Co, condenser work	31
plant improvements	166
Westinghouse Co, contract for destroyer turbines	28
reduction gear	29
Western Electric Co, conference on submarine detection	48
Whitney, Dr. W. R, member of special board	49
Worthington Pump Co, remodeling of plant	28, 166

RETURN TO ➡	CIRCULATION DEPARTMENT 202 Main Library	
LOAN PERIOD 1 **HOME USE**	2	3
4	5	6

ALL BOOKS MAY BE RECALLED AFTER 7 DAYS

DUE AS STAMPED BELOW

REC. CIR. AUG 17 1973   SEP 05 1989

REC. CIR. APR 11 1990

LIBRARY USE

REC. CIR. APR 14 1990

2/15/85 AWS
RECEIVED
MAY 20 1985
CIRCULATION DEPT.

Printed in the USA
CPSIA information can be obtained
at www.ICGtesting.com
CBHW050837220724
11778CB00056B/63